RI

Despite reigning for only a relatively short period of time, Richard III is one of England's most controversial monarchs. His life and rule have inspired a huge amount of literature, not least Shakespeare's great play, and controversy still surrounds his seizure of the throne in 1483, the mystery of the disappearance of the Princes in the Tower, and his defeat and death at the Battle of Bosworth in 1485.

This new biography takes a nuanced view both of Richard III's reign and of the controversies surrounding it, exploring them in the wider context of the period. Defining Richard's character as central to the analysis of his actions, David Hipshon emphasises the need to separate the man himself from the caricature that has so often been painted.

Incorporating new research and previously unpublished material, this book is a must-read for all those interested both in Richard III as king, and in the development of the English monarchy and society at the end of the medieval era and the beginning of the early modern period.

David Hipshon is Assistant Head at St James Independent School in Twickenham. He has published articles in the *Journal of Ecclesiastical History*, *BBC History Magazine*, *History Review* and *Convivium*, and gives many public lectures on medieval themes.

ROUTLEDGE HISTORICAL BIOGRAPHIES

SERIES EDITOR: ROBERT PEARCE

Routledge Historical Biographies provide engaging, readable and academically credible biographies written from an explicitly historical perspective. These concise and accessible accounts will bring important historical figures to life for students and general readers alike.

In the same series:

Bismarck by Edgar Feuchtwanger
Oliver Cromwell by Martyn Bennett
Edward IV by Hannes Kleineke
Gladstone by Michael Partridge
Henry VII by Sean Cunningham
Henry VIII by Lucy Wooding
Lenin by Christopher Read
Louis XIV by Richard Wilkinson
Mao by Michael Lynch
Martin Luther King Jr. by Peter J. Ling
Martin Luther by Michael Mullet
Marx by Vincent Barnett
Mary Queen of Scots by Retha M. Warnicke
Mussolini by Peter Neville
Nehru by Ben Zachariah
Neville Chamberlain by Nick Smart
Emmeline Pankhurst by Paula Bartley
Richard III by David Hipshon
Trotsky by Ian Thatcher
Mary Tudor by Judith Richards

Forthcoming:

Calvin by Michael Mullett
Churchill by Robert Pearce
Hitler by Michael Lynch

RICHARD III

David Hipshon

Routledge
Taylor & Francis Group

LONDON AND NEW YORK

First published 2011 by Routledge
2 Park Square, Milton Park, Abingdon, Oxon. OX14 4RN

Simultaneously published in the USA and Canada
by Routledge
270 Madison Ave., New York, NY 100016

Routledge is an imprint of the Taylor & Francis Group, an informa business

© 2011 David Hipshon

Typeset in Garamond by Saxon Graphics Ltd, Derby
Printed and bound in Great Britain by TJ International Ltd, Padstow, Cornwall

British Library Cataloguing in Publication Data
A catalogue record for this book is available from the British Library

Library of Congress Cataloging-in-Publication Data
Hipshon, David.
Richard III / David Hipshon.
p. cm. -- (Routledge historical biographies)
Includes bibliographical references and index.
1. Richard III, King of England, 1452-1485. 2. Great Britain--Kings and
rulers--Biography. 3. Great Britain--History--Richard III, 1483-1485. I. Title.
DA260.H57 2010
942.04'6092--dc22
[B]
2010027990

ISBN13: 978-0-415-46280-8 (hbk)
ISBN13: 978-0-415-46281-5 (pbk)

CONTENTS

CHRONOLOGY vi
LIST OF PLATES XIV
ACKNOWLEDGEMENTS XV

Introduction 1

1 The Son of York: 1452–1461 19

2 Duke of Gloucester: 1461–1469 46

3 Duke of Gloucester: 1469–1471 67

4 Lord of the North: 1471–1483 91

5 The Usurpation: 1483 119

6 The Reign 1: Buckingham's Rebellion, 1483–1484 143

7 The Reign 2: Governing the Realm, 1483–1485 164

8 The Reign 3: The Politics of Kingship 185

9 Posthumous Reputation 208

Conclusion 244

NOTES 249
FURTHER READING 263
INDEX 267

CHRONOLOGY

Date	Personal	Political	General
1452	2 Oct, born at Fotheringhay		15 April, Leonardo da Vinci born
1453		Henry VI incapacitated	29 May, Ottoman Turks take Constantinople 17 July, battle of Castillon: end of Hundred Years War
1454		Jan, York's 1st Protectorate	
1455		Jan, end of 1st Protectorate 22 May, battle of St Albans: Lancastrian lords killed Nov, York's 2nd Protectorate	
1456		Feb, end of 2nd Protectorate	Turks take Athens
1458		25 March, Loveday at St Paul's	Mathias Corvinus becomes king of Hungary
1459	Taken into the custody of Anne, duchess of Buckingham	3 Aug, James II of Scotland killed at Roxburgh James III becomes king 23 Sept, battle of Blore Heath: Salisbury joins York at Ludlow 12–13 Oct, Rout at Ludford: York flees to Ireland	

Year			
1460	Moves to Baynard's Castle, London	10 July, battle of Northampton: Yorkist victory Sept, York returns from Ireland 30 Dec, battle of Wakefield: York and Rutland killed	Louis XI becomes king of France
1461	Sent to Duke Philip the Good of Burgundy for safety June, returns to England 1 Nov, made duke of Gloucester	2–3 Feb, battle of Mortimer's Cross: Edward defeats Lancastrians 17 Feb, 2nd battle of St Albans: Warwick defeated by Margaret of Anjou 4 March, Edward declared king 29–30 March, battle of Towton: Edward gains decisive victory	
1462	Oct 2 made admiral of England		
1464	Enters the household of the earl of Warwick 1 May, Edward secretly marries Elizabeth Woodville	25 April, battle of Hedgley Moor: Lancastrian rebels defeated 15 May, battle of Hexham: John marquess Montagu defeats Somerset 11 June, 15-year truce with Scotland	Cosimo de Medici dies
1465		13 July, Henry VI captured	League of the Public Weal: Dukes against Louis XI of France

Date	Personal	Political	General
1467			15 June, Philip the Good dies: Charles the Bold becomes duke of Burgundy Japanese civil war begins lasting 100 years
1468		3 July, Margaret of York marries Charles the Bold	John Gutenberg invents printing with moveable type
1469	Leaves Warwick's household and attends royal court Attends treason trial at Salisbury 17 Oct, made constable of England 7 Nov, made chief justiciar of north Wales	26 July, battle of Edgecote: Warwick defeats Pembroke 29 July, Edward held captive at Middleham	Lorenzo and Guliano de Medici assume power in Florence
1470	2 Oct, exile in Flanders with Edward IV 2 Nov, Edward V born in Westminster	12 March, battle of Losecoat Field: Edward temporarily regairs control 9 April, Warwick and Clarence sail for Calais Sept, Warwick lands in Devon 6 Oct, Readeption of Henry VI (to 11 April 1471)	

1471	14 March lands at Ravenspur Fights at Barnet Commands vanguard at Tewkesbury 29 June, granted Neville estates in Yorkshire and Cumberland 4 July, made chief steward of the duchy of Lancaster in the north 12 July marries Anne Neville	Edward returns to claim back throne 14 April, battle of Barnet: Warwick killed 4 May, battle of Tewkesbury: Henry VI's son, Edward, killed 21 May, death of Henry VI in Tower	Thomas a Kempis dies Sixtus IV becomes pope (to 1484)
1473		Birth of Richard duke of York, 2nd son of Edward IV	
1474	Dispute with Clarence		Isabella becomes Queen of Castile
1475	Feb, made sheriff of Cumberland for life	4 July, Edward invades France Louis XI of France goes to war against Burgundy 29 Aug, Treaty of Picquigny	Birth of Michelangelo Triple Alliance: Florence, Venice and Milan
1476	21–30 July, Reburial of York and Rutland at Fotheringhay Edward of Middleham born, Richard's only legitimate son		Caxton sets up printing press in Westminster

Date	Personal	Political	General
1477			5 Jan, Charles the Bold killed at battle of Nancy 18 Aug, Maximilian of Austria marries Mary, daughter of Charles the Bold
1478	21 Feb, made Great Chamberlain of England	18 Feb, Clarence executed for treason	9 April, Pazzi Conspiracy in Florence: Lorenzo becomes sole ruler Ivan III, duke of Moscow, captures Novgorod Turks capture Albania Botticelli paints Primavera
1479			Ferdinand becomes king of Aragon: Union of Castile and Aragon
1480	12 May, made lieutenant-general in the north Aug, leads troops against the Scots	Aug, war against the Scots 23 Dec, Treaty of Arras between France and Burgundy	23 Dec, Treaty of Arras between France and Burgundy
1481			Ferdinand and Isabella begin war against Moors of Spain
1482		3 June, war with Scotland renewed 24 Aug, Berwick surrenders	Portuguese settle in Gold Coast

1483	Jan, made hereditary warden of the Western March	9 April, death of Edward IV	Raphael born at Urbino
	March, given palatinate powers in Cumberland	30 April, coup at Stony Stratford	30 Aug, Louis XI of France dies; Charles VIII becomes king
	April, holds brother's funeral in York Minster	13 June, execution of Hastings	(to 1498)
	26 June, accepts throne	26 June Edward V deposed	
	6 July, crowned Richard III	Sept, rebellion in favour of the Princes	
	Sept, Investiture of the prince of Wales at York	4–10 Oct, Buckingham joins rebellion	
	12 Oct, hears of Buckingham's treachery	2 Nov, Buckingham executed	
1484	April, death of only son, Edward	23 Jan, first and only Parliament begins	Innocent VIII becomes Pope
		1 March, Elizabeth Woodville comes out of sanctuary	(to 1492)
		Sept, Henry Tudor escapes from Brittany to France	
		Sept, 3-year truce with Scotland	
1485	16 March, Queen Anne dies	7 Aug, Henry Tudor lands at Milford Haven	Botticelli paints Birth of Venus
	22 Aug, killed at Bosworth	22 Aug, battle of Bosworth Field: end of Yorkist dynasty and beginning of Tudor dynasty	Ficino translates Plato
			9 Aug, France and Brittany sign peace treaty

The Houses of York and Lancaster

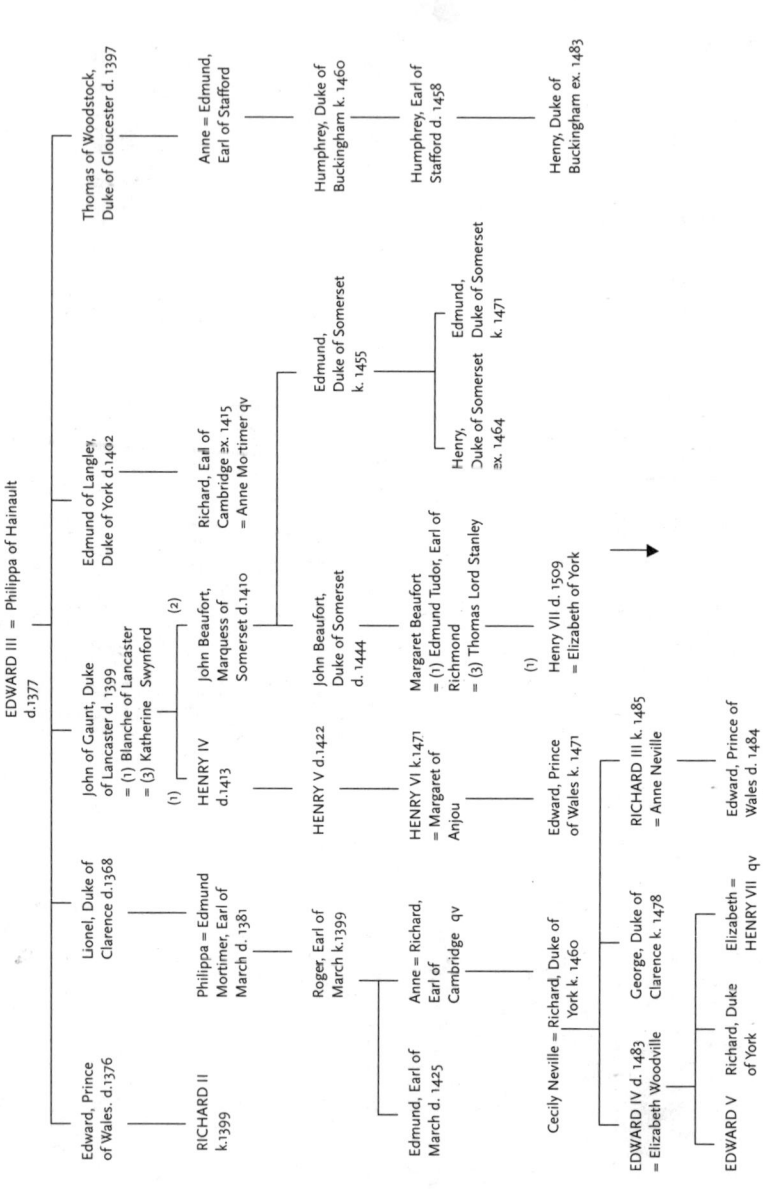

The House of York

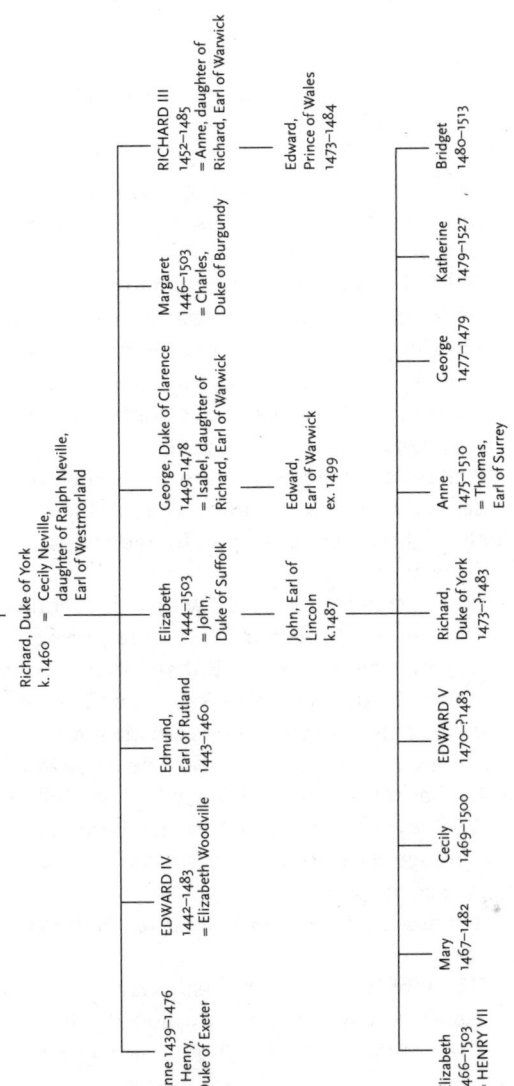

LIST OF PLATES

PLATES (BETWEEN PAGES 176 AND 177)

Image Captions and Credits

1. All that remains of Fotheringhay Castle, Richard's birthplace, with the church, where his father is buried, in the background. Author's own photograph.
2. (Top) Richard's first letter, dated June 1469. Image © British Library Board, Cotton Vespasian F III, no. 19.
   (Bottom) Richard's letter 12 October 1483 requesting the Great Seal. This has a postscript in Richard's own hand referring to the treachery of the duke of Buckingham. National Archives, C 81/1392/6.
3. Richard's teenage signature and motto *Tant le desieree* ('I have desired it so much') on his copy of the romance *Ipomedon*, the story of the perfect knight. Image courtesy Longleat Historic Collections.
4. An illustration of Jean de Waurin presenting his *Chroniques* to Edward IV with Richard second left (the earliest likeness), French School. Image courtesy British Library, London, UK/ © British Library Board. All Rights Reserved/ The Bridgeman Art Library.
5. Richard III, English School. Image courtesy Society of Antiquaries of London, UK / The Bridgeman Art Library.
6. All that remains of the Great Hall at Middleham Castle in Wensleydale, on the first floor, where Richard would have conducted much of his business as Lord of the North. Author's own photograph.
7. Richard III, by an unknown artist. National Portrait Gallery, London.
8. Statue of Richard III in Castle Gardens, Leicester, by James Butler MBE RA. Image reproduced with kind permission of the office of James Butler. Photograph © Emily Kindleysides.

ACKNOWLEDGEMENTS

Writing this book was, at times, a lonely and daunting experience. It would have been quite impossible without the support and encouragement of friends and colleagues too numerous to mention in this short space. I am deeply grateful for all the cheerful words of confidence so naively but opportunely offered. I would particularly like to thank Rosemary Horrox for her sagacity and kindness at the inception of the work. In many ways she unwittingly inspired this offering. I hope that she will not be too disappointed. The team at Routledge have been fantastic. I would like to thank Vicky Peters for her guidance and advice, Emily Kindleysides for her patience and assistance and Bob Pierce for his unflagging encouragement and fortitude. The production team deserve special thanks for all their efforts. Stacey Carter and Rob Brown brought the process to a conclusion with great skill and efficiency and made it all a little less painful than it might have been. I would like to thank all my pupils, past and present, for their inspiration and enthusiasm and my family for their benign goodwill. Finally, as ever, I would like to acknowledge the debt I owe to my wife, Sarah Jane, for her love and support.

ACKNOWLEDGEMENTS

INTRODUCTION

Richard III's reign of just two years and two months has spawned a remarkable quantity of literature, including one of Shakespeare's great plays. Much of this has been focused on the enduring controversy surrounding Richard's seizure of the throne in 1483 and the mystery of the disappearance of his nephews, the two Princes in the Tower. The battle of Bosworth Field has also entered the public consciousness because it has always appeared to represent a defining moment in English history. It was the last time a king of England led his troops into battle and it caused the destruction of one dynasty and the advent of another. The Tudor era began at Bosworth, and the medieval world, represented by Richard and his household knights charging to their deaths, seemed to disappear forever. But the reign is important for other, perhaps more significant, reasons.

Richard's reign had a lasting impact on the nature of monarchy and government in England. By continuing to use the methods his brother, Edward IV, employed in royal administration, the policy of making use of the royal household, particularly in the area of finance and the management of the crown lands to increase royal revenue, was preserved. The promotion of loyal and trusted men from within the household, often of relatively humble origins, was another feature of Edward's reign that Richard adopted and accelerated. In Richard's case this was one of the defining characteristics of the reign. Whereas Edward had elevated these men to the peerage, Richard did not do so and thereby promoted a trend that was to become a feature of the Tudor period. Under Richard these 'new men' began to exercise considerable influence and even to direct policy. They were a new type of courtier and their promotion under Richard began an era in which the power of the nobility was gradually subordinated to a new kind of royal rule.

Much of this was unconsciously achieved by the vicissitudes of fortune. Richard had taken the throne at a time when the possibility of weak kingship had reared its head again. The backdrop to the usurpation, and to Richard's early life, was the turbulence and turmoil caused by the Wars of the Roses. When Richard was killed at Bosworth two years after taking the throne, the inexperienced Henry Tudor had little choice but to continue to exploit the methods of governing he had inherited from his Yorkist predecessors. Richard's reign preserved strong monarchy and increased the speed of the changes in the political class that had been taking place in Edward IV's reign. Of course this occurred in large part despite Richard, rather than because of him. He had not intended to be killed at Bosworth. Nevertheless the outcome was the emergence of a distinct class of royal agents, less dependent on regional hegemonies and valued for their expertise and ability, rather than their birth. We do not know whether kingship would have developed in the same way had Edward V been allowed to grow to maturity and to reign, but if Richard's aim in seizing the throne had been to preserve royal power untrammelled by magnate faction, this was certainly a consequence of it.

As for the fate of the princes and the motives that caused Richard to remove them and make himself king, the mystery will remain and continue to fascinate future generations. All we know for certain is that contemporaries did not know their fate. Whatever became of them, and each person who considers the subject will make their choice from among a range of theories, responsibility for it lies squarely at Richard's door. In deciding to take the throne Richard sealed the fate of his nephews.

The truth about Richard will not be found by describing him as 'a man of his times', but rather by remembering that he was a human being. His motives may have been complex, changing, subject to one influence or another, but ultimately of the same stuff as our own. Perhaps this is one reason why Richard continues to fascinate and inspire supporters and detractors alike: in studying a man under such conflicting pressures, we come close to studying the human being itself.

THE HISTORICAL BACKGROUND: ORIGINS

Richard III was born Richard Plantagenet on 2 October 1452 at Fotheringhay Castle in Northamptonshire. We know this because in a Book of Hours owned by Richard there was a calendar for October in which a careful scribe had added an entry to commemorate the birth. One function of a Book of Hours was to inform its owner of the numerous saints' days and church festivals upon which special masses would be sung throughout the year. These books were beautifully presented works of art, often commissioned by a wealthy patron of at least conventional piety who could afford the handwritten and elaborately decorated manuscript. The first entry for 2 October in Richard's book tells us that it was the feast day of 'Sancti Leodegarius'. This St Leodegar (or St Ledger) was famous for the fact that he had introduced Benedictine monasticism into 7th-century Francia, but he had also, as had many early medieval churchmen, a significant role in the politics of the time. He helped protect, ironically enough, the regency of the boy-king, Chlothar III. Unfortunately there is no evidence that Richard was at all interested in St Leodegar. His feast day would have been commemorated because it was still included in the Sarum Rite, which Richard's foundations followed, but it is unlikely that he knew anything about him. Perhaps it is just as well: the life and reign of Childeric II would have made very unpleasant reading at Richard's court. The Latin entry that has been inserted after Leodegar's name tells us that 'on this day was Richard III King of England born at Fotheringhay Anno Domini 1452'.[1]

Richard is often considered to be a 'northern king' on account of his close association with the north of England, but he certainly wasn't northern by birth. Fotheringhay is in the county of Northamptonshire and firmly situated in the Midlands. Close to the town of Peterborough, it is a mere 85 miles from London up the A1 and only halfway to Sheffield, a town with real northern credentials. York is another 125 miles north of Fotheringhay. Richard moved into the heart of Yorkshire while still a boy and it was certainly in the north that he felt most at home, but his birth place was not in the north. The languid meandering of the River Nene as it wandered slowly through the Midlands and Norfolk towards the Wash provided Fotheringhay Castle with its moat as it passed. The first glimpse of England available to the young Richard, perhaps after clambering up the spiral staircase in the great stone keep and peering gingerly through the battlements, would have afforded him with an extensive panorama of flat, green fields interspersed with large wooded areas stretching for miles towards the horizon. Only the forlorn remains of the mound upon which the keep once stood are left today. Nothing more of the once great edifice remains. The towering fortress that so dominated the land and boasted proudly the power and prestige of the duke of York has all but disappeared. The peaceful but desolate spot has a poignancy made sharper by the knowledge that the great misfortune suffered by Fotheringhay had nothing to do with the fall of the House of York. Warwick Castle and Middleham in Wensleydale are both testaments to the ability of their great seats to survive. A century after Richard III's death, however, it was at Fotheringhay that Queen Elizabeth I had her cousin, Mary Queen of Scots, imprisoned and executed. When James I, Mary's son, became king of England after Elizabeth's death, he vented his deep hatred of the place that had provided the last quiet moments of his mother's life, and razed it to the ground. Having stood mighty and impregnable throughout the Wars of the Roses, Fotheringhay Castle succumbed to the vengeance of the first Stuart king of England. The castle in which Richard was born was 'slighted': a word that hardly does justice to the destruction it brought.

The only written evidence concerning Richard's early years comes from a contemporary poem commemorating all the names of the children born to Cecily Neville, duchess of York. Cecily had 13 children, only seven of whom survived childhood. The verses tell us that of her last seven children only two survived the rigours and risks of medieval infancy. Three sons died, one after the other, before George was born, to be followed by another son who died. Richard was then born and, the poet informs us, 'liveth yit'. Cecily went on to give birth to her last child, a girl who died in infancy. When the poet tells us that Richard was still alive, he may have been suggesting that, given the rather bald survival statistics emanating from Cecily's numerous confinements, Richard was not expected to live for very long. This has led some historians to associate the words with the later stories of his unnatural birth and its associated deformities. There is no evidence to support these tales. The words 'liveth yit' should, first and foremost, be taken as a simple statement of fact. Richard, in other words, was still alive when the poem was written. The poet makes no comment on any of the other 12 children except to tell us whether they were alive or not, and having told us that Thomas 'born was, which sone aftir did pace by the path of dethe to the hevenly place', he says Richard is still alive 'but the last of alle was Ursula, to Hym whom God list calle'. Richard, in other words, was surrounded by death but appeared to be surviving against the odds. This might equally signify a robust constitution as a feeble one. Richard was the fourth and youngest son of Cecily and Richard. Although his parents were both from the upper reaches of the nobility, of ducal rank and royal blood, no one could possibly have predicted that their youngest son would ever become king. To have supposed that two of their sons would become kings would have been unimaginable in 1452.[2]

RICHARD'S MOTHER: CECILY NEVILLE

Cecily seems to have been unfortunate in the number of her losses, but not unusually so. She lost six of her 13 children before they reached adulthood, but her sister Eleanor lost five out of 10, and both sisters fared better than their elder sister, Katherine, who had only three children from all of her four marriages. The records show that large families in which most, or all, of the children survived were not uncommon. Cecily's father, Ralph, had married Cecily's mother only after the death of his first wife, Margaret Stafford, who had borne nine children and only lost one. Cecily's eldest brother, Richard, earl of Salisbury, had 10 children by his wife Alice Montacute, and all 10 survived. Of course survival in the middle of the 15th century was not only dependent on the ability of the mother to bear healthy children. Of Richard earl of Salisbury's four sons, only one survived the vicissitudes of fortune caused by the Wars of the Roses while three were killed in battle. The fourth, George Neville, only survived because he entered the Church and became a bishop. The number of Cecily's children who survived was fairly similar to that of her own mother, Joan Beaufort, who had 14 children, of whom 10 survived.

One cause of difficulty may have been the arduous nature of the constant travelling Cecily seems to have undertaken in her commitment to follow her husband as he undertook various responsibilities abroad. Cecily gave birth to children in places as far apart as Rouen and Dublin. There may have been other, medical problems. The verse telling us that Richard 'liveth yit' begins by stating that Cecily gave birth to her first child, Anne, 'after the tyme of longe bareynesse'. This was in 1439. The poet fails to mention an earlier daughter, Joan, who did not survive and may have been born in 1438. Cecily was betrothed to marry Richard, duke of York, at the age of 9, in 1424, and married him sometime before October 1429. The fact that it took the couple almost 10 years to produce a child strongly suggests some unexplained difficulty. Cecily might only have been 14 at the time of the marriage, which may have caused problems, but this was not an uncommonly young age for aristocratic girls to marry in the Middle Ages. Whatever the cause of her long period of barrenness it casts her subsequent 13 pregnancies in 13 years in an heroic light.

Cecily Neville was born on 3 May 1415 at Castle Raby in County Durham. She signed her own name 'Cecylle' and was known as 'the Rose of Raby' and also 'Proud Cis'. Both these appellations suggest something about her: she was famous for her beauty and her indomitable spirit. Her father, Ralph Neville, first earl of Westmorland, having been well rewarded for services on the Scottish border by Richard II, nevertheless supported the king's rival, Henry Bolingbroke, and helped him usurp the throne in 1399. Cecily's father, in other words, helped to create the Lancastrian dynasty. Ralph had recently married his second wife, Joan Beaufort, who was the half-sister of Henry Bolingbroke. When Henry became King Henry IV, Ralph became one of his chief supporters and a mainstay of the regime. Henry IV's son, Henry V, continued to place absolute trust in Ralph, leaving him behind in England to secure the northern frontier while he, the hero of the battle of Agincourt, was busy conquering France. Cecily's mother, Joan, was the fourth and youngest child of John of Gaunt by his mistress, Katherine Swynford, whom he later married. Joan was his only daughter. John of Gaunt was the third son of Edward III and, as duke of Lancaster, the progenitor of the Lancastrian dynasty. Cecily was, therefore, the great-granddaughter of Edward III. Royal blood flowed in her veins.

RICHARD'S FATHER: RICHARD DUKE OF YORK

When Cecily was 10 years old her father betrothed her to Richard, duke of York, who was then but 14 years of age. Richard Plantagenet, third duke of York, was born on 21 September 1411. His father, Richard earl of Cambridge, was the second son of Edmund Langley, duke of York, who was the fourth surviving son of Edward III. The Lancastrians, descended from the third son of Edward III, would always take precedence and have a stronger claim to the throne than the descendants of the duke of York. The order in which the sons were born determined their seniority. The House of Lancaster would always have had a superior claim to the English throne than the House of York, if it hadn't been for the fact that in 1406 Richard earl of Cambridge married Anne Mortimer. Anne was the great-granddaughter of Lionel, duke of Clarence, who just happened to be the second son of Edward III. What this meant was that any son born to Anne Mortimer and Richard earl of Cambridge would be descended from both the second and the fourth sons of Edward III and be able to trump the claims of the Lancastrians. Anne's first child was a daughter, Isabel, whose descendants were to become the powerful Bourchier family. Her second child was a son, Richard, who inherited her superior claim. Anne died after giving birth to her son but her husband, Richard earl of Cambridge, allied with her brother, Edmund Mortimer, to try to overthrow Henry V and place Edmund on the throne. The 'Southampton Plot' failed and Richard earl of Cambridge was duly executed in August 1415. His son, Richard, was now an orphan, having lost his mother in childbirth and his father at the age of 4.

Somewhat luckily for Richard, a few weeks after these dismal proceedings his uncle, Edward duke of York, was killed in the battle of Agincourt. The victorious Henry V was generous to the little orphan and, rather than completely disinheriting the son of a traitor, he allowed him to inherit the title and some of the considerable lands of his childless uncle who had died so heroically in battle. Richard was to become the third duke of York. The valuable wardship of this now fortunate boy eventually fell into the hands of Ralph, earl of Westmorland and, when he died in 1425, he bequeathed it to his wife Joan Beaufort. Thus it was that Richard, duke of York, was married to Ralph's daughter, Cecily.[3]

To gain a fuller understanding of Richard III it is necessary to have some knowledge of the career of his father and of the impulses that motivated him. The background to his early life in the upper echelons of aristocratic society is illuminated by the blazing trail of the incandescent reign of Henry V. Henry was the archetypal medieval warrior-king, establishing firm order and justice, extending his borders and enriching his subjects with opportunities to exploit the supine weaknesses of his enemies. His victories in France were to become woven into the fabric of English nationhood and self-belief. All future kings would necessarily be judged according to the high standard set by this ideal king. Henry V died in 1422 leaving behind a glorious military reputation, a vast extension of English sovereignty over French territory and a baby son, Henry VI. This son turned out to be so unlike his martial father that his reign witnessed the complete reversal of English fortunes in France and the outbreak of the disastrous Wars of the Roses. In two generations the English saw the sunlit uplands of military glory abroad disappear into the murky bog of bloody civil conflict at home. Initially, the regency of John duke of Bedford, Henry V's brother and the uncle of the infantile Henry VI, was successful in maintaining the English initiative in France and consolidating the achievements of Henry V. It was this man, the duke of Bedford, who, more than anyone else, influenced the future conduct of Richard duke of York and epitomized the hopes and ambitions of the young duke. At the age of 14 Richard duke of York was knighted by Bedford in a ceremony laden with powerful emotional and spiritual meaning. The young Richard swore to serve his lord, the duke of Bedford, faithfully and truly, even unto death. Bedford for his part, having become the liege lord of his protégé, swore to protect him and defend him as became a good lord. They were bound together in a relationship of mutual advantage and dependency that placed enormous emphasis on the highest human virtues and ideals. For the fatherless Richard, this would have been one of the defining moments of his life.

RICHARD DUKE OF YORK IN FRANCE

Both of Henry V's surviving brothers, John, duke of Bedford and Humphrey, duke of Gloucester, spent their lives committed to preserving English possessions in France and thereby defending their great brother's legacy. It was to prove an uphill and ultimately fruitless struggle. When Bedford died in 1435 English hopes took a severe blow. They had lost one of their ablest commanders and a man whose integrity and leadership were to be sorely missed. His mantle passed to Richard, duke of York. The 25-year-old duke had inherited vast estates stretching from Wales to Lincoln and from Yorkshire to Sussex. His lands in Wales, the Marches and Ireland gave him independent wealth and power. Many of Bedford's men transferred their services to York and the council appointed him lieutenant governor of France, at first only temporarily but then in 1440 for a five-year term. He attempted to retain as much of England's French territories as possible under the misapprehension, shared by all optimistic contemporaries, that King Henry VI would come of age and assume personal rule. His presence in France would reignite memories of his father and serve to inspire the English captains with hope and enthusiasm. Tragically for them, and happily for the French, this never happened. Henry VI turned out to be quite incapable of providing leadership of any kind, and certainly not of the military variety. Those closest to him, particularly Cardinal Beaufort, Cecily's cousin, realized this and tried to make the best of a bad job. The aim of the Beaufort-dominated council was, increasingly, to secure peace with France in order to secure Normandy and Gascony.[4]

This was a policy York would always struggle to accept. As a young lieutenant governor he had restored English authority in Normandy and put the French king to flight. A failure by the royal administration in England to support his efforts in France would inevitably be seen by York as incompetence and even betrayal. By inheriting Bedford's role and his expectations, and through them the legacy of Henry V, York became the last beacon of hope for those who yearned for a return to the good old days. France was the natural enemy, and English rule over the French was the right of all Englishmen whose ancestors had shed their blood in the noble cause. Good governance at home and military success abroad brought prosperity and security to the common weal. With the French monarchy under Charles VII resurgent, however, and the English under Henry VI ineffective, York's values would seem increasingly outdated and impractical. He was already set on a collision course with the Beaufort administration. It was in this way that the Hundred Years War against France became the Wars of the Roses in England. York can be criticised in many ways but ultimately his life was a testament to the tragic futility of upholding a lost cause. His son, Richard, was to inherit some characteristics of his outlook and approach.

York came to be seen by the court in England as a dangerous outsider. He not only had a strong claim to the throne, but his independent position threatened their own security. The problem caused by Henry VI's ineptitude was that decisions emanating from the king's council could always be viewed as partisan. It was perhaps inevitable that decisions did indeed become motivated by self-interest as much as by the needs of good government and sound policy. The fear of accusations of corruption was often sufficient to justify measures that might damage opponents and strengthen the power of supporters. A weak king allowed the natural tensions and rivalries that always existed among the higher nobility to descend into bitter feud.

York was successful in maintaining English authority over Normandy and became increasingly frustrated by the failures of the Beaufort-dominated council to prosecute the war with the same degree of success elsewhere, particularly in Gascony. A marriage alliance had been concluded between Henry VI's court and Charles VII of France, which saw the king of France's niece, Margaret of Anjou, become Henry VI's queen. York was prepared to negotiate with France, indeed he had been negotiating a marriage between his own son, Edward, and one of the daughters of the king of France, but only from a position of strength. If there was to be peace in France it was to be to the lasting advantage of English interests there. There should be dynastic security for English landowners and their tenants to support the military endeavours of her soldiers. York's stay in France, meanwhile, produced a crop of infants for his wife, Cecily. Edward, Edmund and Elizabeth were all born there in successive years from 1442 to 1444. More important, York's sons, Edward and Richard, would inherit their father's assumptions about France. It was a military playground to be exploited by the English for glory, land and profit. It was also lawfully and rightfully, they believed, an inheritance of the English crown. This assumption was to cost Richard dear in the end. The French backed his enemies in 1485.

YORK VERSUS HENRY VI

In the end the manifest incompetence of Henry VI's regime, dominated by Edmund Beaufort, duke of Somerset, and the failure of the government to either bring the war in France to a successful conclusion or to back York's efforts to do so, led to the beginning of dynastic conflict. York was incensed by the retrenchment of the Beaufort council and his manifest exclusion. Henry VI was a weak king without an heir and the duke of York believed that his descent from the second son of Edward III gave him the right to be recognized as the heir to the throne. Henry

VI's council were determined to prevent this happening. Quite when York began to think of himself as an alternative to the non-king miserably malingering on the throne is not at all clear. He did not seriously advance this claim until 1459, but he was resolutely determined by 1452 to force the government to recognise his legitimate claim to be the heir presumptive. Its deliberate failure to do so was a direct assault on his noble dignity and royal lineage. York was angry at the way Edmund Beaufort dominated the government, despite losing Normandy to the French. As he explained in a letter to the city of Shrewsbury in February 1452:

> the said Duke of Somerset ... laboreth continually about the King's highness for my undoing, and to corrupt my blood, and to disinherit me and my heirs, and such persons as be about me.

Again, the reference to the corruption of his blood is one that has echoes during the usurpation of 1483. Richard III seems to have inherited this concept of pure blood and the legitimacy it bore.[5]

York raised troops and marched on London but in the tension and confusion in the capital he was again out-manoeuvred by Somerset and forced to make a humiliating climb-down at Dartford in 1452. York was allowed to present a petition to the king outlining his grievances but had to take an oath of loyalty to the king in St Paul's Cathedral. He returned to Ludlow to nurse his grievances, but was pursued by Somerset. The king washed up with his entire Somerset-dominated court at Ludlow in July 1452 to hear indictments against trouble-makers in recent disturbances. This could only be seen as a deliberate threat to York, many of his personal retainers being exposed to the charges brought against them by the royal commissioners in the county. The show of lordly unity and royal power on York's own doorstep must have been a carefully planned assault on his perceived pretensions. In the light of these dangers York moved to Fotheringhay in early August and remained there for several months while Somerset consolidated his position and reduced York's lordships and offices wherever and whenever he could. Cecily, as ever, was with her husband at Fotheringhay. It was in these dangerous and difficult circumstances, with her thwarted, angry and anxious husband at hand, that the duchess of York gave birth to her fourth surviving son, Richard.

THE WIDER CONTEXT

The backdrop to Richard's 32 years and 10 months of life was to be the bloody civil war known as the Wars of the Roses, between the Lancastrians and the Yorkists. This would shape his upbringing and character in incalculable ways. He was directly involved in the fighting from the age of 17, or even a little earlier, and in the thick of battle twice. His father and a brother were killed in the fighting, while another brother was to be executed. Relatives and friends were lost and two ignominious flights into exile had to be endured before peace was eventually restored. His brother Edward IV established the fortunes of the house of York and restored the authority of the crown after a catastrophic period of Lancastrian misrule under Henry VI. During this golden period Richard was given extensive command over the north and established himself as a regional magnate greater than any before in English history. This was the background to the shocking events of 1483 when Edward IV died leaving a 12-year-old boy to inherit the throne.

There was, however, an even bigger stage upon which all these events were being played. When the Hundred Years War was coming to an end, in the first year of Richard's life, and the Wars of the Roses were starting, in his third year, Europe itself was undergoing significant changes. When Richard was not yet 1 year old, Constantinople, the capital of the Eastern Roman Empire, fell to the Turks. Refugees from the east had been flooding into Europe bringing new ideas with them. A Renaissance had begun to flower in Italy, centred on the Florence of the Medici, which was to reach its zenith during Richard's reign. There were even greater changes taking place across the world. Exploration was in its infancy but already opening up a wider world. The technology to produce gun powder was beginning to have an impact in warfare and was to change the military structures of Richard's world. Artillery and handguns were becoming a feature of a new kind of warfare. The printing press had also been successfully adopted in northern Europe and was to have a massive impact on the spread of ideas. This was a changing world in which inherited values might begin to appear threatened or might be abandoned and considered obsolete. All this may have been unconsciously felt by Richard as he learnt the arts of war and command, of diplomacy and government. His father certainly stood for the values of what was already a bygone era when Richard reached manhood. If we examine Richard's character and behaviour closely we often see an image of the duke of York behind the choices he made and the people he trusted. We know what happened in the fateful year of 1483, but we don't know why Richard acted then in the way he did. It may, however, be significant that the father he so revered had staged a coup of his own, 24 years before. He had failed and died in the attempt, but the reasons the duke of York acted in the way he did had some echoes in the actions of his son.

A NOTE ON THE PRIMARY SOURCES FOR THE REIGN

There are contemporary accounts of the events before and during Richard's reign. Richard lived at a time when the number of letters and vernacular chronicles written by merchants and the gentry class was increasing. At the same time the staple of medieval history, the monastic chronicles written in Latin, were in serious decline. This has left us with a lack of a broad objective account of the period, but nevertheless with some useful, often idiosyncratic and local, material. We can also benefit from the foreign interest in events in England and the consequent record left by continental visitors. On top of all this there are routine administrative documents that shed light on the workings and intentions of government officials and their bosses.

The most important account of events comes from the chronicler known as the Second Continuator of the Croyland, or Crowland, Chronicle. This appears to be a continuation of the monastic chronicles for the Fenland abbey of Croyland in Lincolnshire, but it is in fact a sophisticated piece of historical writing by an intelligent and very well-informed government official. He had inside knowledge of the operation of the court of Edward IV and was an eye-witness to several key events close to the king. He had a professional interest in, and experience of, politics, diplomacy and the workings of chancery. Although he was anonymous, a reasonable case has been made for identifying him as Henry Sharp, a high-ranking chancery official who attended council meetings and went on diplomatic missions for Edward IV. He wrote the whole account in 10 days in April 1486. The first thing that needs to be said about him is that he was noticeably critical, hostile even, to Richard. He disliked northerners in general, which did not improve his objectivity, but he particularly distrusted and disliked Richard. There are a number of possible explanations for this prejudice, the first of which is that his successful career at the court of Edward IV appears to have been in decline during Richard's reign. More significantly, he seems to have identified himself with the personnel at the heart of Edward's regime. The turmoil of Richard's usurpation adversely affected the world of the Croyland chronicler. In particular, there is evidence in his text of a familiarity with Edward's children and, given that Richard's usurpation was not in their best interests, this may be the source of his disapproval.[6]

As the Croyland chronicler was bringing the clerical tradition of monastic chronicles written in Latin to a close, so a new form of historical writing was emerging in the form of civic narrative histories designed to appeal to the new literate class of laymen. The first appeared in the capital and are known as the 'London chronicles'. These are compilations of various writers, each adding their own knowledge and experience to an annalistic framework. They make no attempt at commentary or analysis, merely recording whatever seemed important to the leading citizens of London. Rumour and superstition are mixed arbitrarily with concrete fact, and all is centred on London and its interests alone. There are three versions of these chronicles, all closely related and probably drawing on a lost original source. Their value lies in their ability to reveal to us the prevailing climate of opinion at crucial moments during the confused weeks of the usurpation. They are known as *Vitellius A XVI*, the *New Chronicles of England and of France* and the *Great Chronicle of London*. The first was probably *Vitellius A XVI*, written in the early 1490s. It gets its ungainly name from its shelf reference in the British Museum, where it is properly referred to as *British Museum MS Cotton Vitellius A. XVI*. The *New Chronicles* and the *Great Chronicle* were probably written by the same man, Robert Fabyan, before 1502. Fabyan, or Fabian, was a citizen of London, a master of the Draper's Company, who rose to become an alderman of the city and then, in 1492–3, a sheriff of London. The *New Chronicles* are often referred to as *Fabyan's Chronicle*. Although he died in 1513, he lived and worked in London during the crucial period, 1483–85, and his record of events gives us a first-hand account by an eye-witness. All three differ, the *Great Chronicle*, in particular, adding views on the fate of the princes and Richard's culpability, but all are also interrelated. This is valuable contemporary material but it has to be used with caution. It contains inaccuracies, inconsistencies and basic errors, with a pronounced tendency to treat rumour as fact. Furthermore, the signs of having been written up in the reign of Henry Tudor are evident.[7]

Of the foreign visitors to England who wrote about political events, by far the most important is Dominic Mancini. His *Usurpation of Richard III* is the closest contemporary account of the events surrounding the usurpation, and is critically hostile to Richard. The original title of the work reads *De Occupatione*, rather than *Usurpatione*, having been mistranslated by its discoverer and first editor, C. A. J. Armstrong. This difference, first pointed out by Jeremy Potter in *Good King Richard?* (1988), has been seized upon by Ricardians as evidence of both Armstrong's prejudice and Mancini's reluctance to call the usurpation anything more than an occupation. There may be something to be said in both cases, but nothing will change the fact that Mancini portrayed Richard's seizure of the throne, through his 'insane lust for power', as a brutal and outrageous usurpation. Mancini was an Italian cleric trained in the humanist tradition and came to England in 1482 as part of some sort of diplomatic mission. His actual role in London is something of a mystery, and he may even have been a spy, but he was in the pay of his patron Angelo Cato, archbishop of Vienne. Cato himself was a councillor of Louis XI of France, who would have been keen to get information on events in England. Mancini was recalled to France shortly after Richard's coronation on 6 July 1483, probably to enable him to write his account. He is by no means impartial and his work contains factual errors, but it is nevertheless a contemporary history of enormous value. His knowledge seems to have been gathered from a combination of public pronouncements, rumour and information gleaned from fellow Italians. Mancini mentions one of these, a certain Dr Argentine, who happened to be the physician to Edward V and was probably one of the last people to see the boy alive. Mancini is unlikely to have been able to speak any English but John Argentine, though English himself, spoke fluent Italian having lived and trained in Italy for many years. With an informant so close to the entourage of the princes in the Tower it is probably not surprising that the account of the usurpation was so hostile to Richard. The manuscript was lost for centuries until it was discovered in 1934 in the municipal library at Lille, by C. A. J. Armstrong. The immediate impact of the discovery, and its publication in 1936, was the revelation that there was widespread hostility towards Richard well before the Tudor propaganda machine began to creak into life.[8]

Another foreign observer, more distant geographically but more astute politically, was Philippe de Commynes, a councillor at the court of Louis XI of France who, like Mancini, was persuaded by the ever-curious archbishop Cato to write his *Memoirs*, between 1488 and 1504. Commynes is a well informed commentator but has opinions of his own that he is all too happy to share. He, like Mancini, viewed Richard with considerable distrust and suspicion. There have been suggestions that this was because their patron was keen to hear a good story, preferably showing the Yorkist government of England in a bad light, and both Mancini and Commynes were willing to oblige. It is possible that Cato was motivated as much by a love of intrigue as of plain facts, but at least our two foreign correspondents were in tune with the common report. They were both writing with a little hindsight but they certainly reveal a common understanding of the events they describe and the contemporary European perspective on Richard. We have no cause to doubt that what they wrote was what they believed.[9]

The private correspondence of gentry families, reflecting both the growing importance of this class of society and improvements in levels of literacy in the 15th century, throw some light on the events of the period. The correspondence of four families has survived, but by far the most voluminous and significant is that of the Paston family from Norfolk. The Paston letters allow us to follow the fortunes of three generations of the Paston family from the 1440s to the 1480s. In their particular case local preoccupations involved them, often reluctantly, in affairs on the national stage. Their interests were still very much parochial and personal but they allow us to see how such families attempted to navigate safely through the troubled waters of the 15th century. Much of their correspondence relates to the period before Richard became king and only four letters have a bearing on his reign. There is even less relevant material in the collections of the other families. The Plumptons of Yorkshire have left us only three letters dated from Richard's reign, only one of which has material relating to national events. The Stonors of Oxfordshire and Berkshire were also preoccupied with their own local interests but their papers do contain two intriguing newsletters written from London in June 1483. The Cely family of London wool merchants have left us with their letters and business papers too but these are, frustratingly, nearly all bereft of newsworthy information apart from a brief summary jotted down in the turmoil of June 1483.[10]

In addition there are administrative records, both national and local, that enable us to witness the routine operations of government and occasionally to draw conclusions from them. Often these tell us very little of national importance but sometimes they are able to indicate the will of the political masters behind the bureaucratic ministrations of the salaried officials. Many of these have been calendared and printed. The most relevant tend to be the *Calendar of the Patent Rolls*, recording the issuing of grants, instructions and commissions in 'Open Letters' sealed with the Great Seal. This seal was kept by the chancellor and used on all official documents leaving his department, the chancery, giving them the authority and authenticity of royal proclamations. The *Calendar of Close Rolls*, on the other hand, were closed, and meant only for the eyes of the addressee. Before these documents reached the chancellor and his officials they might be discussed, recorded and issued by the king himself in his chamber. The document would then be sealed either by the Privy Seal or by the Signet with instructions on whether to send the letter open or closed, or to by-pass the chancery altogether. A great deal of this material exists in a collection known as *British Library Harleian MS 433*. There are also insights to be gained in the interaction between royal government and the localities in records such as the duchy of Lancaster archives and the York civic records.[11]

What all this might suggest is a rich variety of original sources offering the prospect of an unambiguous narrative of events. Quite the opposite is in fact the case. It is the yawning gaps in the evidence, the crucial silences and the lack of corroboration that strike historians and hamper their efforts. Furthermore, much of the evidence is tainted with prejudice and hindsight and has to be treated with caution. This is one of the reasons why the reign of Richard is so controversial and subject to so many different interpretations. What the original sources do not provide is unequivocal evidence of motive and it is precisely the question of motive that is so important to an understanding of the usurpation of 1483 and the subsequent fate of the princes in the Tower. Without that evidence it is hardly surprising that so much of the writing about Richard III has been mere speculation. We can make informed assumptions about his motives, but in the end we can never be absolutely sure we are right. Even if we achieve a consistent portrait of his character, one that manages to account for his actions before and after he became king, we will not have accounted for the inconsistencies with which most human beings are endowed. Because Richard's behaviour appears to have been unpredictable at a key moment in his life, both his contemporaries and his historians have found it impossible to provide a definitive account that will stand the test of time. It is however possible to examine the influences acting upon him and to draw some conclusions from them.

1

THE SON OF YORK:
1452–1461

CASTILLON 1453

Richard was born at a dangerous time for his father and for the whole family. He would, no doubt, have been blissfully unaware of the storm clouds gathering over the House of York during his early years. The first battle between Somerset and York took place when Richard was only 2 years old. No one at that time realized that this was the beginning of the Wars of the Roses, a prolonged and protracted conflict costing thousands of lives, but the growing tension and political volatility would have been apparent to all. Richard grew from infant to boy in this climate, but, from what we can tell, spent his early years in the usual secure aristocratic environment a child of his rank might expect. He was 6 years old when the peace and security of the nursery were shattered by the realities and dangers of armed conflict.

In the first few months of Richard's life, Somerset's star was in the ascendant. The three areas of major concern – disorder in the shires, military losses in France and the succession question – were all apparently being resolved. The king's itineration and the hearing of the commissions of oyer and terminer gave a reasonable semblance of the reassertion of royal justice in the localities. John Talbot, earl of Shrewsbury, had arrived at Bordeaux on 17 October 1452, with a relatively small force, to find the gates of the town flung open to greet him. The rest of Gascony seemed only too glad to welcome the English back. As for the succession issue, the best of all outcomes seemed in prospect with the news that the queen, Margaret of Anjou, was pregnant. Against all the odds it was possible that Henry VI had produced an heir. To consolidate his grip on power, and to give added security to the Lancastrian regime, Somerset had promoted the king's two half-brothers, Edmund and Jasper Tudor, to the ranks of the peerage, making them, in November 1452, the earls of Richmond and Pembroke respectively. They were then richly endowed with the lands formerly held by the dukes of Bedford and Gloucester. As Richard prepared to experience his first Christmas and the long dark nights of winter, Somerset must have felt the warm glow of security and success enveloping the royal household.

On 17 July 1453 John Talbot, earl of Shrewsbury, was catastrophically defeated at the battle of Castillon and all English hopes in Gascony destroyed. Talbot had been rather too confident in the ability of his men to defeat the French whenever they encountered them. At Castillon he had been taken completely by surprise when 300 cannon had opened fire from behind a well-defended palisade, with deadly results. Cannon could out-fire archers by a hundred yards and Talbot's knights were equally helpless against the onslaught of burning iron. Talbot had glimpsed the future; the roar of the guns at Castillon not only shocked the English troops but they also sounded the death knell of the Middle Ages. The English commander became one of the very last victims of the Hundred Years War. As one of the cannon balls hit his horse and caused it to fall on top of him, at least the injured Talbot, now forced to wait helplessly while the French charged out of their battlements, had the satisfaction of being killed in the more traditional manner, by a battle-axe.

Talbot's death was a consequence of a reinvigorated French monarchy under Charles VII being pitted against the pathetic military virtues of Henry VI of England. The battle of Castillon represented the culmination of the disintegration of English authority in France, not its cause. The consequences of the defeat were profound on both sides of the Channel. In England, factionalism, bitter recrimination and local feuding increased and flourished in the climate of uncertainty emerging from royal failure. The twin personal responsibilities of the monarch – peace at home and success abroad – had been disastrously abdicated. It is no coincidence that less than two years elapsed between the battle of Castillon, the last battle in the Hundred Years War, and the battle of St Albans, the first battle in the Wars of the Roses. Failure of English arms abroad was to contribute to the causes of a bloody civil war which, in turn, was to provide the turbulent backdrop to Richard's life. War against the common enemy for the glory and posterity of the whole realm was to be transformed into an insidious, endemic violence that tore friends and families apart, destroyed justice and converted aspiring ranks to the idolatry of self-interest. This was the changing world in which the youngest son of the duke of York grew to manhood.

As news of the English defeat in France in 1453 filtered through in early August, its impact was compounded by another calamity closer to home. Possibly as a consequence of hearing the news that English hopes in France were at an end, Henry VI suffered a severe mental breakdown. News of the king's incapacity spread as quickly as news of the defeat at Castillon. Then, in October, the queen gave birth to a son. From this time the constitutional crisis caused by the king's incapacity would be shadowed by the queen's determination to secure the succession for her son, Prince Edward.[1]

YORK MADE PROTECTOR

York realised that compromise was necessary and on 15 March 1454 he recognised Prince Edward as heir to the throne. The infant was promptly created prince of Wales, five months late, and earl of Chester. Two weeks later York was offered the post of protector. In 1422, upon the untimely death of his father, Henry V, the infant Henry VI had been given joint protectors in the form of his uncles, Gloucester and Bedford. Over 30 years later he was once more under a protectorate. What made the situation even more ironic was the fact that Prince Edward, it was proclaimed, would succeed to the protectorate when he reached the age of discretion. Monarchy in general was protected in this way, and, in particular, the Lancastrian dynasty. A broad consensus accepted the authority of the duke of York to lead a council that would rule while, and only while, the monarchy was in abeyance. One telling feature of the arrangement is the presumption that it would not be Henry who would be restored to his former power, but his son. No one seems to have predicted Henry's rather extraordinary recovery.

Looking forward 30 years, suggestive parallels emerge. When the duke of York's son, Richard, 2 years old during his father's first protectorate, was to face a constitutional crisis in 1483, he also was to challenge a court faction lead by the queen. Then, too, there would be a young Prince Edward. Once again a protectorate would provide a temporary solution. Excluding York from the counsels of the king and the avenues of power in 1453 led to sharp divisions among the nobility and the potential for endemic violence to descend into war. A solution of sorts was found in 1454, even if it was to be destroyed by the king's return to health. In 1483 Richard, then duke of Gloucester, sought the retention of his already existing power, security from powerful and possibly malicious opponents, and a wider, if vague, consideration for the public weal. In York's case, Prince Edward was so young that it was possible to believe that a long-term solution to the crisis might emerge over time. In Richard's case it was precisely this emollient time factor that was missing. Prince Edward of 1483 was 12 years old and could already voice his own opinions. Richard's solution in 1483 was to swiftly end the protectorate and to usurp the throne. If his father in 1454 genuinely accepted the legitimacy of Prince Edward, his own claims were never too far from his mind and were to surface soon enough. Richard duke of Gloucester would have a precedent to follow when he claimed the throne.

The real problem was not so much that in January 1455 Henry miraculously regained his wits, such as they were, but that in so doing Queen Margaret took control of the reins of government. Somerset was released from the Tower, York's protectorate brought to an end and a determined attempt was made to exercise power from within the narrow confines of the royal household once again. During his year as protector York had not only restored a semblance of order in the north and west, but he had also rewarded his allies sufficiently to give him some insurance for the future. Salisbury had been made chancellor and Warwick, Salisbury's son, had become convinced that York could protect him from his own disputes with Somerset. These two Nevilles, brother and nephew of Cecily, had become supporters of York. York could not have dreamt that King Henry would regain his faculties, but York's failure to deal with the duke of Somerset during his protectorate was to haunt him for the rest of his life. If Somerset had been reconciled in some way to the new order he might not have emerged from the Tower quite so determined to destroy York and the Nevilles. On the other hand the solution York's son adopted in 1483, disposing of threats and potential threats quickly, may, with hindsight, have prevented a bloody civil war, but went too far beyond the judicial norms for the duke of York to chance. Constitutional propriety still meant much in 1454. In the end, however, both were forced to prosecute their claims in battle.

THE FIRST BATTLE OF ST ALBANS

Richard was just 2½ when his father and the Nevilles gathered their armed retinues and prepared to march south against the king. Margaret and Somerset had summoned a great council to meet at Leicester in May 1455, and it was clear that they were determined to destroy their enemies. The young child ensconced in his nursery at Fotheringhay would have been blissfully unaware of the anxiety and commotion around him. His older brothers, on the other hand, would have had some understanding of what their father was about to do. Edward was 13 and Edmund 12, both already earls and both already established in their own households with their own retainers. Aristocratic youths grew up very quickly in the 15th century. Edward, earl of March, had already accompanied his father to London at the head of his own Welsh troops and with his brother Edmund, earl of Rutland, had attended a great council of the realm in February 1454. Their youngest brother Richard is unlikely to have seen much of these busy earls. Similarly, the elder girls, Anne and Elizabeth, had already left the roost. Anne had been married since 1449 to the rather unstable Henry Holland, duke of Exeter, and Elizabeth, though only 11 years old, would have been living in another aristocratic household, possibly that of the de la Pole family into which she was shortly to marry. Richard's remaining siblings, Margaret aged 9 and George aged 5, were, like Richard, still with their mother. The tensions between their father and the Lancastrian regime led by Somerset were about to erupt into violence and bloodshed.

The first battle of St Albans, so named to distinguish it from the second battle that took place there six years later, was little more than a brief clash between the armed retinues of a few lords. It might have sunk into the oblivion of barely recorded skirmishes if the poisonous seeds it sowed had not borne fruit four years later. It has become notorious as the first battle in the Wars of the Roses but its true significance lies in the words of York's subsequent declaration in which he attempted to justify his manifest treason. He had been forced to take up arms against the king, he argued, in the first place to exercise his right of self-defence, but also to seek and do justice. Royal authority, in other words, was not sufficient in itself to compel loyalty. Its failure to exercise justice had led to disorder throughout the land. The king himself had 'to be reformed'. Furthermore the battle has rightly been viewed as a turning-point because it unleashed an unstoppable blood-feud that could only be satiated by death. Feud had its own horrific conventions in which entire kin-groups were held responsible for the actions of their members. Injury could only be requited by injury, insult by insult and murder by murder. This was the law of the jungle that every civilised society strove to avoid. The first battle of St Albans released the furies and they lurked and lunged for the next 30 years. Aristocratic conventions, built over years through education and religion, were paper thin in the face of the onslaught of primal emotion engendered by feud.

As York and the Nevilles intercepted the royal party at St Albans, a desperate attempt was made to effect a reconciliation. Somerset was dismissed from his recent appointment as constable of England, and the duke of Buckingham, sagacious and trustworthy, attempted to negotiate with York's party. York wanted nothing less than the arrest of Somerset once more, on charges of conspiring to influence the king against him. Although there can be little doubt that this is precisely what Somerset had been doing, Buckingham could not comply. The king had already pardoned Somerset for similar offences when the duke had been released from the Tower a few months earlier. Only the king could undo a royal pardon and, in a tacit admission of the tight grip the queen and Somerset had on the royal person, no action against Somerset was possible. Not by legal means, that is. As Buckingham stalled and waited for the reinforcements that had been urgently summoned, York returned to his troops camped outside the walls of St Albans. All peaceful options had been exhausted; what was to become known as the Wars of the Roses was about to begin.

Given that only about 5,000 men took part in the battle and that total casualties on both sides were only about a hundred, what is striking is the number of lords who were killed. Clifford, Northumberland and Somerset were all killed, and lords Wenlock, Dudley, Stafford and Dorset all wounded. Stafford was Buckingham's son and close to the royal party. To show how real the danger to the king had been, one need point no further than to the fact that King Henry himself appears to have received some sort of scratch from the glancing blow of an arrow. An aristocrat fighting in the Hundred Years War would not have expected to have been killed or wounded in battle. He was far too valuable as ransom to be harmed by the enemy. Carefully nurtured chivalric traditions had emerged to ensure that such casualties were light and unintended. A nobleman in danger on the battlefield would offer his assailant an article of his clothing and this would guarantee his safety, and the financial reward of his opponent. Breaches of this convention were rare because it mutually benefited everyone. At St Albans in 1455 they were cast to the winds. There would be no security or reward in giving quarter in a civil war. To allow one's enemies to live would be to invite retribution and revenge rather than recompense. Somerset fled to the Castle Inn but, realising that he was cornered and that there was no escape, stepped out to confront York's men and bravely fought to the death.

York's declared position was that, as a true liegeman of the king, he and his supporters had acted to remove traitors from about the king's person and to restore good government to the realm. To demonstrate their loyalty a crown-wearing ceremony was staged at St Paul's on Whit Sunday, 25 May 1455, and parliament was summoned to assemble on 9 July. The parliament which duly met, apart from condemning York's enemies, did attempt to make a new start by issuing a general pardon to everyone else who had taken part in the battle. It also set up committees to begin the process of reform, particularly in the areas of defence and of royal finances. Nevertheless the world in which the duke and his supporters moved had changed forever. The new government had been imposed by force and the tensions that had exploded into violence at St Albans now simmered beneath the surface. The sons of the dead would always seek revenge and be implacably opposed to York. All appeals to unity and the rule of law would be undermined by the illegal spilling of blood. The marvel is not that the first battle of St Albans is remembered at all, but that it took another four years for major hostilities to be renewed. Civil war was now inevitable.

DESCENT INTO CIVIL WAR

In November 1455 the king became ill again. He was too incapacitated to sit on the throne in parliament and York was already acting as his lieutenant there. A more defined office, 'Protector and Defensor of this land' would give him the authority he needed to act. The speaker, York's retainer William Burley, proposed that York be made protector once more and, not without some hesitation, the lords assented. York's second protectorate only lasted three months, from 19 November 1455 to 25 February 1456, when the king appeared to recover his wits, but in that time Queen Margaret emerged as a new force in politics. Her opposition to York and determination to oust him from power would provide the background to the renewal of armed hostilities. An attempt was made to reconcile the two factions and a 'Loveday' was organized on 24 March 1458, possibly at the instigation of Henry VI. The two sides walked arm in arm through the streets of London for a service of unity and concord in St Paul's Cathedral, but even as the procession moved up Ludgate Hill their armed retinues stood at the ready to defend their leaders in case of treachery. The fundamental divisions remained; York could not reform the government without royal authority and this was now in the hands of Margaret of Anjou. While this situation persisted York was left in increasing danger and would have to take steps to protect himself. The two camps that formed around the chief protagonists were now recognizably Yorkist and Lancastrian.

Margaret had moved the court to the Midlands. She was uncomfortable in London, a city full of merchants and their guilds keen to preserve their trading rights and the financial advantages that stability and good government would bring. These guilds, particularly the Company of the Staplers, preferred to support the duke of York and his apparent sympathy with their interests. In particular, the removal of the duke of Somerset and the appointment of the earl of Warwick as captain of Calais had already brought them the prospect of recovering their investments in the garrison. By 1458 the Yorkists had identified themselves with the interests of the citizens of London in a way that was to become a feature of their future conflicts with the Lancastrians. Combined with the strength of the Calais garrison, this gave them an advantage that was to prove decisive. Margaret increasingly relied on the sons of the three lords killed at St Albans. Henry Beaufort, the son of Edmund Beaufort, was a minor until 1457 but was now the duke of Somerset. Henry Percy had become the third earl of Northumberland after his father, the second earl, had been killed, and John Clifford had become the ninth baron Clifford after the demise of his father, Thomas. The desire to avenge the deaths of their fathers was a potent force when combined with the determination of the queen to rid the court of the influence of York.

BLORE HEATH

In the summer of 1459 Queen Margaret calculated that the time was right to act decisively against the duke of York and his supporters. A great council was summoned to meet at Coventry in June, but York, the Nevilles and their most prominent supporters were not invited. In their absence the Yorkists were indicted. Both sides began mustering and arming troops. The duke of York was at his castle at Ludlow in Shropshire, close to the Welsh border. Warwick set out from Calais with a contingent of the garrison while his father, Salisbury, set out from Middleham. As the Yorkists attempted to rendezvous, the Lancastrians used their strategic advantage in the Midlands to disrupt their communications and attempt to intercept them. Warwick narrowly evaded Somerset's army and reached Ludlow in good order. Salisbury, however, in difficult terrain and narrow roads, was being stalked by Margaret's armies and was finally intercepted.

On 23 September 1459, at Blore Heath, between Newcastle-under-Lyme and Market Drayton, the two armies clashed. Salisbury was outnumbered two to one but had several advantages. The Stanley brothers, the most powerful men in the region, were archetypal trimmers who spent the years of conflict between the Lancastrians and the Yorkists avoiding unnecessary involvement unless it was to their decided advantage. William was the more incautious of the two and could be dangerously impulsive, while Thomas rarely committed himself until he could see for certain which side was winning. They had built up a substantial power-base in the north-west and, throughout the ensuing dynastic struggle, secured their own interests at every opportunity. They were single-mindedly consistent in this regard. Their behaviour at Blore Heath in 1459 was almost exactly replicated at Bosworth in 1485,

26 years later. Before the battle, Margaret had summoned the Stanleys to her aid. As she waited, with Thomas lord Stanley sending her missives assuring her of his intention to lead her forces, Salisbury marched past unmolested. William Stanley, in more dynamic mode, threw in his lot with Salisbury. Not to be outdone, Thomas wrote to Salisbury after the battle congratulating him on his victory. He was later to regret this slip and learnt to be even more circumspect in the future. Blore Heath was a full-scale military encounter with dreadful loss of life. Salisbury won and was able to reach his objective and rendezvous as planned with York, but he had been so severely mauled that the appearance of his army in Ludlow might well have dismayed the duke. Even after Warwick arrived, their combined forces meeting at Ludlow were fewer than hoped and the main Lancastrian armies were still in the field and menacingly close.

THE ROUT OF LUDFORD BRIDGE

During the evening of 12 October 1459, after more desultory attempts at negotiation had failed, the Yorkists once again found themselves facing royal banners advancing on Ludlow. The Calais garrison brought over by Warwick was deeply unhappy about opposing the king in battle and promptly defected to the Lancastrian side. Without these troops the Yorkist position was untenable. They faced a royal army containing the dukes of Somerset, Buckingham and Exeter, the earls of Arundel, Devon, Northumberland, Shrewsbury and Wiltshire, accompanied by many other high profile lords. The king and queen, somewhere at the back, provided the moral imperative that held many lords in thrall and which Trollope, captain of the Calais garrison, could not resist.[2]

At about midnight York, Salisbury and Warwick, along with York's eldest two sons and a few of their closest servants, 'stole away out of the field'. They abandoned their camp under the pretext of seeking refreshment in Ludlow, and simply fled. Their banners were left flying before their tents, and their troops, insofar as they had any notion of what was going on, were left in readiness to engage the enemy in the morning. York, with his second son Edmund, earl of Rutland, fled to Ireland, while Salisbury, Warwick and York's eldest son Edward, earl of March, made their way to Calais.

The parliament that met on 20 November 1459 rather predictably attainted the Yorkist lords. They were accused of treason and their lands forfeit to the crown. Margaret was determined to finish off the job of destroying York and his allies. The assembly became known by the Yorkists as the 'Parliament of Devils', so severe was the extent of the indictments and confiscations. The majority of lords had made their choice. If York wished to reform the way in which royal power was exercised, and in particular purge the crown from the undue influence of the queen and the malign presence of the latest duke of Somerset, they would not support him. They were united in recognition of the need to restore royal authority, but they were not prepared to remove the queen or the king's ministers. Kingship must not be dictated to by powerful lords. The queen appeared to be strengthening the monarchy, while York could now be charged with attacking it. The parliament made it very clear that the justification York had used, that he promoted the common weal, was a responsibility that could only be performed by the king. Certainly they all knew that the king was weak and that something had to be done about it to prevent chaos, but the queen and her chosen lords were beginning to restore law and order. To do what York had done, to demand that the king exercise his kingship in a particular way, was to come too close to attacking the institution of monarchy itself. The personality of the king and the exercise of royal authority were too closely bound together to be separated without serious damage to the body politic. The need for collective security far outweighed the need to indulge in constitutional experiments. These had always been attended by danger and uncertainty.

York's flight at least simplified the issues. He could either accept his fate, the consequence of taking up arms against the king, or he could fight his enemies to restore his ancestral rights. If he chose the latter it would be plain that he would have to countenance an attack on the king, and that this attack might well lead to the king being overthrown. If the queen had always suspected that York's claim to be the heir presumptive had been a threat to her husband and her son, there could be no doubt now that York's royal blood would become a major factor in the ensuing struggle. The 'Rout of Ludford', which saw no clash of armies, or even any military engagement at all, was nevertheless a major turning point. Henceforth York could only be secure by removing the king and establishing his own alternative.[3]

While the duke of York was in Ireland the queen attempted to undermine his position there by appointing the earl of Wiltshire the new lieutenant of Ireland. York was popular in Ireland, however, and his security was not threatened. In Calais the earls of Warwick and Salisbury with York's eldest son Edward, earl of March, were also in a strong position, despite the attacks on the garrison made by the duke of Somerset. Having nominally replaced Warwick as captain of Calais, Somerset was able to take the town of Guines and send out ineffectual skirmishing parties, but he could not dislodge Warwick, another popular figure with a growing reputation, from the formidable garrison at Calais. The Yorkist lords were safe and gathering strength.

The same could not be said for the family York had abandoned in Ludlow. His wife, the duchess Cecily, and his three younger children, Margaret, George and Richard, were effectively left to their fate. At the age of 7 Richard briefly emerges from obscurity to be found in Ludlow at the mercy of his father's enemies. Margaret was 14 and George 10, perhaps better able to gain some understanding of the vicissitudes the family endured over the next nine months. Of young Richard we only know that he went with his mother and siblings as she threw herself on the mercy of the king. It is difficult to ascertain the true extent of the danger they faced. Richard's father and two older brothers had fled the realm and been declared traitors. His father's properties and accessible wealth were forfeit to the crown. More than 20 of his most prominent supporters were condemned in the Act of Attainder. The future prospects of the house of York must have seemed bleak to any objective observer. It is, nevertheless, possible to exaggerate the danger Cecily and her young brood faced. She was able to travel with her children to Coventry and submit to the king. She was granted the not inconsiderable sum of 1,000 marks per annum and a declaration that she and her children had not offended against Henry VI. A lady from the higher ranks of the nobility had less to fear than most from public disorder and dynastic upheaval. A strong element of protection was still offered by the social bonds and the military and religious proprieties current at the time. Cecily also had the advantage of having been able to make the acquaintance of Margaret of Anjou when the queen was on her way to England for the first time. There is no reason to believe that their friendship, even if only a matter of courtesy and courtly protocol, did not now work in Cecily's favour.

Cecily's situation, despite the protection of conventional mores, was nevertheless unenviable. Her sister-in-law, the countess of Salisbury, was attainted with her husband, and many may have thought that the duchess was fortunate to be treated with such exceptional generosity. What is more, it could not have been anything less than a precarious and dangerous crisis that confronted her on the day following her husband's flight. One chronicler described 'the misrule of the kings gallants at Ludlow'. The soldiers of the king's army, having found their way to Ludlow unopposed, broke into the town and got completely drunk. They 'went wet-shod in wine, and then they robbed the town, and bare away bedding, clothes, and other stuff, and defouled many women'. Not for the last time Margaret was unable, or unwilling, to control the excesses of her troops. There must have been at least a risk to Cecily's personal safety, and that of her children. While it is true that it would have been far more dangerous for York to have attempted to take his entire family with him, not least because it would have hampered the flight and made detection and retribution more likely, Cecily cannot have enjoyed submitting herself to the mercy of the king and promising to pray that her husband would also submit himself to the king's grace. She was taken into the keeping of her sister Anne and her husband, the duke of Buckingham. Although a chronicler describes her being kept 'full straight with many a rebuke', she was more likely to have been treated with respect and consideration; the duke of Buckingham was an honourable and distinguished man. She was, nevertheless, confronting a decidedly uncertain future. The prospects of her 7-year-old son, Richard, had also sunk remarkably low in a very short space of time.[4]

NORTHAMPTON

The next 18 months, Richard's seventh and eighth years, were among the most dramatic and turbulent in English history. In that relatively short space of time the youngest son of the duke of York witnessed, in turn, the danger and opprobrium brought upon his house by his father's precipitous flight, followed by a rapid renaissance in the family fortunes. This was quickly followed by a dire calamity, which entirely wrecked the chances of the family achieving security and brought them perilously close to ruin, only to be succeeded by a final twist that saw them reach the highest pinnacle of power. It could not have been a more topsy-turvy sequence of events, nor could the margins between failure and success have been closer or attended with greater consequences. England was about to endure the dreadful descent into a civil war that all had hoped to avoid. It was to rip apart those political and social conventions, so carefully nurtured over many years, whose preservation had been the primary concern of the governing aristocracy for centuries. Not for over 300 years had a conflict between fellow-countrymen been so violent and protracted. In five battles, in the space of just eight months, the last being the bloodiest battle ever fought on English soil, the Yorkist lords and their Lancastrian opponents fought to the death.

On 24 June 1460 Warwick and Salisbury sailed from Calais and landed in England with 2,000 men. Margaret's distrust of the city of London had exposed the capital to the Yorkist lords. They were, not without difficulty, eventually admitted to London. The Londoners had no real stomach for an overt show of support for the Yorkists that might bring retribution from Queen Margaret. They would have preferred to remain neutral but allowed Salisbury and Warwick to pass through the city after tense negotiations. The Lancastrian leaders retreated to the Tower and held it against a Yorkist siege. Leaving Salisbury to conduct the siege and to hold London, on 5 July Warwick moved north, accompanied by the duke of York's eldest son Edward, earl of March, gathering support as he went. Margaret remained with her 6-year-old son Prince Edward at Coventry, while Shrewsbury and Buckingham, taking the feeble king with them, marched to intercept the Yorkist earls at Northampton. On 10 July 1460, in pouring rain, the Lancastrians were overwhelmed in little more than an hour. Casualties were surprisingly light given that as many as 30,000 men took part in the battle; probably as few as 300 men, mostly Lancastrian, were killed. In a telling twist to the chivalric conventions of medieval warfare, Warwick had issued orders for his men to spare the king and the commons. His targets were the Lancastrian lords. Unlike conventional war where the nobility were protected by elaborate and lucrative protocols, civil war unleashed the spectre of tribal vendetta and private feud. From the very beginning, at the first battle of St Albans, it was clear that the lords would pay the heaviest price. Humphrey, duke of Buckingham, was among those killed, along with John Talbot, earl of Shrewsbury, and the lords Beaumont and Egremont. It was only seven years since Talbot's famous father had been killed by the French at the battle of Castillon. His father's death, defending English interests in southern France, had seemed a noble, if disastrous, way to end a life of honourable military service. In the rain and mud at Northampton, honour and glory were in short supply.

The king, not for the first time, was found in his tent, no doubt somewhat bemused. As they had at St Albans in 1455, the Yorkist lords knelt in obeisance before him and professed their loyalty and obedience. Margaret and Prince Edward escaped northwards on hearing tidings of the battle, their hopes shattered, the triumph at Ludford a distant memory. The king was taken, effectively a captive, to London. Warwick was very much in charge and the driving force behind events. For the first time the 31-year-old earl, later to be known as The Kingmaker, was in command of the kingdom. The duke of York, throughout these dramatic events had, somewhat strangely, remained in Ireland. Whatever agreement York and Warwick may have reached in Ireland concerning joint action, it does not seem to have materialised in the summer of 1460. If Warwick gained his first fateful taste of real power in the two months between the victory at Northampton and the arrival of the duke of York in England, he also studiously avoided any suggestion that his actions were designed to unseat the reigning monarch. When York arrived the joint agenda rapidly unravelled. York had clearly had enough of Henry VI and would no doubt have preferred this vacuum at the seat of power to have been summarily despatched by a sword blow at Northampton. The battle had cleared the way for York's return but it had left an intractable political dilemma. York's two protectorates had demonstrated clearly enough the impossibility of either ring-fencing the king with a partisan selection of lords or operating a more broadly-based conciliar system. The queen would be back and York's position undermined again. This time the duke appears to have envisaged an altogether more radical solution.

While the duke was taking his time in Ireland, his wife Cecily's domestic arrangements changed. Her sister Anne had lost her husband, the duke of Buckingham, at the battle of Northampton and Cecily, their former 'guest', was now free. John Paston, newly elected MP for Norfolk, took the opportunity to ingratiate himself with the Yorkists by offering Cecily and her three younger children a large and comfortable house in London to stay in while she awaited the arrival of the duke. The house

in Southwark had belonged to John Fastolf, recently deceased, one of the
richest men in the kingdom. Paston, Fastolf's lawyer and trusted
confidant, was an executor of Fastolf's will. He not only had access to the
luxurious London house, but also needed powerful support to win his
claim to be the chief beneficiary of the disputed will. The 7-year-old
Richard will have experienced a journey from a castle in the Midlands to
a mansion by the Thames in London, and perhaps have been conscious of
a change in the family fortunes. They had been in their new residence
only two days before Cecily received tidings of her husband's landing, on
8 September at Redbank, on the north-west tip of the Wirral. Within a
few more days she received a request to join the duke at Hereford and
left London at once. Her children stayed behind, visited, we are told, by
the earl of March who 'cometh every day to see them'. The 18-year-old
Edward was now a successful military commander and the premier lord
in the capital. He must have been an impressive and reassuring visitor.
Even when Warwick had been leading events, he had negotiated with
the king's heralds before Northampton in the name of the earl of March.
Edward's earldom outranked Warwick's.[5]

Before Cecily reached the duke of York, he had already met Warwick
at Shrewsbury where they spent four days together. It is not known what
they discussed, but one or two weighty matters were of pressing concern.
Soon after the duke's arrival in England he began to act as a man intent
on claiming the throne. The commissions he issued to summon his own
retainers made no mention of the king, and even omitted the regnal year
in their dating. Warwick must have pointed out to the duke that all his
own successes had been achieved in the name of reform and in the king's
name. Although Warwick would benefit from a change of dynasty, he
was aware of the fact that his current support had been garnered under
the guise of removing 'evil ministers'. He would have known that
support for removing the king himself could not be guaranteed. Even
his own father, Salisbury, now the king's chamberlain, could not be
expected to support a usurpation. We will never know whether Warwick
counselled York to take the throne or advised him not to do so, but very
soon after their meeting York was receiving petitions from assemblies of
gentry at Ludlow to take the crown. It is scarcely credible that York was
acting without the agreement of Warwick. They had met in Dublin and
must have considered these things. The likelihood is that, faced with
York's determination to prosecute his right to its fullest extent, Warwick

counselled caution. The duke took his time on his way to London, clearly hoping that support would be forthcoming.

THE ACT OF ACCORD

As York made his slow progress towards the capital he had borne before him the arms of Lionel, duke of Clarence. This blatantly revived the claims of York's mother, Anne Mortimer, the great-granddaughter of Lionel, the second son of Edward III. When Richard II had lost his throne to John of Gaunt's son, Henry IV, in 1399, the claims of the third son, John of Gaunt, duke of Lancaster, had superseded those of Lionel. Lionel had only had a daughter, Philippa, and her son, Roger Mortimer, earl of March, had been killed in the year before Henry IV had usurped the throne. Richard II, the only son of the Black Prince, had died without heirs. To revive the claims of Lionel's line was to forage deep in the mouldy undergrowth of royal lineage. Henry IV's son, Henry V, had overcome the shaky foundations of his royal heritage by defeating the French at Agincourt. To the world at large there could be no clearer divine endorsement of the Lancastrian dynasty than such a mighty victory. So strong was this sense of heavenly sanction that it had been impossible to dislodge his son, Henry VI. Henry's mental instability had not been sufficient grounds for removing him, nor had two defeats in battle at which he was personally present. The duke of York's father, Richard earl of Cambridge, was the son of Edmund Langley, the fourth son of Edward III, and he had married Anne Mortimer, thus uniting the second and the fourth lines. The Lancastrians represented the third line and York might feel his royal credentials were better than theirs, but legally this was a nonsense. Both his father and his maternal grandfather had been attainted for treason and been convicted traitors.

York had chosen, it would seem, to advance his claim to the throne on the grounds that Henry VI was no longer worthy to reign. He could not possibly claim that Henry had never been the rightful king. He was moving towards the throne in the hope that popular support would allow him to depose an unkingly king. This was a highly dangerous precedent. Edward II had been deemed to be 'unworthy', but the usurpation of 1327 had been effected by his own son. There had been no change of dynasty. Richard II had lost his throne to his cousin,

Henry IV, in 1399, a man who had been deprived of his inheritance. Henry's genuine grievance against the arbitrary rule of the king and his abuse of royal authority gave his seizure of the throne the semblance of righteousness. It had nevertheless opened up a whole can of worms. Rebellions and treachery lurked behind every corner until Henry V conquered France. Nobody wanted to return to that dark moment when the worthiness of a king had been judged by a subject. York was doing precisely what Henry Bolingbroke had done in 1399. To remove a king because he had not reigned justly could only be done by powers above the reach of mortals. The laws of inheritance, upon which every lord and peasant depended, could not be altered to incorporate a criterion of 'worthiness'. If Warwick had serious misgivings about proceeding on these grounds, it would seem that York either did not share his qualms or had buried them in a sense of the justice of his cause. As he entered London he displayed the full arms of England 'without any diversity', and had his sword borne upright before him in the manner of a legitimate monarch. Warwick had summoned parliament, which duly awaited his arrival.[6]

The extraordinary scene that followed merely served to highlight the extent to which the duke of York had misjudged the mood of the people of England. He advanced into the packed parliament chamber and headed directly for the throne, which was situated underneath a canopy. Placing his hand upon the cushion there, as if to sit down, he turned to face the astonished lords and commons. Perhaps he expected an exclamation of approbation or even a spontaneous acclamation. Instead he encountered a strange but tangible silence. He had gone too far. The uncomfortable impasse was broken by the archbishop of Canterbury, Thomas Bourchier, who rose up and asked the duke if he wished to speak with the king. Bourchier had become a dependable Yorkist, supporting the Nevilles throughout York's absence, but this rather crude attempt to take the throne could not be countenanced. As he made clear by his tentative enquiry, there was still a crowned monarch in the royal apartments behind the parliament chamber. York was incredulous. He had not expected to be so completely thwarted at the very moment when his high hopes and ambitions were supposed to be endorsed. He exploded in anger, declaring that he knew of no man in the kingdom who should not rather come to see him than he go to see them. He then stormed off towards the royal apartments, ordering his guards to smash open any locked doors barring his way. According to one witness, he took up lodging in the king's own apartments while the king retreated to the queen's quarters. There the duke busied himself preparing for his coronation.[7]

The lords stalled for time. They were concerned at the growing unease outside the palace of Westminster and the refusal of many of their number to break their oaths of allegiance. Warwick attempted to persuade the duke of York's son, Edward earl of March, to speak to his father, but he refused. The archbishop, Thomas Bourchier, and the chancellor, George Neville, bishop of Exeter, were also reluctant to confront the duke. In the end Warwick's brother, Thomas Neville, managed to gain the duke's assent to a debate of the issue by the lords in parliament. York submitted a petition outlining his claim to the throne by lineal descent. The lords submitted the petition to the justices who declared that the matter was too high for their expertise. The lords passed it on to the king's sergeants and attorneys-at-law who responded, not unreasonably, by pointing out that if the matter were too high for the justices it was certainly beyond the competence of ordinary lawyers. The lords could not avoid debating the issue and taking upon themselves the responsibility vested in the High Court of Parliament. They concluded that the house of Lancaster's long tenure of the throne, their own oaths taken to Henry VI and various acts of parliament presented obstacles to York's claim. York replied through his own attorneys that the only bar to his right was a single act of parliament from the reign of Henry IV. His own claim rested on the right of legitimate inheritance, that is 'God's law, and all natural laws', which superseded an act of parliament: an act that parliament itself had the power to revoke. York's moment had passed. By shifting the emphasis to legitimacy rather than to worthiness his claim could not succeed. The lords managed to broker a compromise by which York had to accept that Henry's title to the throne 'could not be defeated' and that he would remain king, but York and his heirs would succeed him. On 31 October 1460 the Act of Accord was agreed. York was to receive a substantial annual income as the recognized heir presumptive. The suspicion that he had been temporarily bought off hangs over the proceedings.[8]

The Act of Accord represented an uneasy truce. The duke of York, 10 years older than the king, could hardly have remained satisfied at the prospect of having to live longer than Henry VI in order to succeed him.

On the other hand it played into the hands of his enemies by shifting the balance of the scales of justice in their favour. It was too late to claim that Henry IV had been a usurper and that his dynasty was therefore illegitimate. Time had to play some part in these matters. There was an indefinable point at which what once had been a novel claim became, through accepted usage and common observance, a customary and settled legality. No inheritance was safe if every skeleton in every closet could be dragged out for all eternity. The real problem York now faced was that he had given the queen the incentive to carry on the fight and also the sympathy for her plight by which she might regain support. A fugitive with a small group of companions, she had been robbed and humiliated on her travels into Wales. Now she had an ace up her sleeve. She had with her the disinherited son of the reigning king, the grandson of the great king Henry V. If Henry VI was a lost cause, his 7-year-old son represented a new dawn for Lancastrian hopes. Almost as soon as the Act was ratified trouble began to bubble up across the land.

WAKEFIELD

Richard, the youngest son of the duke of York, was just 8 years old when his father set off from London, with the earl of Salisbury and Thomas Neville, to deal with 'rebels' ransacking his estates in the north. It was to be the last time that he would see his father alive. The duke took with him Edmund, earl of Rutland, his second son, and Edmund's farewell to Richard was also to be his last. York had underestimated the level of Lancastrian resistance. Margaret had secured the assistance of Jasper Tudor, earl of Pembroke, in Wales and had taken ship for Scotland where she had enough security to muster assistance across the north. The earl of Northumberland and the lords Clifford and Roos were joined in Hull by John Neville, of the hostile senior branch of the Neville family. The earl of Devon had raised his retinues in the south-west and the duke of Somerset had landed from France and occupied the city of York. The duke of Exeter and the earl of Wiltshire rallied to Margaret's cause. As the duke of York moved north, his eldest son, Edward, was sent to Wales to confront Jasper Tudor. Cecily and her three younger children were again left alone and in a state of uncertainty. They could hardly have imagined the nadir to which their fortunes were about to sink.

When York reached his castle at Sandal, just outside Wakefield, he may already have been surprised at the degree of hostility he faced. There were more Lancastrian lords converging upon him than had faced Warwick at Northampton. Nothing could have more clearly demonstrated how York's behaviour had lost him support. After 38 years of Henry VI's misrule, there was no popular inclination to unseat him. If York had satisfied himself with a third protectorate he may have been in a better position, but the general feeling was that he did not have a mandate to stake a claim to the throne. Christmas at Sandal 1460 must have been a dour affair. York was short of victuals and effectively besieged in his own back yard. On 30 December York sallied out of his castle, perhaps to forage for supplies, perhaps into a carefully sprung trap. He may have been fooled into thinking that a large force of 8,000 men under John, Lord Neville, was arriving to relieve him. This army had been raised by a commission of array issued in York's name. The senior branch of the Neville family was staunchly Lancastrian and had allied with the Percys. The presence of Salisbury, the head of the junior branch, would have been sufficient to turn a family dispute into a significant factor in the turbulent national politics of 1460. York, however justified he must have felt in taking up arms against the king and his government, could only be seen by other lords as the head of a personal faction. York's force was swiftly surrounded and outnumbered. He was 'caught like a fish in a net' and killed. As he recognised the danger engulfing him, York sent away his son Edmund, earl of Rutland, under the guard of his tutor, Sir Robert Aspall. It was to no avail; as they crossed Wakefield Bridge they were spotted by Lord Clifford. While Edmund pleaded for his life, Clifford plunged a dagger into the young man's heart with the words, 'By God's blood, thy father slew mine, and so will I do thee and all thy kin.' Men like Clifford could not have cared less about the legitimacy of York's claims. Feud generated its own force, fuelled by the compelling needs of family honour and the settling of scores. It had been five years since Clifford's father had been killed by York at St Albans. The younger Clifford would only live to enjoy his revenge for another three months. Salisbury's son, Thomas, was also killed and, the following day, Salisbury himself, having been captured, was publicly beheaded in Pontefract. One tradition recounts that Margaret ordered the severed heads of her enemies to be placed on Micklegate Bar in York, 'so that York may look on York'.[9]

MORTIMER'S CROSS

The death of the duke of York, fighting bravely to the last, brought to an end the aspirations and complex motives of one of the last great English magnates to serve with merit in France. He had been ruined by the implacable hostility of Queen Margaret and the obstinate reluctance of his fellow peers to countenance the removal of an anointed king. Ironically it was his death that handed the initiative back to the Yorkists. The lack of legitimacy that had dogged his campaign was a flaw that could no longer be exploited by the Lancastrians. York's son, Edward earl of March, was not only recognised by parliament as the rightful successor to Henry VI, but could also justly claim to be fighting for his own endangered inheritance, the duchy of York. The events of the next few weeks enhanced his claims and removed the main obstacles to the throne.

When news of York's death reached Edward he was in his Marcher earldom recruiting forces to fight for his father's cause and suppressing Lancastrian uprisings in Wales. He determined to take these forces to assist Warwick in the defence of London but was prevented from doing so by the news that James Butler, earl of Wiltshire, had landed in south-west Wales with a force of French, Bretons and Irish. Wiltshire had joined up with Jasper Tudor, earl of Pembroke, and Jasper's father, Owen, and they were marching towards Edward at Hereford. On 2 or 3 February 1461 the two armies clashed at Mortimer's Cross, a few miles south of Edward's castle at Wigmore, and the 18-year-old duke secured a decisive victory. It is said that an astrological, or meteorological, phenomenon preceded the battle and that this led Edward to adopt the sign of the sun in splendour as one of the badges of the house of York. Punning in the choice of imagery for badges was a common practice, and when Shakespeare opened his play about Richard III with the famous lines, 'Now is the winter of our discontent/Made glorious summer by this son of York', he utilised the juxtaposition of images that had probably been intended by Edward. The young victor was not only conscious of bearing the legacy of York as the son of the duke, but he was also a new generation, a new dawn and a bright hope for the future. After 38 years of the reign of Henry VI, in which the realm seemed to have descended into a never-ending darkness of benighted violence, Edward's choice of emblem demonstrated an astuteness and political acumen so manifestly lacking in his father.[10]

Jasper Tudor and the earl of Wiltshire had both escaped after the battle of Mortimer's Cross, but Owen Tudor was not so lucky. Taken to the market square at Hereford for execution, he could not believe he was going to be put to death. Perhaps the husband of Queen Katherine, the former wife of Henry V, had not realised that the old protocols that had served to protect the nobility in conventional warfare no longer applied. St Albans had put paid to that, with the battles of Blore Heath, Northampton and Wakefield eradicating any remaining traces of chivalric etiquette. Owen Tudor, grandfather of the future Henry VII, blithely assumed he would not be harmed until the moment when he saw the axe and the block. If he still had doubts about his intended fate they were removed when his collar and red velvet doublet were ripped off. Gregory's Chronicle tells us that, 'Then he said, "That head shall lie on the stock that was wont to lie on Queen Katherine's lap", and he put his heart and mind wholly unto God, and full meekly took his death.'[11]

THE SECOND BATTLE OF ST ALBANS

Meanwhile Margaret had sprung into action following the defeat of York at Wakefield. She had crossed the border from Scotland, perhaps bringing some Scottish troops with her, and met the Lancastrian lords in York. Determined to complete the ruin of her enemies she then set out for London. On the road south she did her cause immense damage by allowing her troops to forage and plunder in lieu of pay. The Croyland Chronicle described how the panicking population poured into the Fenland abbey with all their possessions, in order to escape the marauding soldiers. Margaret's forces came to within six miles of the abbey and the chronicler believed that only divine intervention had spared it. His account may well be poorly informed and unnecessarily dramatic but it is supported by all other contemporary accounts. Clement Paston wrote to his brother, John, that the northerners 'rob and steal and are planning to pillage all this country'. The papal legate, Coppini, reported that the Lancastrians performed 'countless acts of cruelty', and Abbot John Whethamstede recorded at St Albans his frightening experience of witnessing a 'northern invasion' worse than any of those perpetrated by Attila the Hun. However exaggerated these reports may have been, and they are all tainted by Yorkist agendas, they nevertheless indicate that

Margaret had lost the propaganda war. In the public imagination she had become a heartless foreign invader.[12]

Warwick led an army out of London to confront the Lancastrians at St Albans, and on 17 February 1461 the town endured its second battle in just six years. Warwick had brought Henry VI with him and so, ostensibly, fought in the name of the king he had attacked in the first battle and had done so much to destroy in the intervening years. The truth was that Henry VI's cause was one that no longer commanded support. As if to highlight this very fact, Gregory's Chronicle describes Margaret's troops donning the livery of the prince of Wales. Margaret was fighting for her son, not her husband.

If the reasons for the defeat of the duke of York at Wakefield are something of a mystery, then Warwick's defeat at the second battle of St Albans is equally puzzling. The most likely explanation is that poor reconnaissance caused his vanguard to be surprised and overwhelmed by the Lancastrians before Warwick himself could intervene. The chronicler William Gregory actually fought in the battle and was very impressed with all the new-fangled artillery at Warwick's disposal, much of it accompanying the Burgundian contingent Warwick had engaged. He could not, however, account for the fact that it was all to no avail in the battle. A similar question may have arisen in the minds of Richard III's surviving troops at Bosworth. If artillery was becoming increasingly popular, there was still some way to go to train men to use it effectively. The fact that no Yorkist lords were killed suggests that Warwick did not engage the enemy himself but simply lost the initiative and fled. His brother, John Neville, Lord Montagu, had attempted to resist the entire Lancastrian force despite being hopelessly outnumbered. By the time Warwick returned at the head of a cavalry force, it was too late. Montagu had been defeated and captured. As night fell Warwick abandoned the field and moved west to seek out Edward, the new duke of York. Margaret regained possession of the hapless king and there seemed no obstacle to the achievement of an important strategic objective: the control of London.

FLIGHT

With London now at the mercy of Margaret and her Lancastrian adherents, Duchess Cecily saw fit to despatch her two younger sons abroad to safety. George, aged 11, and Richard, now aged 8, were sent across the Channel to the court of Philip the Good, ruler of the Burgundian Netherlands. Duke Philip was not only a trusted friend of the Yorks but also the wealthy lord of a powerful state. There is no extant information about the vicissitudes of the journey endured by the boys, but they were still at Sluys on 17 April 1461 when the duke sent emissaries to escort them to his ducal palace at Bruges. By this time the fortunes of their house had been transformed by the triumphs of their brother Edward, and it would seem likely that the duke had kept the exiles at arm's length for the two months that had elapsed since Warwick's defeat at St Albans. He may have been sympathetic to their plight but they were the sons of a defeated rebel from a kingdom in turmoil. Cecily's own situation was unenviable. If she had been left to the mercy of her enemies at Ludlow in 1459, the cataclysm that had engulfed her since the battle of Wakefield can scarcely be imagined. At the latter battle she had lost her husband, her son Edmund, and her brother Salisbury. Even if news of Edward's victory at Mortimer's Cross, 2 February 1461, had reached her in London before the second battle of St Albans on 17 February, its implications were by no means obvious. Edward had secured his own safety but the threat to London and the Yorkists was far greater in the week after the second battle of St Albans than at any other time.

After the battle and Warwick's escape westward, there was no effective protection for Cecily against Margaret. Warwick's brother, John, Lord Montagu, had been captured at St Albans but had been spared execution. The two men who had been executed, Lord Bonville and Sir Thomas Kyriell, had been household retainers of Henry VI who had been wooed by Warwick. Margaret had no mercy when it came to treachery against her family. Lord Montagu's survival can perhaps be attributed to the fact that Margaret could sympathise with a man who was merely being loyal to his own family, or, more cogently, because Edmund Beaufort, Somerset's brother, was still being held captive by the Yorkists. To kill Warwick's brother would have been to invite savage reprisals. This unusual restraint could not be expected to extend to the main rivals for the throne. Clifford's murder of Cecily's son, Edmund, in the aftermath of the battle of Wakefield, was a grim reminder of the nature of the dynastic conflict now coming to its climax. Margaret's son, Edward prince of Wales was only 7 years old at St Albans but she had placed him at the forefront of the judicial proceedings following the battle. Henry VI, once more united with his family, had knighted the young prince on the field and the executions that followed were performed in the prince's name. Margaret seemed to envisage a new era of Lancastrian rule that would see her husband as titular head of the dynasty while her son learnt the ropes and increasingly took the reins of government. If her husband had lost his authority, then a visible revival of royal power would be provided by her son. Richard and George were scions of the house of her deadliest rival; there were many in Margaret's entourage who would not hesitate to cleanse the body politic of these poisonous vestiges.

To Richard and his brother George, having left a fearful London with its armed and riotous mobs swirling through the streets, entering the world of the duke of Burgundy must have been an extraordinary experience. Philip the Good was famous for his love of chivalry and pageantry, his ostentatious displays of wealth and hospitality and his rigorous adherence to ceremony, protocol and courtesy. His towns were crammed with merchants and financiers made rich by the profits of the cloth trade and keen to outdo each other in decorating their large town houses with the latest tapestries and paintings. Duke Philip provided a haven for both business and art. His court boasted scholars and books, choirs and musicians, knights and diplomats. They came to be at the most fashionable court in Europe where respect for the ancient world blended with a fascination for the novel. The Italian Renaissance had worked its magic here and a sense of freedom, of civilization and of purpose filled the air. In the brief interlude that Richard and George spent as guests of Philip, they may have gained a hint of the world that England might have enjoyed if it had not been riven by internecine strife.

The younger sons of the erstwhile duke of York were not to know how fragile the stability was of this Burgundian wonderland. With a resurgent France and the death of Philip, Burgundy would begin its inexorable decline. The young Richard was fortunate to see Burgundy in its prime, and to feast and be entertained at its lavish court, before the glorious pageant faded, leaving scarcely a rack behind. We cannot know the impact on him of the four months spent in exile, but there is evidence of Burgundian influence in Yorkist England. Cultural and military ideas were certainly exchanged, but perhaps, too, Richard's later diplomatic leanings were born at this time. It was, after all, in the Netherlands that Richard was first treated like a prince of the royal blood and experienced the dramatic shift in the fortunes of his family that elevated him from the ranks of poor fugitive to the upper echelons of aristocratic privilege.

2

DUKE OF GLOUCESTER: 1461–1469

EDWARD THE KING

As February 1461 drew to a close Queen Margaret made her fateful decision to retreat northwards despite having defeated Warwick at St Albans and appearing to have London at her mercy. She may have feared being trapped in the city by the fast approaching victorious army of Edward. Leaving London to the heir of York was to present him with an opportunity he could not miss. On 27 February 1461 Edward, with Warwick at his side, entered the City of London with, according to the eyewitness, Robert Fabian, 'a great power of men ... the which was of the citizens joyously received'. As Margaret had possession of Henry VI the Yorkists could no longer claim to be acting on his behalf and with his authority. This inconvenient fiction was readily discarded and the process of creating a new king began in earnest. Richard, duke of York, had come to London in 1460 to claim the throne and been rebuffed. His son, however, had altogether stronger grounds on which to stake his claim. In the first place he had a legitimate claim to the throne. By the Act of Accord in October 1460 he had been recognised as heir to the throne by Parliament. The murder of his father at Wakefield and the seizure of York's estates in the north were such breaches of faith on the part of the king that his former subject, Edward, no longer owed him allegiance. Secondly, by joining Margaret after the second battle of St

Albans, Henry had abandoned the terms of the Accord and thus forfeited the right to rule. His heir, Edward earl of March, was thus the rightful king of England.[1]

The truth was that these legal constructions would have counted for nothing if it were not also the case that Edward was both popular and victorious. The 19-year-old earl was conscious of his public image and appeared to be in touch with common concerns. He brilliantly exploited his public persona and deliberately sought, and gained, the approbation of the commons in a way his father had never been able to manage. A proclamation issued on 6 March announced that any adherent of Henry VI who submitted within 10 days would be pardoned, except for those with an income of more than 100 marks a year. Here was a deliberate attempt to separate hostile magnates from their more lowly retainers. Furthermore, Edward could now attack the person of Henry VI as being 'unworthy' to reign. It had taken nearly a decade of manifest incompetence before the thick fog of sanctity that protected the Lord's anointed had finally drifted away to reveal the bedraggled puppet sitting on the throne.[2]

Three days after they had entered the city, a muster of supporters was organised in St John's Field. The wrongs perpetrated by Henry VI were asserted and the crowd asked 'whether the said Henry were worthy to reign as king any longer or no'. They duly responded, 'Nay, Nay', and were asked if they would have Edward, earl of March, as their king, to which 'they cried with one voice, Yea, Yea'. Captains were then appointed to convey the glad tidings to Edward who was lodged at Baynard's Castle, the York family's London residence beside the Thames. He, of course, demurred until prevailed upon to accept by the wise counsels of the chancellor, George Neville, bishop of Exeter, and Thomas Bourchier, archbishop of Canterbury. As far as Robert Fabian was concerned, Edward had been duly 'elected and admitted for king'. The archbishop of Canterbury's role is significant. It was he who, five months earlier, had effectively prevented the duke of York from taking the throne. He appeared to have no qualms in this case.

The next day, Monday 2 March, the articles of Edward's title to the throne were proclaimed throughout London and on 3 March a meeting took place at Baynard's Castle of all the lords that could be mustered. Calling themselves a council they 'agreed and concluded that Edward, duke of York, should then be king'. This was a partisan group, of course, and hardly representative of all the peers of the realm, but the presence of Thomas Bourchier, archbishop of Canterbury, Richard Beauchamp, bishop of Salisbury, George Neville, bishop of Exeter, John Mowbray, duke of Norfolk, Richard Neville, earl of Warwick and the lords Ferrers and Fitzwalter with Sir William Herbert of Raglan and 'sundry others' gave Edward a strong political platform. The following day, Thursday 4 March, Edward was formally made a king in a series of elaborate rituals. Beginning at 9 am at St Paul's, Edward was proclaimed king in a solemn service at which a *Te Deum* was sung, a sermon preached by George Neville and acclamations received. He then processed through the city to Westminster Hall where he took the oath, donned the robes of royalty and the cap of estate before sitting on the king's marble bench in chancery. From the 'King's Bench' he personally pronounced his title to the throne and, swearing to 'keep the realm and maintain its laws as a true and just king', was again acclaimed by the assembled company. Proceeding through the palace of Westminster he was taken across the way to Westminster Abbey. At the west door he was greeted by the abbot proffering the sacred sceptre of St Edward, 'which he grasped'. Moving in procession to the high altar he made obeisance before the Lord and offered prayers at the shrine of St Edward before sitting on the coronation seat itself. Only one thing was lacking and that was the crown. In effect, Edward had been made king at a coronation ceremony that had omitted the coronation. This meant that the anointing with holy oil, the unction, had also been shelved for the time being. Commentators have noted the brilliant stage-craft employed in these solemnities that had made Edward king in fact and in name, but not in totality. Edward, like all kings before him, would be king before being crowned. The coronation could, and should, wait. There may have been a hint of hesitation about taking this final step but, considering that another crowned monarch was still at large in the realm, it made sense. The Croyland chronicler believed that Edward preferred to receive the ultimate sanction from God by victory in battle: 'However he would not at present allow himself to be crowned, but immediately, like unto Gideon or another of the judges, acting faithfully in the Lord, girded himself with the sword of battle.'

The reign of Edward IV, the brother of the two young exiles in the Netherlands, had begun. Richard had not been present at these solemnities, but the parallels with the events of 1483 are striking. Richard was to overawe London with an army, to be petitioned at

Baynard's Castle and to proceed to the King's Bench and the Abbey. Both displaced existing monarchs and had the most powerful magnate in the kingdom at their side. It wasn't sufficient in either case.[3]

TOWTON

The length of Henry VI's reign, nearly 40 years, and the determination and concerted effort needed to replace him serve as reminders of the dangers and difficulties exposed by usurpation. Edward only achieved a measure of security after considerable bloodshed in three battles over the next three years. Only by the killing of his main Lancastrian opponents was he able to enjoy a degree of stability. Even this was not sufficient to prevent a rebellion eight years after his accession which forced him to flee the kingdom and fight to regain it. Two further full-scale battles ensued before Edward was firmly established on the throne. In other words it was to take five major battles and more than a decade before Edward IV could rule without the threat of a Lancastrian resurgence. In some ways his own path to the throne had been mapped out by the usurpation of 1399, when Henry IV had unseated his cousin Richard II. York's attempt to take the throne in 1460 had been justified on the grounds that Richard II should not have been supplanted by the Lancastrians. In Edward's first Parliament his title to the throne was based precisely on this premise. Both Edward's usurpation and the difficulties he faced subsequently, clearly demonstrate the inherent problems caused by the removal of a king. It was not only considered abhorrent and unnatural by all ranks of medieval society, but also illegal and irreligious. Peace, security and prosperity, the very aims of communal organisation, were always threatened by an attack on the summit of power. Judicial procedures, commissions of the peace, Acts of Parliament, offices, privileges, oaths, writs and charters, the whole panoply of instruments upon which settled administration and justice depended, were disrupted and undermined by challenges to the throne. The rarity of the success of these usurpations in English history indicates the latent fear and dread they evoked. Having occurred, they always left a legacy of insecurity and a constituency of opposition.

The second half of the 15th century saw two usurpations in succession, that of Edward IV and that of his brother, Richard III. When we consider the later usurpation it will be important to do so in the context of the earlier one. Edward was finally able to accuse Henry VI of 'unworthiness', but he needed and depended on strong financial and military support from London and the south. These regions had become the heartlands of Yorkist support, while Margaret of Anjou and her Lancastrian supporters had become increasingly identified with the north. When it came to regional conflict, it was the south that had the resources, and the advantages of proximity to the seat of power, to influence the outcome. In the later usurpation Richard had all the problems associated with deposition, which would have arisen in any case, combined with two major disadvantages. Unlike Edward he was dependent for his support on the north, and unlike his older brother he was unable to accuse the incumbent king of incompetence and injustice. The 'unworthiness' of Edward V could never be based on his personal failings and proven inability to reign, because he never exercised supreme authority in his own right. It could only be based on a declaration of his illegitimacy. Richard in 1483 may have felt himself to be in a similar situation to that of his father in 1460 when the inability of the king to prevent the duke from being excluded from the royal council was deemed sufficient to remove him. The weakness of Richard's claim to the throne in 1483 and his identification with the north contrast markedly with Edward's situation in 1461. It takes a long period of settled rule, and a measure of good fortune, to establish a successful dynasty. In retrospect Edward failed, but he could never have imagined that his work would be so quickly destroyed after his death.

The importance of the backing of London, and the Church, was made immediately apparent when Edward was able to raise £4,000 in the first three days of his reign. The money came from loans secured from merchants and from religious houses. The Londoners had already lent the Yorkists £4,666 in the previous 10 months. These were enormous sums of money, each equivalent to about a fifth of the income a late medieval monarch might expect to raise from customary dues in a year. Edward also had support from Duke Philip of Burgundy, who sent a contingent under the banner of the dauphin of France, Louis. The dauphin, heir to the throne of France, was at odds with his father, Charles VII, and virtually exiled in Burgundy. He therefore supported the anti-French Yorkists along with Duke Philip. Louis' father was to die shortly after these events and the reign of his son, Louis XI, was to coincide precisely with that of Edward IV of England, both dying in 1483. In the event, Edward was fortunate to possess such an ally at this stage of his reign. Louis was to prove to be a very tricky opponent in years to come.[4]

There could be no doubt about Edward's determination to do battle with the Lancastrians. On 5 March the duke of Norfolk left London to recruit an army from East Anglia. On 8 March Warwick left with commissions of array to raise levies from 10 counties stretching as far north as Yorkshire. On 11 March Lord Fauconberg marched out with the foot soldiers from Kent, London and the Welsh Marches, and on 13 March Edward himself left the capital with his mounted knights. He met the duke of Norfolk at Cambridge and Warwick at Nottingham and the combined force headed north to rendezvous with Fauconberg. The Yorkist strength may have reached between 25,000 and 30,000 men as they headed for Pontefract in Yorkshire where a massive Lancastrian army, probably even bigger, had mustered.

The two armies first clashed at Ferrybridge, nine miles south of Towton, on 28 March. The Lancastrians had destroyed the bridge over the River Aire and, with a force led by Lord Clifford, attempted to prevent the Yorkists from crossing. Edward ordered Lord Fauconberg to cross the Aire at Castleford, three miles upstream from Ferrybridge, while he attacked Clifford from the south bank of the river. Attempting to escape from the trap about to encircle him, Clifford's men were overwhelmed and killed. Edward had at least avenged the murder of his brother Edmund, brutally slain by Clifford on Wakefield Bridge three months earlier. Edward's army crossed the river and moved into position in front of the Lancastrian position at Towton. Nothing more clearly illustrates the sharp division of the country brought about by the civil war than the strength of the support both sides could command. The Yorkists presented two dukes, Suffolk and Norfolk, while the Lancastrians two of their own, Somerset and Exeter. The Yorkists paraded two earls, Warwick and Arundel, matched by the three Lancastrian earls, Northumberland, Devon and Wiltshire. Both armies also contained a single viscount and about a dozen lords each. The Lancastrians, however, commanded an impressive depth of support from among the lesser peers, knights and gentlemen that the Yorkists could not match. A large proportion of the aristocracy of England was about to engage in a decisive struggle for mastery, but the strength of support for the Lancastrian king would not be overcome in a single day.

This was, of course, a battle fought in the name of two rival kings. There was, displayed for all to see, one glaring difference between them: Edward IV was calmly and vigorously commanding his troops while Henry VI was in York with the queen and Prince Edward, awaiting news of the outcome. That news, when it arrived, signalled the end of Henry's painfully long reign. As dawn broke on Palm Sunday, 29 March 1461, in an atrocious winter storm of blinding snow and bitter cold, one of the largest and bloodiest battles ever fought on English soil began. It continued until nightfall with heavy casualties on both sides. The late arrival of the duke of Norfolk, turning the left flank of the Lancastrian army, eventually proved decisive. After determined resistance the Lancastrian line was routed and then massacred as the ranks tried to escape. The earl of Northumberland was killed on the battlefield, and the earls of Devon and Wiltshire, though they managed to flee from the field, were inexorably hunted down and duly executed. William Gregory reported that 42 Lancastrian knights taken prisoner were executed at the end of the day. Contemporary estimates of casualties are notoriously unreliable, ranging from a widely reported 28,000 to a much lower figure of 9,000, but a figure approaching 20,000 is not inconceivable.[5]

With all the chief protagonists from both sides of the conflict either present on the battlefield or in close proximity to it, this was the showdown that had not been achieved in the other battles. Only at the first battle of St Albans in 1455 had all the key players been present, and then the conflict had only amounted to a struggle to gain control of the king's person. The Yorkist victory at Towton was decisive because it endorsed Edward's usurpation of the crown. Such a conclusive demonstration of support and power, in a battle in which the armies fought unequivocally for rival kings, bestowed on the victor the sanction from heaven that only God could grant. Nevertheless, Edward might have hoped for a greater tally of Lancastrian leaders among the dead or captured. Not only had Margaret escaped, fleeing back to Scotland with Henry VI and Prince Edward, but the dukes of Somerset and Exeter had also escaped. Prospero di Camulio, the Milanese ambassador, writing a few days after the battle to Francesco Sforza, duke of Milan, perceptively remarked, 'if the King and Queen of England with the other fugitives … are not taken, it seems certain that in time fresh disturbances will arise'.[6]

For the time being, however, England had a capable and effective monarch for the first time in almost 40 years. Duke Philip of Burgundy, who had actively supported Edward's cause, could now bring Edward's fugitive brothers to the ducal palace at Bruges. Richard and George experienced an extraordinary change in their fortunes. Instead of being the outcast, fatherless exiles they had been a few months before, they were now princes of the blood royal, the brothers of a reigning king.

EDWARD IV'S FIRST REIGN

Richard and George were still lodged in some obscurity at Sluys when news of their brother's victory arrived on about 12 April 1461. They were taken on 17 April to Bruges by the duke's emissaries and the papal legate, to be received in state and entertained by Duke Philip. The duke's court was arguably the most lavish in Europe and his patronage of goldsmiths, jewellers, artists and musicians combined with his love of chivalry and courtly etiquette to offer a spectacle of aristocratic splendour few could match. He had created his own order of chivalry, the Order of the Golden Fleece, in imitation of Edward III's creation of the Order of the Garter, and he was as renowned for his fabulous tournaments as he was for his extensive library. The two English princes spent no more than six weeks under his magnificent hospitality, and it is impossible to gauge the impact such a visit may have had on them, but it is worth noting that Richard never subsequently wavered in his support of Burgundy. Another feature of Richard's future career was his implacable hostility to France, an enmity which both of his brothers, Edward and George, were willing to set aside if the need required. In this trait he resembled both his father, the duke of York, and his host at Bruges, Philip, duke of Burgundy. Philip's own father, John the Fearless, had been notoriously betrayed and slain at a meeting with the dauphin, Charles, soon after to become Charles VII of France, on a bridge at Montereau in 1419. This was the Philip who had captured Joan of Arc and handed her over to the English to be burnt at the stake. He shared much in common with the erstwhile duke of York in his tireless efforts to wage war on France, a cause that had frustrated them both. Duke Philip was elderly by the standards of the day, 64 years old, and his rule marked the apogee of Burgundian power and influence. The young Richard had witnessed the greatest flowering of its ducal might and never fully realised that he had seen it at its zenith. In commerce, music, art, military technology and education, Burgundy was an exemplar to other courts, but it was also an anachronism a resurgent France was soon to expose.

The boys returned to England in early June 1461 via Calais. They were received with ceremonial pageantry at Canterbury and London where the main business was preparation for the coronation of their elder brother. The great ceremony had been brought forward to 28 June because the Lancastrian rebels were causing considerable difficulties on the northern border. Margaret of Anjou, having escaped to Scotland after the battle of Towton, had enlisted Scottish help by issuing orders for Berwick to be surrendered to them. On 25 April 1461 it was duly handed over after more than a century of English rule. It was to remain in Scottish hands until 1482, when Richard, duke of Gloucester, was to recapture it for his brother Edward. Margaret was also willing to cede Carlisle on the western march to the Scots, and a force was heading in that direction. Lancastrian lords, Roos and Dacre, were raiding beyond Durham, and a French fleet under the command of the seneschal of Normandy, Pierre de Brézé, had landed a French force on the island of Jersey and was threatening to launch an invasion of England on Margaret's behalf. Jasper Tudor, earl of Pembroke, and Henry Holland, duke of Exeter, still held castles in Wales in defiance of Edward's authority. The new king faced a considerable task to establish his rule throughout the realm and to restore order to areas that had become violent and lawless as Henry VI's reign had descended into chaos. It would take three years of vigilance, endeavour, military campaigns and good fortune before the new Yorkist regime was truly established. The atmosphere in London may have been jubilant and tinged with relief after the serious threats its citizens had endured in recent times, but holiday celebrations at the end of June would have been seasoned with the poignant underlying tension of uncertainty. The instability and fragility of the new government serve as a reminder of the difficulties attendant on the deposition of a king.

On 26 June Richard was admitted into the Order of the Bath. This was the second highest rank of knighthood among the orders of chivalry. Two days later he attended the coronation of his brother in Westminster Abbey. On the same day, George was made duke of Clarence. He was not only senior to Richard in years but also in rank. Clarence, as he now became known, was the heir apparent, and would remain so until Edward produced his own children. Richard was by no means forgotten, however, and, shortly after his ninth birthday was made duke of Gloucester on 1 November 1461. Despite the difficulties still facing the regime and the roller-coaster ride their fortunes had endured over the previous year, the transformation from youngest son of a duke to the rank of royal duke saw Richard propelled from the branches to the summit of the aristocratic tree. He was now the third highest ranking individual in the kingdom. The titles of the dukedoms conferred upon the two boys were significant, even if they conferred no lands or authority in themselves. Clarence was the dukedom conferred on Edward III's second son, Lionel of Antwerp, and Gloucester was the title held by Edward III's fifth son, Thomas of Woodstock. There could be no doubt that Edward IV intended to convey the message that he was the direct descendant of Edward III and his family was reclaiming its rightful inheritance. The ducal titles of Edward III's other sons, those of John, duke of Lancaster, the third son, and Edmund, duke of York, the fourth son, were already in Edward IV's possession. When Henry of Lancaster had become King Henry IV he had retained the duchy of Lancaster as part of his own ancestral rights. The dukedom had passed to his son, Henry V, and then to his grandson, Henry VI. Not only did Edward IV claim to inherit the duchy of Lancaster because he was king, but he also retained the dukedom of York in the same way. These were invaluable assets to the new king, and he was to exploit them to great advantage, but they also completed the tally of royal dukedoms formerly held by the sons of Edward III.

The dukedoms of Clarence and Gloucester had also been conferred on the brothers of Henry V. In Richard's case, his two predecessors as duke of Gloucester had both met untimely ends at the hands of their enemies. Both Thomas of Woodstock and Humphrey had been outspoken critics of their respective contemporary political regimes, and had paid high prices for it. Both had also inspired cults dedicated to the posthumous restoration of their reputations. Unbeknown to Richard this habit was not to end with the second duke. In February 1462 Richard was admitted into the Order of the Garter, the senior order of chivalry, and, on his 10th birthday 2 October 1462, was made Admiral of England, Ireland and Aquitaine. These honours were commensurate with his status, but Richard also needed endowments that would bring him the financial rewards he would need to meet the costs of a princely upbringing. Edward seems to have experienced difficulty in conferring lands on Richard that were sufficient to meet his needs. On 12 August 1462

Richard was granted extensive estates in Yorkshire, west Wales, Essex, Suffolk and Cambridge, but over the following 15 months most of these were restored to their former owners or their heirs. The Honour of Richmond in Yorkshire had to be handed over to Clarence after the older youth protested and demanded it be granted to him, rather than Richard. Clarence had received vast estates in comparison to Richard, but Richmond in Yorkshire was to be taken from his poorly-provided brother and added to them. Perhaps Clarence wanted the estates he had received from the confiscated lordships of the earls of Northumberland and Wiltshire, which covered extensive tracts of Northumberland, Durham and Yorkshire, to be a jurisdiction untrammelled by the intrusion of his younger brother. It is an odd episode and suggests a precocious petulance on Clarence's part, which was to develop over time. Richard was given the forfeited estates of Henry Beaufort, duke of Somerset, on 20 December 1463, but these did not raise a great deal of revenue. The main source of his income before coming of age was from the duchy of Lancaster lordships of Bolingbroke in Lincolnshire and Pickering and Barnoldswick in Yorkshire, amounting to an annual value of £1,000. Compared to the revenues of Clarence, perhaps four times this sum, it was not extravagant and precisely met the expenses Edward paid to Warwick for Richard's upkeep. The diverting and exploiting of the revenues of the duchy of Lancaster for royal purposes of this kind provides an illustration of the advantages Edward discovered in acquiring the Lancastrian inheritance. It also began Richard's long association with the duchy.[7]

At first Richard lived in the royal palaces of London, in the royal household or that of his mother at Baynard's Castle. He appears fleetingly in the records for Greenwich and may have stayed for a time in the household of Thomas Bourchier, archbishop of Canterbury. From 1461 to 1465, from the age of 8 until he was 12, Richard, knight and royal duke, lived a life close to the centre of power but almost invisible to the historical record. In 1465 he moved into the household of his mighty cousin, the earl of Warwick, to complete his education by boarding in an aristocratic household, as was customary for the sons of the nobility. Again we have no record of his activities in these formative years. An Exchequer receipt tells us that Richard Neville, earl of Warwick, received £1,000 in 1465 for the costs and expenses of maintaining the king's brother, Richard duke of Gloucester, and the wardship of Francis,

Lord Lovell, at Middleham. Lord Lovell was to become a lifelong friend of Richard, so loyal that he was to die fighting for him two years after Richard himself was dead. Middleham Castle was to become a favourite haunt of Richard, and his northern home and base in later years. It would seem that these three years were to have a significant impact on Richard's future loyalties. It was at this time that Richard met Warwick's 10-year-old daughter, Anne. On 22 September 1465 he was in her company at the ceremony held in York to celebrate the enthronement of archbishop George Neville. She was to become his wife in due course.

No doubt Richard's love of the north began at Middleham in 1465, but it was also fostered by his early association with Warwick's important retainers, the men who assisted the earl in the management of his estates and his military, administrative and judicial functions. John Conyers, Thomas Metcalfe, William Parr, John Huddleston, and James and Robert Harrington were all close associates of Warwick in the north and members of a tight-knit group of upper gentry who were all later to be closely associated with Richard. The lesser nobility of the north who operated within Warwick's affinity, the Scropes, Fitzhughs, Greystokes and Dacres, were also to become Richard's men in the course of time. The young duke may have encountered them while visiting Warwick's other principal northern strongholds at Barnard Castle, Penrith and Sheriff Hutton. He was at Warwick Castle in early 1466, and visited York with his guardian in 1468, suggesting that he was not entirely based at Middleham. Although we have no knowledge of Richard's movements, training or education at this time, we can discern the development of a character trait. He was loyal to men he had encountered in his early life, and they were loyal to him.[8]

On 25 October 1468 the duke of Gloucester received a grant of the confiscated Hungerford estates, again not amounting to a very lucrative settlement, perhaps only £500 a year, but at least a recognition that the duke had reached his 16th birthday and would need an independent household. Although there was no fixed rule on the subject, in common with other aristocratic youths at the time, Richard, at the age of 16, could have been deemed to have come of age. He was to spend more time in the company of the king from henceforth. In January 1469 Thomas Hungerford and Henry Courtenay were tried for treason at Salisbury and subsequently executed. The king presided over the trial in person and Richard took a prominent role in the proceedings. In February he was removed from Warwick's custody and appears to have joined the royal household. He was with the king in June 1469 when Edward set out with other prominent members of his household on pilgrimage to Bury St Edmunds and Walsingham. Whether the difficulties Edward was experiencing in his relations with Warwick suggested to him that this would be an opportune moment to bring his brother closer to the court is not known, but the move was certainly timely. The simmering resentment harboured by the king's powerful cousin was about to explode into open rebellion.

THE CAUSES OF WARWICK'S REBELLION

Trouble had been brewing between the earl of Warwick and the king since Edward had married Elizabeth Woodville in May 1464. In the years following his accession Edward had been content to allow the Neville family, headed by Warwick, to reap the rewards of the Yorkist triumph they had helped to secure. Immediately after the battle of Towton, Edward had confirmed Warwick as great chamberlain of England, captain of Calais and keeper of the seas, warden of the Cinque Ports and warden of the west march. In addition he was made warden of the east march and steward of the duchy of Lancaster. He received liberal grants of the lands confiscated from the defeated Lancastrians, including parts of the Percy estates in Yorkshire. When one includes his own earldom of Warwick and the inherited lands of the Despenser family and the earldom of Salisbury, he was by far the largest landowner in England apart from the king. His wealth and authority impressed foreign observers who all concluded that the earl was the real ruler of England. Philippe de Commynes reported in his *Memoirs* that the earl of Warwick 'governed King Edward in his youth and directed his affairs. Indeed, to speak the truth, he made him king and was responsible for deposing King Henry'. The governor of Abbeville remarked wryly in a letter to Louis XI, that the English 'have but two rulers: M. de Warwick and another whose name I have forgotten'. Warwick certainly ruled the north and had command of the king's forces at land and sea. His brother, George, bishop of Exeter, was made chancellor in 1461 and archbishop of York in 1464. Another brother, John, was made a baron, Lord Montagu, in 1461 and earl of Northumberland in 1464 while Warwick's uncle, William, Lord

Fauconberg, was created earl of Kent. Warwick may well have felt that he was 'director of the Yorkist regime'.[9]

Edward IV was one of the most eligible bachelors in Europe and it was expected that he would marry a foreign princess, as most of his predecessors had done. Warwick, during the summer of 1464, was negotiating with Louis XI of France for just such a marriage. Louis' own daughter was too young to be considered but he offered his sister-in-law Bona of Savoy instead. Louis was keen to improve relations with England and his flattery of Warwick was considered to be the best method of achieving this goal. Warwick was also confident in his own judgement and authority and went so far as to organise a conference to meet at St Omer on 1 October 1464 to finalise a treaty. The king's council met at Reading in September 1464 to discuss, among other things, the English policy at the conference. It was at this council meeting that Edward stunned the assembled company of lords, ministers, advisers and servants, with the news that he was already married. He had met Elizabeth Woodville in April 1464 and at some time between then and the council meeting, clandestinely and without consultation, he had married her. She was the impoverished widow of a Lancastrian knight and her credentials were ludicrously inadequate for becoming the queen of England. Her husband, Sir John Grey, had been killed at the second battle of St Albans fighting for Henry VI and had left her with two small sons. She was also about four years older than Edward. Apart from the fact that she must have been attractive, and possibly beautiful, there would have been very few royal counsellors who would have had the audacity to find anything to recommend such an unlikely union.[10]

The immediate consequences of the astonishing revelation that the king had secretly married a low-born woman were not as significant as the lasting damage the marriage inflicted on Warwick's relations with the king. In the first place Warwick had been humiliated. The conference planned for St Omer was abandoned and all the careful negotiations for a French marriage rendered fruitless. Secondly, Elizabeth Woodville was only too keen to find suitable grants of land, offices, titles and marriages for all her five brothers, seven unmarried sisters and other relatives. It was only a matter of time before this process of promoting new men and cementing new political alliances would noticeably diminish Warwick's influence at court. Warwick may have been able to swallow his initial shock and disappointment at the king's youthful impetuosity, in the knowledge that he was far from alone in not being consulted about the king's marriage, and that the king's manifest indiscretion had not been a deliberate attempt to undermine the Neville ascendancy. Nevertheless, an increasingly pro-Burgundian foreign policy and the influx of Woodville courtiers proved fatal to Warwick's ambitions.

In fact Warwick had misjudged his young protégé. Edward had depended on the Neville family in general, and Warwick in particular, to become king, but he was not exclusively obliged to them. Philippe de Commynes was quite wrong to assert that Warwick had made him king and deposed Henry VI. Warwick had lost the second battle of St Albans while Edward had won the battle of Mortimer's Cross. Warwick could be ponderous and defensive in battle and it was clearly the offensive tactics of Edward himself that allowed them both to prevail at Towton. It is also notable how many of the knights who had shared the new king's company from the Rout of Ludford to the victories at Mortimer's Cross and Towton were ennobled at the outset of the new reign and took prominent roles at court. William Herbert, formerly one of Warwick's men, had fought for Edward at Mortimer's Cross and marched with him to London. He became earl of Pembroke, chief justice and chamberlain for south Wales and later chief justice of north Wales. His power in Wales was so great that he could be described as the king's Welsh viceroy. Warwick's own ambitions in Wales were thwarted by Herbert's spectacular promotion. Almost as extraordinary as William Herbert's rise to power was that of Sir William Hastings, who was to become Edward's chamberlain, adviser and boon companion for the entire reign. He had been with Edward at Mortimer's Cross and knighted by him at Towton. The estates with which he was endowed created a massive lordship in the Midlands, allowing him to control a great central swathe of territory through Leicestershire, Warwickshire and Northamptonshire. Again this restricted Warwick's own ambitions, this time within the parameters of his own earldom. Other faithful friends were rewarded. Sir John Wenlock became Lord Wenlock, having been with Edward from Calais to Towton. Sir Walter Blount became Lord Mountjoy and treasurer of England, having also been with Edward in exile at Calais before being knighted at the battle of Towton. Sir Walter Devereux was knighted at Towton and created Lord Ferrers. Sir John Howard, who was to become Lord Howard, was also knighted at Towton. John lord Audley, had been with Edward at Calais. These men were to become the bedrock of

Edward's government. A combination of shared danger, companionship, reward and trust made such men essential. Warwick failed to realise that he was part of a new structure, not the creator of it.

Edward has been criticised for being too conciliatory towards his enemies, a policy that dangerously backfired in the cases of Ralph Percy and Henry Beaufort. There were many Lancastrians indefatigably opposed to the Yorkists who nurtured grievances too deep for the balm of reconciliation to reach. When Ralph Percy had finally been surrounded by his enemies at Hedgeley Moor in 1464 he had consoled himself with the thought that at least he had 'saved the bird in my bosom'. He had not betrayed his king, Henry VI. The civil war between the Lancastrians and the Yorkists had exposed the body politic to narrow polarisation and the bigotry of partisanship and factionalism. Edward had to begin the process of healing the wounds and rebuilding confidence in a central authority in which all could trust. Nevertheless he chose to surround himself with those whose loyalty was proven and unconditional. The devotion to a cause he believed to be right had cost Ralph Percy his life. He could have been accommodated within the Yorkist regime but he refused to accept the proffered hand. This quality of loyalty was not as common as the cruder motivations of ambition and self-interest. Edward needed it and nurtured it.

There are parallels in the way Edward exercised kingship and the way his brother attempted to do so in 1483. The emphasis on personal retainers and members of his former council was a feature common to both, as was the effort to reconcile former enemies. Edward was only partially successful in this sphere but had time and the circumstances to learn from his errors. Richard was not so fortunate and became boxed into a corner early in his reign. Edward's secret marriage to Elizabeth Woodville was to become the central plank upon which the legal case for the deposition of her son, Edward V, was to rest. Richard was to claim that the marriage was unlawful and her son illegitimate. The power of some of Edward's Woodville adherents was also to become a major issue in the reign of Richard III and he was to find that the elevation of Hastings was to create a loyalty that could not be broken except by summary execution.

The swift marriages of the queen's siblings only served to emphasise the fact that a new affinity was being created around the king, to Warwick's growing consternation and discomfort. Not only were suitable marriages for his own two daughters harder to come by, but some of the marriages bound the new elite closer to the king. William Herbert, the son of William, earl of Pembroke, was married to Mary Woodville, the queen's sister. Another sister, Anne, was married to William viscount Bourchier, the son of Henry, earl of Essex. More serious, from Warwick's point of view, was the marriage in October 1466 of the queen's elder son, Thomas Grey, to Anne Holland, the daughter of the duchess of Exeter. The duchess was the sister of Edward IV and this highly advantageous marriage had already been promised to Warwick's nephew, George. When Henry Stafford, the young duke of Buckingham who was to play such an important role in the usurpation of Richard III, was married to Katherine Woodville, yet another sister of the queen, Warwick found that the prospects for finding eligible husbands for his daughters were considerably reduced. The only viable candidates left were the king's brothers, George and Richard. Edward persistently refused to countenance any suggestion of this kind. Warwick has been accused of having overweening ambition and of being the archetypal over-mighty subject, but there can be little doubt that the marriage of his daughters Isabel and Anne, 14 and 10 years old respectively in September 1466, was a major and legitimate concern. Edward's determination to prevent Warwick's daughters from marrying the royal dukes may have been inspired by the prospect of useful foreign marriages, such as the king himself singularly avoided, but it is worth noting that he was happy to allow his brother Richard to marry Warwick's daughter Anne, after the earl of Warwick was dead. Edward was casting off the yoke of dependence on Warwick, establishing a court of his choosing and, perhaps without realising it, creating a deadly enemy.

Warwick's perception of the Woodvilles as grasping upstarts without pedigree was only partially justified. In fact Elizabeth's mother, Jacquetta of Luxemburg, was a great French princess who had been married to John duke of Bedford, the brother of Henry V. When he had died she had certainly married beneath herself – a dowager duchess was not supposed to marry a mere knight in her husband's entourage – but Richard Woodville should not be written off as a nobody. Having served with one of the greatest captains in the glory days of English supremacy in France and having married a duchess who was herself the daughter of a count, he could certainly fill the role of elder statesman and father-figure to the young king, the role Warwick believed belonged exclusively to him. Richard Woodville, now Earl Rivers, was also able to make good use of his wife's connections with the Netherlands in negotiations with Burgundy, and Edward clearly found his advice and company congenial.

THE BATTLE OF EDGECOTE

While Edward was on his pilgrimage to Walsingham, with the 16-year-old Richard in attendance, he became aware of serious disturbances in Yorkshire under the leadership of a rebel calling himself Robin of Redesdale. It soon became apparent that this was not simply a local riot. There had been violent mobs congregating and marching in the north for much of the spring. Taxation was high and there was general discontent about the king's failure to restore law and order. It was even evident to the king that Warwick was very popular. It was only when Robin of Redesdale issued a manifesto demanding the removal of the king's favourites that it became clear that this was a well-organised rebellion of Warwick's northern retainers. At the same time, in early July 1469, Warwick crossed to Calais with George, duke of Clarence, Archbishop George Neville and the earl of Oxford. There, on 11 July 1469, Clarence, the brother of the king, was married to Isabel, the daughter of Warwick, in a marriage expressly forbidden by Edward. The following day Warwick issued his own manifesto condemning the evil ministers and covetous rule of those about the king and summoning supporters to meet him at Canterbury on 16 July. Edward responded immediately by calling up troops from the West Country and Wales under William Herbert, earl of Pembroke, and Humphrey Stafford, earl of Devon, and sending Earl Rivers and his two sons away for their own protection. As Warwick marched through London and on towards Coventry, Edward moved to Nottingham to await the arrival of his own retainers.

While the earls of Devon and Pembroke were attempting to keep their rendezvous with Edward, Robin of Redesdale was heading south to join up with Warwick and Clarence. John of Warkworth was quite sure that 'Robin' was in fact 'Sir William Conyers', and most commentators agree that he was probably Sir John Conyers, a kinsman by marriage of Warwick and his steward at Middleham. Bypassing Nottingham he collided with a reconnaissance force led by Pembroke's brother, Sir Richard Herbert, and bloody conflict was inevitable. On 26 July 1469 at Edgecote near Banbury, Pembroke and his Welsh men-at-arms were overwhelmed in a fierce struggle. It is likely that as many as 2,000 Welshmen were slaughtered at Edgecote. Edward had so organised the muster that Devon's troops consisted mainly of archers while Pembroke's were predominantly foot soldiers and cavalry. The two armies did not combine against the rebels and Pembroke was left without any cover for his flanks. Outmanoeuvred and surrounded he was captured with his brother and taken to Northampton. The earl of Devon had argued with Pembroke the day before the battle and this may have been the reason why his forces were not engaged. He fled to Bridgewater in Somerset where he was lynched by a mob. Pembroke and his brother were executed on Warwick's orders on the day after the battle. William Herbert pleading for the life of his younger brother adds poignancy to the whole sordid business. For good measure the third brother, Sir Thomas Herbert, was rounded up and executed at Bristol. The unmerciful and illegal nature of their deaths, the bitter fruit of rivalry and jealousy, characterised Warwick's behaviour during his brief ascendancy. A few days later Earl Rivers and his second son, Sir John Woodville, were hunted down in the Forest of Dean, captured at Chepstow and executed. Making clear his antipathy to everything Woodville, Warwick also arrested the queen's mother, the dowager duchess of Bedford, on charges of witchcraft. Warwick was settling scores and summarily removing his rivals, in most cases without even the pretence of legality.

As news of the defeat of the royalist troops reached the king, his retainers fled and his support evaporated. He was found in Olney in Buckinghamshire with just a small escort. Warwick sent his brother, George, archbishop of York, the man Edward had removed as chancellor, to arrest the king and bring him to Coventry as a prisoner, from whence he was taken to Warwick Castle. The Nevilles appeared to have gained control of the kingdom. Warwick issued orders to the king's council in Edward's name and sent out writs summoning a parliament to meet at York on 22 September. It is clear that he preferred to have a compliant king under lock and key, as he had with Henry VI after the battle of Northampton in 1460, and to rule the kingdom himself in the king's name. Edward was moved from Warwick to Middleham, another of Warwick's strongholds, but it was rapidly becoming clear that this bizarre arrangement for governing could not be sustained. Uncertainty and rebellion had unleashed the inevitable horrors of violence and lawlessness in many localities. Warwick could not bring order to the realm without the authority of the king. If he had intended to depose Edward at the September parliament then events, and the king's own resourcefulness, outstripped his plans.

Perhaps the most troubling aspect of the turmoil inflicted on the Yorkist government by Warwick's rebellion was the treason of Clarence. The king's brother had been wooed by Warwick, persuaded that he shared the earl's alienation and disaffection, and was now irretrievably bound to him by ties of marriage. Warwick had managed to wed his eldest daughter to one of the most eligible bachelors in Europe, but Clarence also gained by the match. Warwick was unlikely to produce a male heir and Isabel could expect to inherit a substantial portion of her father's vast estates. These would fall to Clarence in right of his wife and create for him a vast holding throughout the Midlands and the north. It may even have been a little disappointing to Clarence to behold Warwick brutally and systematically destroying his enemies while at the same time allowing Edward to keep his throne. Warwick may have planned to take things further; it was at this time that rumours were circulated suggesting that Edward was not the legitimate son of the duke of York, but for the time being any planned deposition was shelved. If Edward had been deposed at this point then Clarence would almost certainly have been the next king. A serious northern rebellion, however, threatened both Warwick and Edward; the moment passed. Raising the necessary county levies to deal with the insurgency required royal authorisation and Edward was able to negotiate his release. The rebellion was suppressed and the parliament cancelled. Edward called a council meeting to York on 29 September and then progressed to Westminster side by side with Warwick.[11]

If Clarence had been swayed by the blandishments of the earl of Warwick, his brother Richard had not been so adversely affected, despite being in Warwick's care for the past four years. There was clearly a marked difference in their characters, evident during these events and consistently reaffirmed thereafter. It is not known where Richard was when Edward was captured at Olney, nor where he went when the king was incarcerated, but he was summoned as soon as Edward had secured a partial freedom and joined him in the north before accompanying him on the march to London. The march itself must have presented an interesting spectacle of amity to observers. Warwick had just killed the queen's father and brother and polished off two of Edward's closest friends. A show of friendly cooperation was attempted but it seems to have fooled nobody. The Croyland chronicler, who seems to have known the king well, believed that there probably remained 'deeply seated in his mind, the injuries he had received and the contempt which had been shown to his majesty'. Meanwhile, Clarence's blatant disregard of his brother's injunction against the Neville marriage provided a contrast to the fidelity of the king's younger brother. As the duke of Gloucester turned 17 it was increasingly apparent that he had the credentials to take up a more prominent and significant role in Edward's administration.[12]

3

DUKE OF GLOUCESTER: 1469–1471

THE PROMOTION OF RICHARD

Richard, duke of Gloucester, had already received substantial holdings in Cheshire and Lancashire before Warwick's rebellion. In May 1469 he had been given a collection of duchy of Lancaster land, including the lordships of Clitheroe, Liverpool and Halton. His intrusion into this region was resented by the Stanley family, who had been steadily acquiring an unassailable hegemony in the north-west, and was to result in violent conflict between Richard and Stanley in the coming months. Edward's problem had been to provide Richard with an endowment befitting his status without damaging the interests of his other lords. Warwick's rebellion, by destroying some of Edward's prominent adherents, had unexpectedly provided a solution. The earliest surviving letter of Richard dates from June 1469 when he wrote from Castle Rising in Norfolk to Sir John Say, chancellor of the duchy of Lancaster, asking for a loan of £100. Richard had been asked to accompany the king as he moved north to deal with the disturbances fomented by Warwick. There is evidence that he was recruiting men while he was in East Anglia, and Edward always expected his lords to retain men at their own expense, but Richard's predicament was obvious. He explained to John Say that he had been called into the 'north parts' to his 'great cost and charge, whereunto I am so suddenly called that I am not so well purveyed of money therefore as behoves me to be'. It was just as much in Edward's interests to have a trusted duke with sufficient means to supply large numbers of men, as it was in Richard's. The remedy was supplied, unwittingly, by Warwick's murder of the Herberts. Richard provided an interesting postscript to his letter to Say, written in his own hand: 'Sir J Say, I pray you that you fail me not at this time of my great need as you will that I show you my good lordship in that matter that you labour me for.' Richard was already sufficiently close to the king and of such high rank that his lordship was worth securing, even for a man as well-connected as John Say. The neat well-educated hand that provided this postscript unwittingly reveals a medieval world of mutual dependence.[1]

Warwick's execution of William Herbert, earl of Pembroke, had removed a rival whose power in Wales had conflicted with Warwick's interests in the region. It had also done enormous damage to royal authority in the principality. Edward had worked hard to utilise Herbert's strong local connections to provide a unified sphere of royal control over a region notoriously difficult to govern. The immediate impact of Warwick's rebellion was to take much of Wales and the Welsh Marches out of royal control. Warwick began to take some of the offices previously occupied by Herbert, making himself chief justiciar of south Wales, for instance, and helping himself to the control of four castles. Edward was not only anxious to prevent Warwick from profiting in this way, and keen to provide for his brother Richard, but he was also determined to preserve intact the network of lordships created by Herbert. On 17 October 1469 Richard was created Constable of England, in succession to the late Earl Rivers. This post carried enormous legal and social responsibilities, with, among many other duties, the authority to conduct and preside over treason trials. It was not only a measure of the trust Edward now reposed in his younger brother, but it also gave a clear signal to Warwick. The duke of Gloucester was to fill the principal offices held by Warwick's erstwhile rivals. On 7 November 1469 he began the process of replacing Herbert with Richard by making the young duke justiciar of north Wales for life. On 17 November he was made chief steward of the duchy of Lancashire lordships in south Wales and, later in the same month, chief steward of the principality of Wales and the earldom of March. From as early as October Richard had been given the responsibility of restoring order in Wales. For the next four months he was heavily committed to the task and engaged with royal powers to raise troops, reduce castles and bring all those in revolt to justice. In the space of a few months the king's younger brother had evolved from a landless minor in the royal entourage to a powerful lieutenant subduing rebellion in one of the most difficult territories of the realm. His emergence as a force in Edward's new dispensation came at the cost of disturbing the ambitions of two important magnates, Thomas lord Stanley and the earl of Warwick. In early 1470 Richard was to clash with both.

LOSECOAT FIELD

An uneasy truce held sway during the winter of 1469–70 but Warwick and Clarence could have had little doubt about Edward's determination to continue to pursue his own policies and to reduce the power of the rebels. A further showdown was inevitable. Warwick may have been able to accept Richard's vigorous insertion into office in Wales but when Edward began the process of restoring the Percys in Northumberland, further substantial losses were unavoidable. In October 1469 Henry Percy, the fourth earl of Northumberland, was restored to his estates in Cumberland, Northumberland and Yorkshire, and Warwick and Clarence were not compensated for the lands they forfeited. On 25 March 1470 Henry Percy was restored to the earldom, replacing John Neville. The Neville ascendancy was broken and their ancient rivals were once more pre-eminent in the north. Edward had understood that peace in the north could be most securely guaranteed by a Percy restoration, but the risk was almost reckless. The immediate casualty was John. While he was the brother of Warwick, and perhaps may have expected some fall-out from recent events, he had also been one of Edward's staunchest and most reliable allies. Edward attempted to offer him sufficient compensation, and on paper there can be no doubt that the package was generous. John was promoted to the rank of marquess, second only to the highest rank of duke, and his son, George, was created duke of Bedford and betrothed to the king's own daughter, Elizabeth. John was also given substantial estates in the west country formerly held by Humphrey Stafford, earl of Devon. None of this proved adequate. John had not considered his promotion to the earldom of Northumberland a temporary affair. He had worked hard to restore royal authority in the region and proven capable and successful. The Percys may have been the traditional lords of an inveterately conservative area, but they had rebelled time and time again. Losing the earldom for which he had given so much was a step backwards, and such retrograde career moves were very difficult to swallow among the upper nobility of the 15th century.

By February 1470 Warwick was prepared to rebel again, this time with the intention of deposing Edward completely. A diversion was staged in Lincolnshire when Richard lord Welles and his son Sir Robert attacked and destroyed the house of Sir Thomas Burgh, master of the king's horse. The aim seemed to be to draw Edward away from London and trap him between the northern insurgents and Warwick's Midlands retainers. Edward moved swiftly north, his renewed vigour perhaps taking everyone by surprise. Lord Welles obeyed a summons to appear before the king after being offered a pardon. According to Warkworth, Edward commanded Welles to send a letter to his son, and all those gathered with him, saying 'that they should yield them to him as to their sovereign Lord, or else he made a vow that the Lord Welles should lose his head'. Robert Welles made a desperate bid to rescue his father, only to be completely routed by the royal army at Losecoat Field between Stamford in Lincolnshire and Empingham in Rutland. As the rebels faced Edward's army, the king executed Welles for all to see. His son was captured and also executed, again in front of the entire army. Compassion, conciliation and perhaps also complacency, had been put aside and replaced by ruthlessness. By the end of the day, 12 March 1470, it was very clear to Edward that the rebellion had been the work of Warwick, and, even more so of Clarence. As the rebels had charged into the face of the royal cannon, they had cried, 'A Warwick! A Clarence!' The livery jackets of both conspirators were littered across the field and captured rebels, including an envoy of Clarence, confessed that it was indeed Clarence, aiming to become king himself, who had called them to arms. Edward moved to York, restored Henry Percy in Northumberland and declared Warwick and Clarence his 'great traitors'.[2]

GLOUCESTER VERSUS STANLEY

While Edward had been busy dealing with the rebellion, Richard had also encountered difficulties in the north-west. Thomas lord Stanley had apparently not taken too kindly to the intrusion of a royal duke into a region over which he had built an impressive degree of control. On 12 November 1469 Stanley had been ordered by Edward to pay all the sums due to Richard from his new duchy of Lancaster appointments. The warrant under the duchy of Lancaster seal went so far as to order Stanley to pay all the revenue due from his office as receiver of the duchy in Lancashire and Cheshire, directly to the duke of Gloucester. Richard had been granted two honours, Clitheroe and Halton, which had formerly belonged to Stanley. He had also been granted the forestserships of Amounderness, Bowland and Blackburn, which had also formerly been held by Stanley. The fact that Stanley had continued to collect the fees from these offices is not surprising: he tended to run the region as he saw fit, with a marked penchant for treating royal warrants as advisory rather than compulsory, but he must have baulked at having to hand over the revenues of his receivership. It may be that Thomas lord Stanley's marriage to Eleanor Neville, Warwick's sister, had given Edward cause to suspect his recent loyalties, or simply that, in need of funds to raise troops, he had asked Stanley to divert the money to defray Gloucester's costs. It is quite clear, however, that Richard was equally determined to exercise his new prerogatives, and that conflict between the two was more than likely.

While Edward was pursuing Warwick and Clarence, it became evident that Richard had been in some sort of armed conflict with Stanley. Edward issued a proclamation at York on 25 March 1470, the same day on which he denounced Warwick and Clarence, referring to the 'variance late fallen between his right entirely beloved brother the duke of Gloucester and the lord Stanley'. Edward ordered that no man should 'distress, rob or despoil any of his subjects', but if he had been wronged in the disturbances caused by the conflict between the duke of Gloucester and the lord Stanley, he 'should sue his remedy by the course of the king's law'. A clue is given as to what may have happened by a grant issued by Richard, the day after Edward's proclamation, and signed 'at Hornby'. Hornby Castle in Lonsdale had been the scene of a 10-year dispute between the Harrington family and the Stanleys. The Harringtons were a powerful gentry family with lands in east Lancashire and Yorkshire. They were kinsmen of both the Huddlestons and the Pilkingtons who also had disputes with the Stanleys. All were strong supporters of the Yorkist regime. Sir Thomas Pilkington was sheriff of

Lancashire and his cousin, John, had been sent from Edward's household to assist Richard in his work in Wales. Sir John Pilkington was to become the duke of Gloucester's chamberlain while his brother, Charles, was to become a knight of the body when Gloucester became Richard III. John Huddleston had been associated with Richard as an original member of his ducal household and he and his brother and two sons were to become among Richard's closest servants. He was a cousin of the Harrington brothers and had already been imprisoned with James Harrington for failing to deliver Hornby Castle to Stanley. These were powerful members of the upper gentry with extensive lands and offices in Cumberland, Yorkshire, Lancashire and Gloucestershire. With Richard duke of Gloucester as their lord, they could make serious trouble for Stanley. On 26 March 1460 Richard duke of Gloucester was a guest of the Harringtons at Hornby. He may have intervened to prevent Stanley from using the general state of lawless insurrection to seize Hornby. Whatever the reasons for his presence there, it signified an important change in the disposition of power in the region and a blatant provocation to Stanley.[3]

At the battle of Wakefield in 1460, Thomas Harrington and his eldest son, John, had been killed fighting for the duke of York. John had two daughters who were infants and co-heiresses of the Hornby estate. James Harrington, their uncle, took custody of the girls and occupied Hornby in order to preserve the family inheritance and prevent Stanley from getting his hands on it. The castle held a commanding position on a hill overlooking the River Lune and the approaches to the city of Lancaster. It was of enormous strategic value to Stanley, guarding the route east into Yorkshire and north into Cumberland. In 1466 Stanley obtained a grant of the wardship of the two girls and, arranging their marriages with his second son, Edward, and a nephew, John, claimed the Harrington lands for his family. This was by no means the end of the matter however, because James Harrington, with the support of his brother Robert, dug his heels in and refused to surrender either the castle or the girls. Edward IV, despite his sympathy for the plight of the Harringtons, could not allow the most powerful magnate in the region to be flouted, and ordered the Harringtons to surrender their estate. This had still not been achieved by 1469, despite the arbitration of the earl of Warwick in 1468. Stanley had been using every method, both legal and illegal, to wrest Hornby from the Harringtons, but they had powerful friends. Robert Harrington, for instance, had his own dispute with Stanley because he had married Isabella Balderstone and thus acquired the hereditary bailiwicks of Blackburn and Amounderness. Stanley had refused to allow Robert to exercise this influential and lucrative jurisdiction in Lancashire. Isabella's sister, Jane, was married to John Pilkington, brother of Sir Charles Pilkington. The Pilkingtons and the Harringtons together were a substantial force, able to raise hundreds of retainers to defend their rights. With the duke of Gloucester now taking an active interest, and to the detriment of Stanley, a local feud began to take on national significance.[4]

If it had not already occurred to Stanley that he might profit from a Warwick-sponsored change of regime, his involvement was certainly anticipated by the earl of Warwick himself. Unsettled by defections to the king from among his Yorkshire tenants, Warwick, with Clarence still in tow, crossed the Pennines hoping to secure Stanley's support. Stanley chose not to show his hand at this stage, possibly too preoccupied with events at Hornby. Warwick and Clarence fled south pursued by Richard, who had been ordered by Edward to raise men in Gloucestershire and Herefordshire against the traitors. Warwick and his family took ship at Dartmouth in early April and on 1 May, after spending some weeks attacking shipping, they were granted refuge in France by Louis XI.[5]

THE FLIGHT OF WARWICK AND RECONCILIATION WITH MARGARET

King Louis was quick to exploit the political turmoil in England and, staging one of the most unlikely of reconciliations, brought Margaret of Anjou and Warwick together. Both had done enough damage to the interests of each other to cause permanent enmity, but their needs now coincided and joint action was their only hope. An anonymous French chronicler, who appears to have been an eyewitness to the events, makes it clear that the king of France was instrumental in overcoming Margaret's profound hostility to Warwick:

> Whereunto the said king being present agreed himself to be surety for all the premises with good will, praying the said queen that at his request she would pardon the said Earl of Warwick, showing the great love that she had unto him

[Louis], and that he was bounden and beholden to the said earl more than to any other man, and therefore he would do as much and more for him than for any man living.

The queen still took a great deal of persuading but, 'after many treaties and meetings', Warwick went on his knees to ask for her pardon and, after some hesitation, she 'graciously forgave him' on 22 July 1470.[6]

The parties agreed that Warwick would lead an invasion of England, with French backing, restore Henry VI to the throne and give his second daughter, Anne, to Prince Edward, the son of Henry VI and Margaret of Anjou. It apparently took 15 days to persuade Margaret to allow the betrothal of Prince Edward and Anne Neville, and she refused to allow them to be formally married until Warwick had performed his side of the bargain and restored her husband to the English throne. Nor would she accompany Warwick on his expedition, but would follow later when her husband was firmly back on the throne. It would seem that she did not rate Warwick's chances very highly. Few objective observers would have disagreed with her private assessment of the probability of a successful Lancastrian restoration after a decade of Yorkist rule. Nevertheless, perhaps more out of desperation than anything else, Warwick descended upon the coast of Devon on 15 September 1470, with French archers, money and some ships. He was accompanied by John de Vere, the earl of Oxford, Jasper Tudor, the former earl of Pembroke, and Clarence. The earl of Oxford's long and implacable hostility to the Yorkists began in 1462 when his father and brother were executed for plotting against Edward IV. He had already been implicated in another plot in 1468 for which he was imprisoned in the Tower. He had escaped punishment by exposing his fellow conspirators. If he had been executed in 1468, Henry Tudor may never have become king in 1485, such was his value to the anti-Yorkist cause. He had married Warwick's sister, Margaret, and attended Clarence's wedding in Calais. Jasper Tudor was the uncle of Henry Tudor, and the son of Owen (who had been executed after the battle of Mortimer's Cross in 1461). Jasper had been the defeated commander of the Lancastrian forces at Mortimer's Cross and, having been on the losing side at the first battle of St Albans and again at Towton, was to further develop his reputation for escaping from battles.

The third leading member of Warwick's entourage was the duke of Clarence. His portion of the spoils was to be a restoration to his former lands, with the addition of the dukedom of York. In Warwick's carefully laid plans, Clarence was the weakest link. He had been persuaded to join Warwick, and marry Isabel Neville, with the prospect of an aggrandisement that may have had a regal dimension. The restoration of Henry VI, and also the marriage of his sister-in-law to Prince Edward, would see his position seriously undermined. In due course he would become the brother-in-law of a king, a prospect hardly appealing for a man who was already the brother of a king. For the time being, however, he was trapped by his own treachery and forced to accept the imperative of continuing to support Warwick's shifting agenda.

THE READEPTION

Warwick had timed his landing to coincide with an uprising of his tenants in the north. Although this had not gone to plan, and Edward had swiftly moved to stamp his authority on the northern part of his kingdom, Warwick may have been surprised at the early enthusiasm he encountered. Edward had delayed his return south because, although he had executed their leaders, Warwick's retainers and gentry associates in Yorkshire and Cumberland were causing havoc in the region. The restoration of Henry Percy to the earldom of Northumberland was about to backfire in spectacular fashion. In the long term it was a sensible strategy, but in the short term it almost destroyed Edward. Warwick's appeal to Lancastrian sympathies, rather than to his own Neville interests, had given his campaign a remarkable boost. Henry Percy, grateful to Edward for restoring the earldom to him, could not persuade his retainers to fight for Edward against Henry VI because so many of them had lost kinsmen fighting for the Lancastrians at Towton. They had died fighting with Henry Percy the third, in the cause of Henry VI.

Within days of Warwick's landing, his proclamation in favour of Henry VI brought John Talbot, the earl of Shrewsbury, and Thomas lord Stanley to his banner, with their considerable followings. By the time Warwick had reached Coventry he had amassed an army of about 30,000 men, and far outnumbered Edward's army. High taxation, combined with poor harvests and high inflation, had made Edward's government unpopular. John Warkworth believed that it was Edward's failure to provide 'prosperity and peace' that caused the people to turn against him. They had suffered 'one battle after another, and much trouble and great loss of goods among the common people'. When Edward had called them up to fight for him, despite high levels of taxation, the poor people had had 'to come far out of their countries at their own cost'. In addition, 'many men said that King Edward had much blame for hurting merchandise'. Warwick, on the other hand, was riding on the crest of a wave of popular adulation. By failing to remove Henry VI from the equation, Edward had provided the discomfited and the disillusioned with an alternative.[7]

As he moved south to confront the rebels, Edward waited for the arrival of his trusty lieutenant, John Neville, now Marquess Montagu, with a sizeable army raised by royal commissions. When Montagu's army had approached to within a mile of Edward's camp, the king learnt the dreadful truth. Montagu had betrayed him. In many ways Edward was responsible for turning one of his most able commanders into an enemy. Edward was undoubtedly right in his assessment that only a Percy could keep the north under control, but his handling of Montagu was far too presumptuous. Montagu was a Neville who had striven hard to achieve what every Neville desired: ascendancy over the ancient enemy, the Percys. To be compensated with a marquisate, and a royal marriage and dukedom for his son, was to underestimate the regional dimension to Montagu's ambitions. It meant far more to him, as it did to many of the older noble houses, to hold sway in his heartlands, than to possess honorific titles and blandishments. He had clearly been demoted, however it was dressed up, and the fact that he was Warwick's brother had told against him. When Warwick had been attainted for treason in March, his estates had been forfeited to the crown. This included the earldom of Salisbury, which was entailed in the male line. Because Warwick had had only daughters, Montagu and his son were the heirs of these Neville lands. Edward's cavalier approach to the Neville patrimony owed much to his determination to destroy Warwick, but combined with the restoration of Percy it caused Montagu's hopes to evaporate. John Neville was an honourable man who had served Edward unstintingly and with great distinction. The fact that Edward had warning of his treachery was in part due to the manner in which Montagu formally announced his change of allegiance. Drawing up his troops he publicly declared for King Henry and invited his men to pursue the man they had been commissioned to defend. He gave the reasons for his defection, describing the lands which he had received as compensation for the loss of his earldom as 'a magpie's nest'. One of the host took the opportunity to warn Edward who, trapped between two armies, fled to Bishop's Lynn in Norfolk.[8]

On 2 October 1470 Edward abandoned his kingdom and set sail for Burgundy with a few companions who included Anthony, earl Rivers, William, lord Hastings and Richard, duke of Gloucester. Richard had joined his brother in July to assist in the suppression of the rebels in the north. His effectiveness is perhaps attested by his appointment on 26 August 1470 as warden of the West March towards Scotland. This was a post previously held by the earl of Warwick and had been in the Neville family for over 70 years. Gloucester appeared to be about to profit from Warwick's fall and to adopt the Neville mantle in the north. Five weeks later Richard's promising career was brought to a premature end in the precipitate flight of his brother. On the very day that Richard boarded ship for a dangerous voyage and uncertain future, he reached the age of 18. He would have had little cause to celebrate. Throughout the next seven months he was to share the dangers and hardships of exile, and the subsequent struggle to restore Edward's kingship. For the time being, the reign of Edward IV was over.

A few days later, on 6 October 1470, Henry VI was taken out of the Tower and put back on the throne. Moving in a matter of moments from being *persona non grata* to being the most important figure in the kingdom might have confused even the sanest of individuals, but Henry probably had little comprehension of the unfolding drama. Warkworth reported that when Henry was taken from his keepers he:

> was not worshipfully arrayed as a prince, and not so cleanly kept as should seem such a prince, [but] they had him out, and new arrayed him, and did to him great reverence, and brought him to the palace of Westminster, and so he was restored to the crown again.

The unprecedented peculiarity of the situation is reflected in the accounts of contemporary writers. The Croyland chronicler noted:

> Now all laws were once more enacted in the name of this king Henry, and all letters patent, writs, mandates, chirographs, and instruments whatsoever were published with a twofold mode of annotation in reference to this king's

government, in this manner, 'In the year from the beginning of the reign of king Henry the Sixth, forty-eight, and in the first year of the recovery of his throne by the said king.

Warkworth, writing in English, was also taken by the novelty of the proceedings and recorded the Latin preamble to the new king's official documents, including the phrase *et reademptcionis sue regie potestatis primo*. Thus it was that the period from 29 September 1470, the day Edward was deemed to have abandoned his realm, to his recovery of it on 11 April 1471, became known as the Readeption.[9]

EXILE

Earl Rivers had been able to provide Edward with just three ships in which to escape from the coast of Norfolk. The crossing to the Low Countries was fraught with difficulties, not the least of which was the threat posed by a fleet raised by the Hanse towns. A state of war existed between England and the Hanseatic League, and Edward was harried across the sea by a pursuing squadron of hostile vessels. He arrived at the Dutch island of Texel on 3 October from where he was conducted to Alkmaar to be met by an old friend, Louis de Gruthuyse, the duke of Burgundy's governor of Holland. Edward was penniless and reduced to rewarding the captain of his ship with a furred gown. His brother Richard appears to have become separated from the fugitive king during the crossing and landed further south near the town of Veere in Zeeland with Earl Rivers. He too had been unprepared for such a precipitate flight and had to borrow a few pounds from the town's bailiff. Richard had endured exile before, of course, in 1461, but for at least two of the four months he had spent in Holland as an 8-year-old he had been a guest of honour at the fashionable court of Philip the Good. All was rather different now. Charles the Bold may have been the brother-in-law of his two royal guests but he was most reluctant to welcome them. It was almost three months before Charles agreed to meet the exiles. The duke of Burgundy was far more concerned about the security of his territories than he was about the plight of the Yorkists. He could not afford to endorse the legitimacy of Edward's kingship if that meant finding himself at war with the new regime in England. As it happened he was already providing succour to the Lancastrian exiles, Edmund Beaufort, duke of Somerset, and Henry Holland, duke of Exeter. A Lancastrian restoration might suit him better than a Yorkist one. Edward and Richard became the guests of Gruthuyse at Bruges. The stay must have been congenial in many ways; the governor had been an ambassador at Edward's court and knew the king well. His library and collection of illuminated manuscripts was among the best in Europe and his tastes influenced the English court in Edward's second reign. He was able to provide royal hospitality and agreeable company. Nevertheless the future for the ex-king and his brother looked bleak. The longer they stayed out of England the greater the prospect of a permanent restoration of the Lancastrian dynasty. To return, on the other hand, was highly dangerous and must inevitably lead to a military showdown with Warwick. In 1461 Richard had known within weeks of his arrival in Holland that Edward had become king of England and had defeated his enemies. He had been entertained as a young prince. Now his royal status depended on the fortunes of a brother whose exile he shared. The five months they endured abroad could only have been a distressing and anxious time for them both.

Charles's hand was eventually forced by Louis XI. The duke had sent his congratulations to Henry VI on his restoration to the throne of England, but Charles knew that with Warwick in charge an Anglo-Burgundian alliance was far less likely than an Anglo-French attack. Louis' grand plan was indeed to use the Readeption of Henry VI as a springboard for an English-French attack on Burgundy. On 3 December 1470 he went to war with Charles with the intention of dismantling the Burgundian territories. Warwick was to get Holland and Zeeland in return for English assistance. In early January 1471 Charles agreed to meet Edward and, while reluctant to declare his support openly, he privately provided Edward with £20,000, a few hundred Flemish gunners and several ships. More important, he was able to bring about a reconciliation between Edward and the Hanseatic League. This made a crossing to England a distinct possibility. The Bastard of Fauconberg, Warwick's kinsman, dominated the Channel with his vessels, and any attempt to sail back to England could end in disaster at sea. During February, with Louis XI seizing the Somme towns of Amiens and St Quentin, Charles became increasingly generous. Soon Edward had a sizeable fleet, including 14 ships from the Hanse towns. As March approached, a window of opportunity seemed to open. Duke Francis of Brittany had distracted Fauconberg sufficiently to clear the seas off the coast of Holland. Louis' fleet was preparing to escort Margaret and Prince Edward to England and posed no immediate threat. On 2 March 1471 Edward, Richard and their companions in exile boarded ship at Flushing. The winds prevented them from setting sail for nine days but Edward, having taken his leave of Gruthuyse, refused to disembark. On 11 March they finally crossed to England to confront their enemies and an uncertain future.

EDWARD IV'S RECOVERY OF THE THRONE

Edward anchored off Cromer in Norfolk where he discovered that, with the earl of Oxford now in control of the region, he was not welcome. He headed further north only to be hit by a storm that almost cost him his life. On 14 March 1471, with a relatively small force of about 500 men, and having lost touch with his main supporters, he landed at Ravenspur in Holderness. In 1399 this had been the landing site of Henry Bolingbroke, who was to depose his rival, Richard II, and become Henry IV. When Bolingbroke had landed he had secured his safety and gathered support by claiming that he had only come to reclaim his rightful inheritance, the duchy of Lancaster. Edward followed exactly the same ploy. Instead of announcing his intention to depose Henry VI again, he proclaimed that he had come simply to reclaim his dukedom of York. This bought him time and a little security. It would seem that the people understood the principles of legitimate inheritance, and sympathised with them, far more than they did the dynastic squabbles and dangerous monarchical ambitions that had caused so much violent disruption for so long. Edward's approach may not have fooled everybody but it at least gave them the excuse for offering him no resistance.

Edward spent his first night back in England in a small village two miles from his landing place. On the following morning he was joined by his brother Richard and Earl Rivers with a further 500 men. While they were as yet unopposed there was no rising in their favour either. There was still a great deal to do and considerable danger to face before Edward could regain his kingship. He boldly decided to march to York. The towns of Beverley and Hull refused to open their gates to him and, arriving at York, he was confronted by a similar hostility. The recorder of the city, Thomas Conyers, rode out to warn him that if he approached the city he would be resisted and in danger. Edward had little choice but to press on and take a chance. When he reached York the city would not allow his force to enter, only Edward and 16 supporters. Putting on a brave face, Edward, wearing an ostrich feather representing the prince of Wales, and crying out 'A King Henry! A King and Prince Edward!' entered the city to confront the citizens gathered beyond the gates. Protesting that he had only come to claim what was rightfully his as the son of the duke of York, he was allowed to stay the night. The city relented sufficiently to furnish his men with victuals and lodgings, on the condition that they moved on by noon the following day. Edward, still accompanied by Richard, Rivers and Hastings, and their relatively small retinues, headed south. The truculence of the city of York reflected the unease of a region caught between the Neville adherents of Warwick and the followers of Henry Percy. As he moved towards London, his policy of restoring the Percy heir to Northumberland paid off. The irony was that the Percys were traditionally Lancastrian, and the Nevilles had been Yorkists. Edward exploited the uncertainty and the cross-currents of conflicting loyalties by his bold and energetic action. A clerk, who seems to have been with Edward throughout this arduous time, has left us a highly intelligent and detailed account of Edward's journey and the travails he suffered. His work, known as *The Historie of the Arrivall of Edward IV in England*, explained that one reason the small force was not overwhelmed by insurgents was because people knew well 'the great courage and hardiness that he was of, with the perfect assurance of the fellowship that was with him'. Although the account became 'official' when Edward had copies of it made, the insights with which it is furnished have the ring of truth about them. Edward's victories at Mortimer's Cross, Towton and Losecoat Field, combined with a knowledge of his ability to take swift and brutal reprisals against his enemies if need be, would have given most challengers pause for thought. His 'fellowship', of course, included a young duke who had shown a promising aptitude for military service so far, as well as Rivers and Hastings with their experience and capacity for effective action.[10]

The *Arrivall* also shows that Edward's policy of restoring Percy in Northumberland, while it caused him to suffer disaster initially, was manifestly desirable if the region were to become stable in the long term. As Edward passed close to John Mantagu at Pontefract, the marquess 'in no wise troubled him, nor none of his fellowship, but suffered him to pass in peaceable wise'. The reason Montagu could not act against Edward was because 'he could not have gathered, nor made, a fellowship of sufficient number to have openly resisted him in his quarrel'. Only one man could command the loyalty of the region in sufficient numbers to resist Edward:

> For the great part of the noblemen and commons in those parts were towards the Earl of Northumberland, and would not stir with any lord or nobleman other than with the said Earl, or at least by his commandment.

If the marquess Montagu had attempted to assemble forces against Edward, the people would not have gone to his assistance, 'nor for any commandment of higher authority', while the earl 'sat still'. The men that Montagu could rely on had no quarrel with Edward, while the Percy adherents would have readily torn him to pieces for the damage done to their families at Towton. Because the earl of Northumberland 'would not stir', he had done 'a notable good service' to Edward. The clerk's assessment sheds a light on the strength of magnate power in the localities. The earl's tenants and retainers had their own political views, but would not stir unless called upon to do so by their immediate lord. Even then, they preferred to share their lord's motivation. Montagu's personal disaffection was not sufficient to marshal his forces against Edward, as heir to the duke of York, because his Neville retainers had fought for the duke of York against King Henry.[11]

Edward still had a comparatively small force and his progress south was still a hazardous undertaking. It was only when he reached Nottingham that reinforcements arrived in sufficient numbers to increase his confidence. It was here that Sir William Parr and Sir James Harrington arrived with 600 men. Parr had been a prominent supporter of Warwick and his defection reminds us of the growing importance and capacity for independent political action of the upper gentry. Harrington, from a family that had been early and unwavering supporters of the house of York, had recently been given good cause to renew his faith in the dynasty by Richard's intervention against Stanley at Hornby. The 'two good bands of men, well arrayed and prepared for war' which these 'good knights' brought with them, demonstrates the quality and extent of the 'fellowship' members of the upper gentry could present. It might also be noted that while James Harrington was riding to Edward's aid, his nemesis, Thomas lord Stanley, was still busy trying to get his hands on Hornby. He had managed to acquire a great cannon, by the name of 'Mile End', from Warwick's artillery at Bristol. While the siege of Hornby may have preoccupied Stanley and account for his absence over the next crucial weeks, the cannon does not seem to have been of much use. Harrington had sufficient means to repel Stanley's attack on Hornby, while at the same time riding at the king's side.[12]

At Leicester they were joined by 3,000 men raised by Lord Hastings. Edward now commanded an army. Hastings' contingent reminds us of the unassailable power of an established regional lord. No king could manage to effectively govern the kingdom without the support of such men. Warwick could be in no doubt now that his cousin posed a serious threat to the new regime. He moved from London to his heartlands at Coventry to await reinforcements. With substantial support among the nobility, including the earl of Oxford, the duke of Exeter, the duke of Somerset, the marquess of Dorset, the earl of Devon, the earl of Shrewsbury, Viscount Beaumont and Lord Stanley, not to mention the duke of Clarence, Warwick could bide his time. He was also expecting Margaret and Prince Edward to set sail from France at any moment. Few at this stage would have bet against the earl. A battle against Edward would remove a dangerous enemy even if the future beyond that was far from clear. Edward was aware that he needed to act quickly and decisively. He had little respect for Warwick's military abilities and was rightly confident about his own. Scattering the forces of Oxford, Exeter and Beaumont, who fled at his approach, he turned to Coventry and offered Warwick battle. Warwick refused and turned down the rather audacious offer of a full pardon. He said he would accept only under extensive conditions, which Edward in turn refused. Leaving the earl of Warwick behind him, Edward turned south and made camp at the town of Warwick, aware that Clarence was approaching with his retainers.

On 2 April 1471 Clarence approached from Burford on the Banbury road. On 3 April Edward took his army out of Warwick and advanced to meet his brother. Three miles outside the town they drew their forces up, facing each other in battle order with only half a mile separating their troops. Edward displayed his banners and 'set his people in array'. Suddenly he left his army, 'taking with him his brother of Gloucester, the Lord Rivers, Lord Hastings, and few other, and went towards his brother of Clarence'. As he crossed the space between the two armies, Clarence responded by leaving his own host, 'taking with him a few noblemen'. It was precisely in this form of grand theatre at which Edward excelled. Bold, dramatic and irresistible, such gestures formed part of the repertoire of chivalric pageantry expected of great medieval kings. Clarence had probably been wavering in his support of Warwick ever since the reconciliation with Margaret and the relegation of his prospects in favour of Prince Edward and Anne Neville. Pressure had been brought to bear on him from his mother, duchess Cecily, and his sisters, Anne, duchess of Exeter, Elizabeth, duchess of Suffolk, and Margaret, duchess of Burgundy. Interestingly enough, Polydore Vergil, no lover of Richard, gave the duke of Gloucester a prominent role in the events on the Banbury road, 'as though he had been appointed arbiter of all controversies'. The three brothers embraced, trumpets and minstrels struck up and Edward, leaving his own army behind, followed Clarence into his army of over 4,000 men, still only accompanied by a small retinue of his own. There was general rejoicing and relief as the two armies joined and celebrated peace. As Edward marched on London in the company of his two brothers, there can be no doubt which he trusted most. For nearly a year Richard had shared with him the fearful dangers of flight, exile and perilous return. It would still require two hard-fought battles to secure the throne, and in both of those Richard was to play his part.[13]

LONDON ACCEPTS EDWARD

Once more Edward took bold and decisive action attended by enormous risk. In his rear, John Montagu and Warwick had set off in pursuit. His flanks were harried by the forces led by Exeter and Oxford, who had regrouped, and ahead of him lay the duke of Somerset with his brother, the marquess of Dorset and the earl of Devon. Margaret and Prince Edward had set sail from France on 24 March and were expected somewhere in the south at any time. If Warwick had co-ordinated his forces and acted with commensurate vigour, Edward would have been overwhelmed by superior numbers. As it happened, Edward, never regarding Warwick's military abilities very highly, completely outmanoeuvred the earl, steadily gathered strength, exploited all the divisions and uncertainties in the enemy camp and seized the initiative. As he approached London it became clear that Margaret was indeed about to land in the West Country, but this played directly into Edward's hands. Edmund Beaufort, duke of Somerset, his brother John, marquess of Dorset, and John Courtney, heir to the earl of Devon, had left the capital to meet her, leaving only the hapless archbishop of York, George Neville, in charge. He did what he could to muster support for the flagging regime by placing King Henry VI on a horse and causing him to process through the streets of the city. It was a public relations disaster, achieving the exact opposite of the intended purpose. The author of the *Arrivall* heard that Henry's entourage 'was so little and feeble, as there and then was showed' and 'their might was so little', that the citizens feared for their safety. The *Great Chronicle of London* reported that the archbishop of York had to hold Henry's hand all the way, and there were so few attendants that the progress was 'more like a play than the showing of a prince to win men's hearts; for by this means he lost many and won none'. Edward was approaching with a considerable force and the city fathers did not want to 'sustain harms and damages irreparable'. More important, the king, that is Edward IV, 'had many great and mighty friends, lovers and servitors within the said city'. London had always been a friend to Edward, and his instincts in 1461 and 1471, to secure the centre of government administration and the visible instruments of power, were the same, and equally effective on both occasions. It is notable that his progress south had increased his resources and support with every mile. From the barest threads of help in the north, occasioned by doubt and suspicion on the part of the northerners and dissembling bluff on Edward's, he now all but had his hands on the throne again. Richard, with him all the way in 1471, was to experience the reverse in 1483, and was to be only too aware of the contrast.[14]

On 10 April 1471 George Neville, archbishop of York, secretly abandoned Henry VI and submitted to Edward IV. The citizens of London did likewise and on 11 April Edward entered the city in triumph, led by the Flemish gunners who had accompanied him from the Netherlands and had been with him throughout the last two hectic months. He went straight to St Paul's where Henry VI was lodged in the bishop's palace, and took the old king into custody. One report describes Henry as shaking hands with Edward and saying, 'My cousin of York, you are very welcome. I know that in your hands my life will not be in danger.' It was a unique moment in English history. There was, however, only room for one king at a time; it must have been clear to everybody apart from Henry VI that his optimism was misplaced. Two contemporary accounts briefly report that Edward 'seized' his rival and had him conveyed to the Tower. The Readeption was over.[15]

Edward then visited his wife in Westminster Abbey, where his daughters were also residing, and met his son for the first time. He named him Edward after Saint Edward the Confessor, in whose precincts at the Abbey the boy had been born. When he became Edward V for a brief period in 1483, his mother, Elizabeth Woodville, would find herself in sanctuary at Westminster again.

BARNET: RICHARD'S FIRST TASTE OF BATTLE

Edward IV, meanwhile, did not have much time to enjoy his restoration to kingship; he learnt on Good Friday, 12 April, that Warwick was approaching the city. The following day he rode out of London with Gloucester, Clarence, Rivers and Hastings to Barnet to confront Warwick, Montagu, Oxford, Exeter and Beaumont. He also took with him a man who would not be participating in the bloody business of hand-to-hand fighting: Henry VI. This may have been an insurance policy in case things did not go according to plan.

On Easter Sunday, 14 April, as dawn broke, Edward attacked in a thick mist. The previous evening he had drawn his men up close to Warwick's lines and ordered them to be silent. Warwick's artillery shot over their heads for much of the night, not realising how close the enemy were. The two opposing armies had not aligned directly facing each other so that when they clashed in the morning Oxford's troops on the Lancastrian right overwhelmed Edward's left flank and poured down the hill into Barnet. By the time their captains had managed to regain control of them and march them back to the battlefield, the armies had shifted in an anti-clockwise direction. When Oxford's men approached they encountered Warwick's men who, mistaking Oxford's livery, a star with streams, for Edward's, the sun with streams, opened fire on their comrades. Believing themselves to have been betrayed, they turned and fled crying 'Treason!' John Montagu had been killed and Warwick decided that the day was lost. As he attempted to flee he was trapped in a wood and killed.

The earl of Oxford managed, yet again, to escape, while the duke of Exeter, badly wounded, was not recognised at first and left for dead on the field. He survived but spent the next four years in the Tower. The bodies of Warwick and Montagu were displayed in St Paul's before being properly buried. The indignities inflicted on the corpses of Edward's father, brother and uncle after the battle of Wakefield in 1460 were not repeated.

Edward had been in the thick of the fighting, which had been very severe, and so had Richard. This was the 18-year-old duke's first major battle and he acquitted himself with distinction. No contemporary chronicler records Richard's actions at Barnet but the *Arrivall* ascribes Edward's victory to 'the faithful, welbeloved and mighty assistance of his fellowship'. The Burgundian chronicler, Waurin, described him bearing the brunt of the struggle alongside his brothers, and a Hanseatic merchant recorded in a newsletter shortly after the battle that Richard had been slightly wounded. The Croyland Chronicle and Warkworth do not mention Richard in relation to the battle, but there are two pieces of evidence that suggest that he was in the midst of the fray at Barnet. The first is the circumstantial evidence provided by the fact that Edward gave Richard command of the vanguard at the battle of Tewkesbury, less than three weeks later. It is more than likely that Richard's conduct at Barnet recommended him for such an important military command. The second appears in the indenture drawn up by Richard in 1477 for his religious foundation at Queens' College Cambridge. In return for a grant, the college are to admit four priests who, among their various duties, are to say prayers for the souls of those men who had died in Richard's service at Barnet and Tewkesbury. Two of these, John Milewater and Thomas Parr, died at Barnet. Milewater had been with Richard in Wales in January 1470 and, as receiver general of the duchy of Lancaster lands in south Wales and the March, was likely to have been a trusted member of his ducal entourage. Thomas Parr was the brother of Sir William Parr who had joined Edward at Nottingham with early reinforcements. Another brother, John Parr, was knighted at Tewkesbury and it is likely that all three came together when the Parrs rallied to Edward's cause. Thomas was specifically described as an esquire of the duke of Gloucester when he died. These men, and three others, had fought with Richard and died in his service. He did not forget them. Their deaths and the ferocity of the close combat at Barnet suggest that Richard faced very real danger.[16]

TEWKESBURY: RICHARD'S FIRST COMMAND

On the very day of the battle, Margaret landed at Weymouth in Dorset. Two days after the battle, the news of her arrival reached London. Edward gave himself and his commanders barely a week to recover before setting out to confront the remaining Lancastrians. If his behaviour in September 1470, when he remained in the north while Warwick and Clarence landed in the south, has exposed him to accusations of laziness and sluggishness in response to threats, his speed and boldness in 1471 were formidable. Hastings had written to a friend in 1463 saying that the king preferred 'the chase' to fighting, and in the 1470s this trait became pronounced; but Edward took the lead in five major battles during his career – there are few kings able to match his record of success. Margaret was certainly shaken by news of the defeat of Warwick, which reached her the very next day after the battle. It affected her strategy and put her on the back foot immediately. She recruited support in Dorset, Somerset and Wiltshire, but moved west towards Exeter to garner forces from Devon and Cornwall, rather than risk marching east towards London. Edward left London on 19 April 1471 and awaited the muster of fresh troops at Windsor. He celebrated St George's day, 23 April, in his new chapel of St George at Windsor and set out for the final confrontation on the next morning. Richard's experiences in these few weeks in the spring of 1471 would have been the dream of any aspiring knight in the medieval period. Victorious in battle, he celebrated the feast of the patron saint of soldiers with his warrior king and brothers-in-arms, before setting out with his knights and esquires to confront mortal danger once more. Morale was no doubt high. If Richard had faced the nadir of his fortunes in October 1470, he may well have experienced the zenith in 1471.

Margaret's initial aim was to move north and gather support, in Wales at first and then, possibly, from Cheshire and Lancashire. She had always preferred the north. It was important to do battle quickly so that Margaret did not have time to recruit or cause disruption in the southern counties, but Edward could not afford to let her slip past him and so moved cautiously at first. At last sure that Margaret intended to move north, he pounced. In a single day his entire army marched 30 miles from Abingdon to Cirencester, within a day's march of Gloucester. The Lancastrians needed to cross the River Severn into Wales, where Jasper

Tudor's retainers would join them, but the city of Gloucester refused her entry. She would have to cross further upstream and this meant marching west as well as north. With yet another 30 mile march Edward caught up with her as her army attempted to ford the river at Tewkesbury. On 4 May 1471 Edward advanced to meet the last of his Lancastrian challengers. His ordinance, having been supplemented by the armaments from the Tower of London and Warwick's artillery captured at Barnet, was superior to that of the Lancastrians. Instead of waiting to be blasted to pieces, Edmund Beaufort, duke of Somerset, launched the vanguard of the Lancastrian army directly at Edward. There were so many hedges and ditches that Somerset was able to charge at the flank of the king, emerging from a small hill, and take him by surprise. This was the vital moment in the battle and, judging by the account given in the *Arrivall*, Richard, in charge of the royal vanguard, came to Edward's rescue in the nick of time. Edward 'with great violence put them up the hill, and so also the king's vanguard, being in the rule of the duke of Gloucester'. As Somerset fell back he was attacked by a group of some 200 spearmen Edward had placed in a wood to guard his flank. The Lancastrian vanguard were routed and fled as best they could. Edward turned his attention to the other Lancastrian battle headed by Edward, prince of Wales, and soon put them to flight too. The son of Henry VI, and Margaret's great hope, Prince Edward, 'was taken fleeing towards the town, and slain in the field'.[17]

Somerset's brother, John Beaufort, was killed on the battlefield along with John Courtenay, earl of Devon and John lord Wenlock. The only major rebel to survive was Somerset himself, who had sought sanctuary in Tewkesbury Abbey with many of his desperate comrades. Edward had them all forcibly removed and, on 6 May, Richard, as constable of England, presided over the trial and execution of Edmund Beaufort, duke of Somerset. Margaret was captured the next day and the Lancastrian cause was in ruins. There was still a little unfinished business. On 21 May Edward returned to London in triumph. In his absence the city had repelled a serious assault by the Bastard of Fauconberg, Thomas Fauconberg, the illegitimate nephew of Warwick. Earl Rivers and the citizens themselves had repulsed a horde of rebels from Essex, Kent and Calais, demonstrating the fact that if Warwick had managed to coordinate all the forces of his supporters, Edward would have had little chance to recover his throne. Fauconberg was offered a pardon in return for his submission, which he accepted. He surrendered himself and his fleet to Richard, duke of Gloucester, who placed him in custody. In September, for undisclosed reasons, he was executed anyway. Edward had learnt, and there are hints that his brother had also, that when it came to reasons of state, promises, pardons and protection were not inviolable. On the night of Edward's return to London, Henry VI was finally put to death in the Tower. With the death of Edward, his son, Henry was the last of the legitimate Lancastrian line and his survival would have allowed him to become the focus of plots. His son had been the bigger threat, a fact which possibly accounts for Henry's longevity, but his demise after Tewkesbury was inevitable. Both Warkworth and the Croyland Chronicle hint strongly at Richard's involvement in the old king's murder, and this became a commonplace in the Tudor story. It is, of course, irrelevant who did the deed: only Edward IV could have sanctioned and ordered the execution. Richard had shown many qualities during Edward's flight, exile and recovery campaign: he had been loyal, brave, effective and indispensable. None of these characteristics would have been of any use if Richard had not also been ruthless, decisive, and, when necessary, merciless.

4

LORD OF THE NORTH: 1471–1483

THE DUCHY OF LANCASTER

After Edward IV's remarkable recovery of the throne, a major redistribution of power was necessary to fill the gap left by the death of the earl of Warwick. The Nevilles had been the major supporters of the Yorkists during the overthrow of Henry VI and the deaths of both Warwick and his brother John, left a vacuum in the leadership of wide areas of the north. Richard, already warden of the West March, may have been partly responsible for weaning some of the members of Warwick's affinity away from the earl, during his rebellion, and into Edward's orbit. Some of these men, however, already had connections directly with the king through their duchy of Lancaster offices. The Harrington brothers, for instance, held duchy of Lancaster posts and positions in the royal household. James Harrington was steward of Amounderness in Lancashire and also a knight of the king's household. His brother Robert was bailiff in Amounderness and Blackburn, and also a 'knight of the body'. The man who came with them to meet the king at Nottingham in March 1471, William Parr, was Richard's lieutenant as warden of the West March. John Pilkington, who lent Edward 100 marks at Doncaster, one of the first to give Edward material support in 1471, was a kinsman of the Harringtons, steward of Rochdale in the duchy of Lancaster and brother of Charles Pilkington, usher of the chamber in Edward IV's household. Warwick had been chief steward of the duchy of Lancaster and while he was closely allied to the king he was able to exploit his office to extend his patronage in areas beyond the boundaries of his own estates. Officials of the duchy were ultimately, however, royal officials, often appointed from the royal household. When Warwick rebelled, some of them made a political choice to leave his affinity and support the Yorkist king. It must have been clear to Edward that Richard duke of Gloucester, to whom he owed a considerable debt for his unswerving support throughout the recent ordeals, was the ideal replacement for Warwick, not only as lord of the Neville estates, but also as chief steward of the duchy of Lancaster in the north. The combination would allow a powerful connection to remain intact, but also strengthen the royal element within it.

In June 1471, Richard took the place of Warwick as chief steward of the duchy of Lancaster in the north. The duchy was a strange, anomalous mass of lordships, 'honors', estates, castles, and even towns and cities, across the kingdom. Its lands, and the revenues due from them, were the property of the duke of Lancaster and his heirs. The whole elaborate collection of lands and officials had been created by Henry III to give to his son Edmund. Henry was keen to compensate his second son after the failure of the Sicilian expedition during which Edmund had anticipated becoming king of Sicily. Instead he was endowed with lands confiscated from the earls of Leicester and Derby and granted the honour, county, town and castle of Lancaster, and all the royal demesnes in the county. He became the earl of Lancaster. Through marriage and further forfeitures he added to his estates, which covered many counties in both England and Wales. The whole collection was unusual in the freedom of jurisdiction it gave the earl. These privileges were extended by Edward I to include the exalted powers of seigniorial rights usually only exercised by the king. The writ of the earl, for instance, could not be countermanded by a royal writ in the earldom of Lancaster. Tenants could be tried in the earl's court, fines levied, pleas heard and leases confiscated. Eventually Edward III bestowed on the fourth earl the title of duke of Lancaster and made the county of Lancashire a county palatine. Palatinate powers were royal powers in devolution. When Duke Henry died in 1361, his daughter Blanche inherited his lands and they came into the keeping of her husband, John of Gaunt. John, the third son of Edward III, was duly made duke of Lancaster, and he continued the process of adding to the lordships under the control of the duchy.

Such a vast collection of lands, and the vice-regal powers the duke could exercise within them, must inevitably challenge the authority of the crown if a dispute should arise between the two. In 1399 Richard II confiscated the duchy from his cousin Henry, who had been banished from the kingdom. Henry returned to reclaim his inheritance and, in so doing, deposed Richard and became king himself. Henry IV, perhaps as an insurance policy in case he lost the throne he had just usurped, kept the duchy of Lancaster separate from his crown lands. A charter issued the day after his coronation declared that the duchy of Lancaster could only be inherited by his heirs. With the duke now also the king, the nature of the duchy altered. While palatine privileges still only applied to the county of Lancashire, the royal prerogative now applied to all duchy lands. Appointments and revenues from the lands of the duchy came under the control of the king, but were still administered through his duchy council and its officials. A huge collection of estates, scattered throughout nearly every county of England and Wales, was held together under an administrative system independent of the crown and yet controlled by the king.[1]

When Edward IV, like Henry IV, usurped the throne, he did not disturb the unity that the duchy, despite its complex and disparate nature, had managed to evolve. Edward declared the duchy forfeit to the crown, but also that it would now be held by himself and his heirs. In other words it was a personal, heritable holding but incorporated into the king's possession by act of parliament and embodied in letters patent under the Great Seal of England. Edward kept the administration of the duchy under the control of a council, which met regularly in London, with its own seal, chancellor, stewards and receivers. The revenues from the lands were collected by the receivers in every duchy lordship, passed to the receiver general and, if needed, into the royal household. The officers appointed to posts in the duchy were answerable to their stewards, and they to the chief steward. Patronage and its lucrative benefits flowed through this system directly from the king to the localities. In areas where duchy lands, adjacent to each other, formed a substantial royal interest across a region, the absence of a powerful magnate would allow the lesser nobility and the gentry to look to the crown as their immediate lord. Where a magnate could not offer consistent security and direction, these duchy officials had an alternative to which they could resort.[2]

Edward decided in the aftermath of the battle of Tewkesbury to replace Warwick in the north with Richard, with the intention of strengthening royal control. Throughout the next 12 years Richard was able to use his duchy patronage, his inheritance of the Neville lands and his royal status to create an unprecedented unity of lordship across the north of England. Edward built up other lordships, such as Hastings' in the Midlands and those connected with the Woodvilles in the West Country and Wales, but Richard's grew to an extent that none could match. As well as Warwick's post of chief steward, he also took from Thomas lord Stanley the post of chief steward of the duchy of Lancaster within the county palatine of Lancashire. Stanley already had cause to dislike Richard, but this was a direct intrusion of an unwelcome power into a region the Stanleys had dominated for more than a century. In fact Edward was to recognise the strength of Stanley's lordship in the area and to allow him to retain his authority in the north-west, but the tension between the duke of Gloucester and Stanley remained. Stanley retained the post of receiver in the county palatine, which enabled him to keep control of the revenues in his region. The post of chief steward, however, gave Richard a wide control of patronage in all the duchy lands in the north, with many subordinate appointments within his gift and authority over grants, leases and punishments. In addition, he became keeper of the forest of Bowland straddling the eastern border of Lancashire, and master forester of the duchy forests in Lancashire.

THE NEVILLE INHERITANCE

On 29 June 1471, Richard was granted the Neville estates in Yorkshire and Cumberland that had formerly belonged to Warwick. These included the lordships of Middleham, Sheriff Hutton and Penrith. He received, in addition to the post of Constable of England, the offices of Admiral and Great Chamberlain, formerly held by Warwick. On 18 May 1472, he was made keeper of the royal forests north of the Trent, perhaps to compensate him for the fact that his brother Clarence had prevailed upon the king to give back the office of Great Chamberlain, a post Clarence had previously held. It was to return to Richard in due course. Richard's steady rise to power was to seriously inconvenience Clarence. In the meantime, in December 1471, Richard had been granted the confiscated estates of John de Vere, earl of Oxford, which included no less than 80 manors in Essex worth a princely sum of £1,000 a year. Richard was able to obtain the rest of the de Vere estates by forcing Elizabeth Howard, the earl's elderly mother, to surrender her lands to him in January 1473. He has been criticised for the illegality of this act and, taken together with the 'unscrupulous greed' with which he was able to divest the dowager countess of Warwick of her lands in May 1474, has provided his detractors with plenty of ammunition. There is certainly an element in the early years of Edward's second reign of unfettered acquisitiveness on the part of the duke of Gloucester. He seemed in a desperate hurry to gain the lordship he probably believed he warranted. The evidence for his mistreatment of Elizabeth Howard, however, is all from later Tudor sources. The countess of Warwick, dragged north, removed to Middleham Castle and declared legally dead, might also have her case for mistreatment challenged. Richard had married her daughter and the countess joined them at their main residence. The Lancastrian proclivities of these disinherited ladies must also be taken into consideration. The countess of Warwick had arrived in England with Margaret of Anjou and Prince Henry, to deprive Edward of his throne. The son of Elizabeth Howard, John de Vere, was busy harrying the inhabitants of Cornwall with a hostile fleet while Richard was seizing his mother's lands. These factors do not in themselves justify Richard's behaviour, both ladies had legal rights that were trounced, but they might mitigate the opprobrium of historians.[3]

One impact of Richard's accumulation of Neville lands in Yorkshire and Cumberland was to make him the latest protagonist of the junior branch of the Nevilles in their feud with the senior branch. The problem had arisen because Ralph Neville, earl of Westmorland, had married twice; his second wife, Joan Beaufort, was of higher rank than his first. Joan, the daughter of John of Gaunt, was the grandmother of Warwick the Kingmaker who had exacerbated the problem by switching his support, with his father, the earl of Salisbury, from the Lancastrians to the Yorkists. The senior branch remained staunchly Lancastrian. Richard was able to resolve the issue through a combination of power and good lordship. In 1477, Ralph Neville, the nephew and heir to the elderly 2nd earl, formally agreed to quit the claims of the senior branch and to join the duke of Gloucester as his ally. Richard's dominance could not be challenged without considerable risk, but Ralph would have found the lordship of Richard far more effective in offering protection, and much more appealing in opening up access to the royal court, than fruitless opposition could provide.

Richard was to add to the Neville lands and gradually monopolise the available lordships in the north and the patronage that came with them. In 1474 he received the forfeited Hungerford estates, and added to them in 1478. In February 1475 he was made sheriff of Cumberland for life and in June 1475 he was granted Skipton in Craven from the Clifford estates. He consolidated his position in the north by swapping some of his southern properties for northern ones. His wife, Anne Neville, inherited estates in Derbyshire and Hertfordshire. Richard exchanged these for the lordships of Cottingham near Hull, and Scarborough on the east coast of Yorkshire. In March 1478 Corfe in Dorset, Farleigh Hungerford in Wiltshire and Sudeley in Gloucestershire were exchanged for Richmond and Helmsley, both in north Yorkshire. The duchy lands in Yorkshire, centred on Pickering in the north of the county and Tickhill in the south, included a swathe of adjacent lordships from Pontefract through to Leeds and Bradford, and incorporating the forest of Knaresborough. His interests in Yorkshire brought him to the borders of Lancashire through the forest of Bowland, and into Lancashire and north Cheshire through the master forestership of the duchy forests in Lancashire and his stewardship of the county of Lancashire. Richard had taken over Warwick's Neville affinity and consciously forged an unassailable hegemony north of the River Trent.[4]

MARRIAGE AND TROUBLE WITH CLARENCE

Richard had been granted the lands Warwick had inherited from his father, the earl of Salisbury, and the Montagu lands held by Warwick's mother. The Beauchamp and Despenser lands came to Warwick through his wife, Anne Beauchamp, and passed to his daughters Isabel and Anne. Warwick had not been attainted for treason, so his lands had not been forfeit to the crown. This suited both Richard and Clarence because the lands could be held by parliamentary grant or inheritance, rather than as a gift from the king that might be revoked. Clarence had married the elder daughter, Isabel, and held her sister, Anne, as a ward. Anne had married Edward prince of Wales, during Warwick's attempt to overthrow Edward

IV, but, after the battle of Tewkesbury, she was now a widow. She had only been 14 years old when she had married the 17-year-old Prince Edward and their marriage had lasted only a little over four months. We cannot know the thoughts of Anne concerning the early death of her husband, but she was no doubt well aware of the fact that the whole debacle had been caused by her father's desperate attempt to regain his ascendancy in England. Her next marriage, to Richard duke of Gloucester, agreed upon in February 1472 when Anne was approaching 16 years of age, made much more sense.

Anne Neville was the daughter of Richard's first cousin and therefore Richard's cousin once removed. Although it technically required papal dispensation because the couple were related within the prohibited degrees of consanguinity and affinity, such marriages were commonplace among the gentry and the aristocracy in the 15th century. Dispensation was sought and duly granted. Although Anne and Richard had spent several years of their childhood together at Middleham, and therefore personal attraction cannot be ruled out, the marriage would not have taken place if Anne had not the right to a half share in her father's inheritance. The only difficulty was Clarence's desire to keep the entire inheritance for himself. In order to wrest Anne from his brother's 'protection', Richard would inevitably come into conflict with Clarence.[5]

Clarence, despite his treachery during Warwick's rebellion, had been restored to his lands by Edward, except those restored to Henry Percy, for which Clarence was compensated. Isabel had brought with her all the Beauchamp and Despenser estates of her father and Clarence had no intention of sharing them with his brother. The surest way of preventing this was to keep Anne away from Richard. The Croyland chronicler states that Clarence 'caused the damsel to be concealed'. He tells us that Richard discovered her being kept in the city of London 'in the habit of a cookmaid'. Richard apparently rescued her from this ignominious captivity and removed her to the sanctuary of St Martin's. The chronicler, who was a councillor of Edward IV and not prone to inventing wild tales, wrote that the consequence of Richard's action was that 'violent discussion arose between the brothers'. Clarence agreed that Richard might marry Anne, but refused to countenance a division of the Warwick estates. The matter was referred to the king who sat in judgement in the council chamber while his ducal brothers presented their cases before him. The Croyland chronicler, who may have witnessed the scene himself, said that all present, even the lawyers, 'were quite surprised that these princes should find arguments in such abundance by means of which to support their respective causes'. In fact, the chronicler explained, the three brothers – the king and the two dukes - were possessed of 'surpassing talents'. Richard was to show an interest in law later in his career and it may be possible to infer from the chronicler's record that, like his brothers, he was articulate and intelligent.[6]

At the time of Richard's marriage to Anne, Clarence was created earl of Warwick and Salisbury, perhaps to appease him before the dispute got out of hand. It may be that Edward was hoping to reassure Clarence that his rights would not be affected by Richard's marriage, but in any event Clarence continued to refuse to hand over any land. He became particularly concerned when Richard took their mother-in-law, Anne Beauchamp, dowager countess of Warwick, to Middleham Castle. Clarence was probably convinced that Richard would put pressure on the countess to gain more of her lands. An act of resumption in November 1473 caused Clarence to temporarily lose the estates he had acquired through his marriage to Isabel and may indicate that Edward was losing patience with him. It forced him to accept the compromises embodied in the acts of parliament that settled the dispute. In May 1474 the countess's lands were divided between Richard and Clarence as if she had already died. Richard added to his northern lands and received, among others, the lordship of Barnard Castle in County Durham. In the final settlement in 1475 Richard was given the title to the Neville lands. All the Neville lands were, in fact, entailed in the male line, which meant that, in the absence of any sons of Warwick, they should have gone to his brother's son, George, duke of Bedford, and not to his daughters at all. John Mantagu's son, George, was still a minor and, like the countess, he was deprived of his inheritance by act of parliament. The 1475 act, however, stipulated that Richard and his heirs would only keep their entitlement to the Neville lands while George Neville, or any children he had, were alive. If George died without heirs, Richard's title would revert to a life interest: it would not be heritable to his successors. This was far from ideal from Richard's point of view and left him slightly vulnerable to the cycle of fortune. In fact, unfortunately for Richard, George did die without heirs, in May 1483, shortly after Edward IV had died. This may have contributed to a feeling of uncertainty and unease in Richard's mind at that time, but in 1475 he may have felt that further acts of parliament, or the marriage of George, would resolve the problem. Parliament was simply attempting to preserve the recognised rules of inheritance upon which so many of its class depended. The act discriminated against George Neville, preventing him and his heirs from inheriting his father's lands, while protecting the rights of George's cousin, Richard, Lord Latimer. Richard, duke of Gloucester, can be seen to be attempting to mitigate the worst effects of the 1475 act, first by gaining custody of George Neville in 1480, though he could not protect him from death, and secondly by attempting to gain the wardship of Richard Neville, Lord Latimer. Unfortunately for Duke Richard, and perhaps happily for Latimer, the *de facto* heir of the Nevilles had powerful guardians, notably Thomas Bourchier, archbishop of Canterbury, and he remained out of Richard's reach. Nevertheless the duke did manage to obtain the custody of Latimer's Yorkshire estates.

Richard's marriage to Anne was to produce just one child, Edward of Middleham, born in 1476. He did not survive childhood and died on 9 April 1484. His mother did not outlive her son by even a year, dying herself on 16 March 1485. Although the marriage was not fruitful, in terms of the number of children it produced, perhaps because Anne suffered from ill-health, there is no evidence that the union was anything less than a happy one. Richard had two illegitimate children before he was married, John and Katharine, but none afterwards. There is no record of any infidelity after the marriage: a considerable contrast to the behaviour of his brother, Edward IV. Richard acknowledged both his illegitimate children and provided for them. John of Pontefract was knighted in 1483 and made captain of Calais in March 1485. Katharine was married to William Herbert, earl of Huntingdon, as his second wife, in 1484, with a substantial dowry of 1,000 marks a year. The loss of his son, Edward, was to cause Richard considerable grief, and there is no reason to doubt his own words concerning Anne's death, that he was 'sorry and in heart as heavy as man might be'.[7]

THE FALL OF CLARENCE

George, duke of Clarence, unsteady, unstable, perpetually dissatisfied, eventually exasperated Edward to such an extent that he was executed in 1478. The trouble seems to have been fuelled by an act of resumption which deprived Clarence of some of his lands. The Croyland chronicler's description of the sulking Clarence paints a picture of petulance:

> For that duke now seemed gradually more and more to estrange himself from the king's presence, hardly ever to utter a word in council, and not without reluctance to eat or drink at the king's abode.

As the chronicler admits, the real problem that compounded the estrangement was a coincidence of deaths. Clarence's wife, Isabel, died in December 1476, possibly as a result of giving birth to her second son, and left her husband free to remarry. A few weeks later, 5 January 1477, Charles the Bold, duke of Burgundy, was killed at Nancy in Lorraine fighting against the Swiss. He and Margaret had had no children, but Charles left a daughter, Mary, from a previous marriage. She was now the heiress of the extensive lands of Burgundy, and, at the age of 19, a glittering prize in the European marriage market. Her guardian, and the regent of Burgundy while negotiations for her marriage were taking place, was Margaret, dowager duchess of Burgundy, Clarence's sister. She immediately proposed the marriage of Mary and Clarence in order to strengthen ties between her duchy and England. Edward would not hear of such a scheme. Not only would Clarence become the duke of a major European state, but Mary, descended from John of Gaunt, had a claim to the throne of England and there was no telling what mischief Clarence might create as a result. As Croyland observed, 'So great a contemplated exaltation as this, of his ungrateful brother, displeased the king'. After desultory negotiations, Edward finally agreed to support the candidature of Archduke Maximilian of Austria, heir of the Holy Roman Emperor Frederick III, and Mary and Maximilian were betrothed. Clarence was outraged. Edward had blocked his advancement with all the power at his disposal.[8]

Clarence began to behave in a dangerous and erratic way. In May 1477 a number of arrests were made for treason and a member of Clarence's household was among those executed at Tyburn. Instead of heeding this warning, Clarence burst into the council chamber at Westminster and declared that his man was innocent and had been wrongly hanged. When Edward heard this news he left Windsor and summoned Clarence to appear before him in the palace of Westminster, where, in the presence of the mayor and aldermen of London, he charged

Clarence with conduct 'derogatory to the laws of the realm'. Clarence was taken into custody and parliament summoned for January 1478. There, in person, the king accused his brother of 'unnatural and loathly treason'. Only the king spoke against Clarence and only Clarence replied in his own defence. In fact he did not attempt to answer the charges but merely denied them all and offered 'to defend his cause with his own hand', presumably in ordeal by battle. The king was in no mood to offer Clarence any mercy and parliament duly found him guilty and condemned him. He was executed privately, in the Tower, on 18 February 1478. The Italian commentator, Mancini, first reported the story that Clarence had been drowned in 'a butt of malmsey wine'. He also believed that Richard was 'overcome with grief for his brother' and that he blamed the Woodville faction at court for the execution.[9]

There is no reason to believe that Richard was not dismayed by the events that led to the death of his brother. There is certainly none to implicate him in the deed. This inconvenient detail did not prevent Charles Ross from opining that Richard must have been 'at least an assenting partner in the overthrow of Clarence'. Because Richard's gains from the destruction of his brother were not 'by any means negligible' it is certain that he 'condoned – to say the least – the carefully orchestrated overthrow of his brother'. It is true that Richard managed to obtain the castle of Richmond in north Yorkshire, and he prized the acquisition, but he exchanged land in return for it. His son, Edward of Middleham, was created earl of Salisbury instead of Clarence, and Richard himself was restored to the office of Great Chamberlain which had been taken from him by Clarence, but these may well have been inducements offered by Edward to prevent his younger brother intervening on Clarence's behalf.[10]

Mancini, generally hostile to Richard, would have had little reason for exonerating him from involvement in Clarence's death if he had indeed been complicit. He was convinced that the Woodvilles were the main protagonists in the affair, and he was certainly correct in assuming that they perceived Clarence as a threat. One accusation made against Clarence by the king, that the duke had 'put about that the king was a bastard', would have endangered them all. The suggestion that the king was illegitimate had first been mooted in the rebellion of 1469 and was to briefly resurface in the summer of 1483. Such an accusation is the inevitable consequence of any challenge to the throne and rarely precedes it. It is a tiresome commonplace throughout English history and close to the lips of every traitor in the reign of every monarch. Edward's fabled illegitimacy has nevertheless received unwarranted publicity in recent times. Michael Jones has argued that Edward was indeed illegitimate. This theory has, of course, implications for the usurpation of Richard in 1483. It is based on the notion that the duke of York could not have been present at the time of Edward's conception because he was vigorously pursuing the French king, Charles VII, in a five-week campaign near Pontoise. The duchess, Cecily, meanwhile, is said to have had an affair with an archer at the duke's headquarters in Rouen. Jones concluded that the duke 'was absent at the crucial time'. The contrast between Edward's modest christening in the 'small private chapel in Rouen Castle' and that of his brother Edmund a year later in Rouen Cathedral is cited as evidence to support the theory that Edward was a bastard. In fact the duke of York was rarely more than a day's ride from Cecily throughout the campaign from July 1441 until his official return to Rouen on 20 August. Pontoise, which he secured by breaking the siege on 6 August, is only 40 miles from Rouen and much of the business there was the tedious reduction of a fortress by bombardment and starvation. There would have been ample opportunity to return to Rouen, and there clearly was. Furthermore, there are perfectly reasonable explanations for the contrast in the christenings of the two boys. The Yorks had already had a son, Henry, who had died in infancy. Edward, as was customary, was christened quickly and in the safety of the York household to avoid the risk of his death. When Edmund was born, with a healthy heir already in the nursery, there was less need for caution. It is also possible that the duke of York was contemplating setting up his second son as a Norman landowner, while Edward would inherit the duke's titles and lands in England. A public christening in Rouen cathedral would have been an appropriate way of establishing Edmund in the consciousness of the Norman people, something that was not necessary in the case of his principle heir, Edward. When Edward was just 3 years old his father was negotiating a high-profile marriage for him with a daughter of the king of France. The king, for his part, far from harbouring doubts about Edward's paternity, offered the hand of an elder, more valuable daughter.[11]

Clarence's death may have discomfited Richard. Certainly in the last five years of Edward's reign he spent less time at court and more in the north. Mancini believed that this preference for his northern estates amounted to an estrangement with the court caused by the Woodville involvement in the death of Clarence. There is no evidence, however, of any rift between Richard and the Woodville clan. The duke attended all the state occasions at which he was expected and there is no evidence that he absented himself from the councils to which he was summoned. The amount of time he spent in the north, mainly at Middleham, from 1478 onwards, can be accounted for simply in terms of the amount of business he had to attend to there as leader of an extensive affinity. From 1479, when a truce ended, he was increasingly preoccupied with the Scottish threat, which required his presence on the border. From 1480 open warfare developed between the two kingdoms and the ensuing conflict absorbed much of Richard's attention. There are, therefore, perfectly logical reasons for Richard's apparent distance from the court without having to accept Mancini's belief that Richard needed to 'avoid the jealousy of the queen'. There can be no doubt, however, that Richard threw his energy into his northern responsibilities.[12]

A NORTHERN AFFINITY

When Richard stepped into Warwick's shoes at the head of an already existing Neville affinity, he inherited a network of closely connected families from the gentry community. These had been Warwick's servants and retainers, some of whom, as we have already seen in the cases of the Parrs, the Harringtons and the Pilkingtons, deserted Warwick during his rebellion. Their support, or lack of it, could make a difference when political equations needed balancing. Duchy lordships, and gentry service within them, allowed these families access to service which might bring them rewards within the royal household. Richard's arrival allowed Warwick's retainers to protect themselves from the consequences of Warwick's fall at the same time as strengthening their access to service and patronage. Richard could offer them powerful protection, of a kind that only an active royal duke high in the king's favour could provide, and a wealth of opportunities for advancement. The ever-pressing desire to acquire status and wealth had grown during the recent conflicts, partly as a consequence of a new awareness of their own importance, but also as a consequence of survival. Communities had suffered lawlessness and disorder during the recent civil war and active members of the gentry community now looked to recover their losses, improve their fortunes and to benefit from the opportunities peace and stability could bring. Richard could bring a distinctive unity to this community while benefiting himself from the strength of its already existing connections.

Many of these connections blurred the distinction between the higher gentry and the lesser nobility. The Huddlestons, Harringtons and Dacres, for instance, were closely related. John Huddleston and James Harrington were cousins. The mother of James and Robert Harrington, Elizabeth Dacre, was the sister of Humphrey lord Dacre of Gilsland. His granddaughter, another Elizabeth Dacre, married Richard Huddleston, the son of John. Sir John Huddleston, sheriff of Cumberland, steward of Penrith and sometime warden of the west march, was of sufficient standing for two of his sons to marry into the earl of Warwick's family. He himself married the daughter of Lord Fitzhugh. The prominence of such members of the gentry had much to do with their usefulness in keeping order in difficult territory, and their service in battle. In fact the close relationship between the Huddlestons and the Harringtons had been cemented after the battle of Agincourt when Richard Huddleston had served in Sir William Harrington's retinue and married Sir William's sister. Another connection was with the Parr family: Sir Humphrey Dacre had married Mabel Parr, and there were connections with both the Greystokes and the Fitzhughs, two other families from the lesser peerage. Richard used these men in the border region, and they served him well. Sir Humphrey Dacre became lieutenant of the West March with William Parr. His son, Thomas lord Dacre, became lord warden of the March. John Huddleston was under-sheriff of the same region. Richard Huddleston became receiver, master forester and steward of Cumberland and Lancashire.[13]

Another example of the importance of this rank of society in this particular region, and the strength of the connections they were able to offer, is provided by the Harringtons and the Pilkingtons. Thomas Pilkington, the sheriff of Lancashire for most of the 1460s, and re-appointed in 1482, had married Margaret Harrington, the sister of William Harrington of Lathom. Margaret's brother, William, married Elizabeth Pilkington, the sister of Thomas Pilkington. In other words, the sister of Thomas Pilkington married the brother of his wife. The Harringtons of these marriages were the cousins of James and Robert

Harrington of Hornby and Brierley. The family connection with the Pilkingtons was strengthened when Robert Harrington married Isabel Balderstone, whose sister was married to John Pilkington, the son of Thomas. This John was Richard duke of Gloucester's chamberlain until his death in 1478. His brother, Charles Pilkington, was to become a knight of the body to Richard III and one of his closest associates.[14]

One of the men to become prominent, if not notorious, as one of Richard's most trusted councillors, was Richard Ratcliffe. While relatively unknown before he came to Richard's attention, he rose to become steward of Barnard Castle, sheriff of Westmorland and a Knight of the Garter. He also had connections with the other members of the gentry in Richard's affinity through his mother, who was a Parr. He married into the family of Lord Scrope. Francis lord Lovell, Richard's childhood friend at Middleham, married into the Fitzhugh family. The Fitzhughs, Greystokes, Dacres and Scropes were all linked to each other by marriage and extended the reach of the affinity into the ranks of the aristocracy. Richard lord Fitzhugh, for example, was a nephew of the earl of Warwick. His three aunts had married Lord Hastings, Lord Stanley and the earl of Oxford respectively. Leading members of the gentry could penetrate into this stratum of nobility through fortuitous marriages. Their prominence in Gloucester's service might recommend them to these noble families. There were other families, such as the Strangways, Metcalfes and Musgraves, who were also part of this great northern connection, united in their desire to serve and be rewarded by Richard duke of Gloucester. It was in their cooperation with each other, acting for Richard on various commissions, that their usefulness and their strength lay. These men could get things done. They worked together on commissions of array, on commissions of the peace, on commissions of oyer and terminer, and on the many others that were appointed for specific duties relating to the peace and security of the region.[15]

STANLEY AND PERCY

Richard's lordship united his fellowship into a magnate affinity whose primary function was to secure the resources of a region for the king. Richard was always aware of the need to promote the royal will, to preserve its prerogative, and not to seek to compete with it or oppose it.

He was, in truth, no more than a royal agent; it was from the sovereign power that he derived his own authority. There were times, however, when his own ambition to extend his affinity and to secure a wider and more complete hegemony in the north brought him into conflict with the only two magnates with sufficient power to challenge him. It was at these times that Edward had to exercise a restraining hand, and it was on these occasions that the need for a strong personality at the heart of medieval kingship was so clearly illustrated. These magnates understood that their interests would clash, but, provided that the king was sufficiently astute and firm, were largely content to accept his arbitration. His favour mattered to them.

Richard's growing power in the north in the early 1470s brought him into disputes with the other leading magnates in the region, Thomas lord Stanley and Henry Percy, earl of Northumberland. Richard had been attracting retainers and recruiting men into his service as soon as he was granted the Warwick lands in Cumberland and Yorkshire. It was inevitable that some of these men would have already been retained by other lords. Some may have been paid a fee and others simply a gift or an item of livery, such as a badge. For some, just a promise of future help was enough. In return the feed man would provide the service for which he was required, but others might merely 'incline' to the lord and allow him to count on their future support if it should be needed. To recruit another man's retainer would create a conflict of interest. Many men did indeed serve two masters, but these would have had professional expertise in a field such as law, in which there may have been a shortage of trained practitioners. Others, particularly those serving in the royal household, might prove useful to more than one lord without any conflict arising. For the rest, it was essential to the lord's security and the integrity of his affinity that his retainers were totally committed to his service. When Richard recruited the services of John Wedrington, a line had been crossed and Henry Percy appealed to the king. Wedrington had been a Percy retainer used by the earl as undersheriff of Northumberland. With two equally powerful lords, such as had been the case from time to time in the Neville-Percy conflicts of the recent past, such tensions were difficult to avoid. Henry Percy, for instance, was the steward of the duchy of Lancaster honour of Knaresborough. Richard was the chief steward of all the northern duchy lands, as Warwick had been before him. Wedrington might be a retainer of

Percy, but he was bound to obey the call of the chief steward when his services were required within the duchy. Such a dispute might have led to open warfare between the two lords in the past and the king and council were keen to arbitrate. A judgement was issued on 12 June 1473 in Percy's favour, forbidding Richard to retain any of the earl's men. Within a year, however, Richard not only had John Wedrington in his service, but Henry Percy too. In an indenture drawn up between the two lords on 28 July 1474, Richard agreed not to retain any of the earl's men 'John Wedrington only except'. Henry Percy agreed that he would serve Richard as 'his faithful servant' and accept the duke as 'his good and faithful lord'. The indenture stipulated that only the king, the queen and their heirs, would have precedence over the duke. It was this legal instrument that led Paul Murray Kendall to dub Richard 'lord of the North', and few commentators have disagreed with his assessment. The preamble to the indenture seems to reveal Richard's attitude to his authority. He is described as 'the right high and mighty prince Richard Duke of Gloucester', whereas Percy is addressed as 'the right worshipful lord Henry Earl of Northumberland'. Richard was proud of his membership of the royal kin and made it clear that he outranked Percy. Towards the end of Edward's reign, the distinction between a magnate affinity and an extension of royal power, exercised by Richard, became increasingly less clear in the north.[16]

From 1474 onwards Richard and Percy worked well together. The earl was left relatively unhindered in the east of Yorkshire and in Northumberland, while Richard operated unchallenged elsewhere in the north. This arrangement with the earl may have made it easier for Ralph Neville, earl of Westmorland, to accept Richard's lordship in 1477. There was one area, however, over which Richard was unable to impose his authority. In the west of Lancashire and Cheshire, Thomas lord Stanley was able to successfully resist the encroachment of the duke. Stanley's lordship in the north-west was a strong and effective force in the region. He could raise a body of 5,000 fighting men if need be, and his writ was law over much of his ancestral lands. Furthermore, he was steward of the royal household and regularly in Edward's presence. Edward could not afford to allow such a lord to be driven into opposition, and Stanley had the means to resist Richard. The fight of the Harringtons to retain the castle of Hornby had already attracted Richard's support and the issue was still unresolved in 1472. Edward decided to settle the matter himself and heard evidence from both James Harrington and Thomas lord Stanley in April 1472 before awarding the castle, and the substantial estate that went with it, to Stanley. The Harringtons continued to defy the king and refused to relinquish the property. They no doubt felt emboldened by the friendship and support offered by Richard duke of Gloucester. Edward, however, had made his decision and would not be gainsaid. A powerful commission was appointed in June 1473 to take possession of the disputed lands in order for them to be handed over to Stanley. That this commission failed in its objective may have been owing to the appointment of Richard at its head. The king was forced to issue a proclamation to the sheriffs of York, Westmorland and Cumberland, having heard that the Harringtons:

> gathering to them a great number of evil disposed persons with force of arms arrayed in form of war, having no dread of his laws nor to offend his majesty's realm, now entered into the said castle of Hornby and have stuffed and enforced it with men, victuals and habiliments of war, as the king is credibly informed to his great displeasure, in contempt of his laws, to the worst example to all his well disposed lieges; which his highness will not of his royal duty suffer to remain unpunished.

James and Robert Harrington were to appear before the king within 15 days, wherever he happened to be. Not only the support of Richard but perhaps also the sympathy of the king for two stalwart loyal servants enabled the Harringtons to escape punishment and, incredibly, to continue to resist the royal proclamation. It was not until 10 January 1475 that they finally relinquished Hornby to Stanley. It was in 1475 that Edward, preparing for a grand expedition to wage war on France, was most in need of the support of Stanley and his retainers from Lancashire and Cheshire. The Harringtons received general pardons from the king and some compensation for their losses. They were to remain high in Richard's favour, serving him with distinction in the Scottish campaign, and as important members of his northern affinity. Robert became a member of Richard's ducal council and James served with Richard on commissions of the peace in Yorkshire and as a commander in his army.[17]

The dispute over Hornby is of interest to the student of Richard III because it throws a little light on his relationship with Stanley. The

Harringtons were able to defy Stanley for 15 years, partly with their own strength, partly through their knowledge of their standing in royal favour, but largely, in the last years of the dispute, through the support they received from Richard. This support could only serve to damage relations between the two lords. Richard never trusted Stanley to any great extent, even going so far as to arrest him as a prelude to taking the throne in 1483, and a mutual lack of affection characterises dealings between them. Richard's behaviour throughout the Hornby dispute is consistent with what little we can glean about his character. He was often generous in his support of lesser figures, and he was strongly motivated by a desire to nurture and reward loyalty. There is also a sense of natural justice discernable here. Stanley had the law on his side, in so far as he had been legally awarded the wardship of the Harrington heiresses, but the disinheriting of the Harringtons after the death in battle of a father and a brother, fighting for the duke of York at Wakefield, was a manifest injustice. There can be little doubt that it rankled in Richard's heart. While such issues of contention were not uncommon among the nobility, perhaps even to be expected, especially in areas bordering their respective spheres of influence, they were of special significance after a usurpation. A noble who made himself king might be hampered by the legacy of such disputes.

PICQUIGNY

Ever since reclaiming the throne in 1471, Edward had been planning an expedition to France. Louis XI had not only assisted the Lancastrians during the Readeption, but had been one of the main architects of the Yorkist overthrow. To punish him and gain revenge were powerful motives for mounting a campaign against him, but also his continued support for Edward's enemies provided a pretext. Edward was never foolhardy when it came to money or war, even though he enjoyed extravagant spectacle, and he was careful to raise the necessary funds by taxation. Unfortunately, the returns from the tax collectors were inadequate and Edward resorted to raising money through a scheme known as 'benevolences' by which pressure was exerted on the wealthy to make a donation to the king for the projected campaign, each according to his or her means. He also launched a diplomatic offensive to create alliances with all those states that might influence the outcome. One such treaty, the treaty of Edinburgh, October 1473, between Edward IV and James III of Scotland, secured the northern frontier. This was an essential precaution if an invasion of France by the English was not to be echoed by an invasion of England by the Scots. There is some evidence, however, that Richard was unhappy about this treaty. The Scots claimed that the duke of Gloucester was actually planning to invade their kingdom in 1473. His belligerence and continuing raids across the border threatened to scupper Edward's plans, and the king found it necessary to bring Richard to heel. Again, the bigger picture eluded Richard. His immediate concern was to maintain the aggressive policy on the border that his marcher retainers demanded and expected of a good lord. Finally, the largest expedition ever mounted by an English king against France, according to Philippe de Commynes, was ready to sail.[18]

Richard may have been preoccupied with Scotland, but once it became clear that Edward was serious about invading France and the Scots would not invade, he supported it as fully as he could. Almost all the English nobility followed suit. There were no fewer than five dukes and three earls on the campaign. For the military and chivalric honours many may have hoped to win against the traditional enemy, never had such an opportunity presented itself. The result in terms of glory and renown was ignominious failure. The whole enterprise was predicated on an alliance with Charles the Bold of Burgundy, but in the end he proved far too unreliable and Edward contented himself with wringing a lucrative treaty out of Louis. The Treaty of Picquigny undoubtedly brought substantial financial and diplomatic gains for Edward. The duke of Burgundy's failure to supply the necessary assistance was a consequence of Duke Charles' own military ineptitude and misfortune. He had undertaken a war with the Swiss, which he was reluctant to abandon despite heavy defeats, and had suffered a major rebellion by the duke of Lorraine as well as judicious harrying of his territories in Picardy by Louis XI. When Edward landed at Calais in July 1475 with a massive army of perhaps 20,000 men, the duke not only failed to supply any reinforcements but, rather oddly, refused to allow the English to enter his towns. Without Burgundian backing Edward could not risk an attempt to overthrow the French king. The truth was that Burgundy had reached the zenith of its importance under Philip the Good and the behaviour of Charles merely highlighted the fact that the great dukedom was no longer the power it had once been. England alone could not hope to conquer and hold the kingdom of France. It had become obvious to Edward that even with Burgundian support such an enterprise would fail. The kings of France and England met at Picquigny near Amiens and on 29 August 1475 signed a peace treaty. An elaborate security operation, involving the building of a bridge across the Somme and the erection of a fenced enclosure in the middle, allowed the two kings to physically meet. Philippe de Commynes, a Burgundian, was now working as a councillor for Louis XI and he has left us with a fascinating account of the meeting. One important detail he observed was that 'the Duke of Gloucester, the King of England's brother, and some other persons of quality, were not present at this interview, as being adverse to the treaty'.[19]

Edward faced considerable anger at the inglorious end of such a mighty expedition. Louis was able to bribe most of the English nobility with generous gifts and even Richard was induced to visit the French king at Amiens where he was 'nobly presented both with plate and fine horses'. There was, however, much disquiet. Henry, duke of Buckingham, abruptly withdrew from the expedition before the treaty was concluded. He had, perhaps, been hoping to win renown and lands commensurate with his rank and was disgusted by the lack of martial adventure. Even Hastings found the treaty difficult to swallow and can be found intriguing with Margaret of Burgundy in the latter part of the reign. Richard's disappointment should not be underestimated. His refusal to appear by his brother's side at Picquigny was a very public announcement of his dissent. He had won his spurs at the battles of Barnet and Tewkesbury and here was that golden opportunity to gain fame and honour on the fields of France that had so stirred the imagination of previous generations. To put aside the bitterness of civil war and to fight for England on foreign soil was the dream young knights had entertained for two decades. Edward might be content with a 75,000 crowns pay-off (£15,000), an annual pension of 50,000 crowns (£10,000) and a jointure of £60,000 yearly for the marriage of Elizabeth, his daughter, to the dauphin, but there were many who were not. When Edward returned to England he faced bitter criticism. He was forced to remit three-quarters of the taxation granted for the expedition and to speedily put down disturbances in the south and west. He may have failed to realise how strong in the public imagination was the lure of foreign conquest and the restoration of English pride in arms. Many soldiers marched off in disgust to join the duke of Burgundy. They felt cheated by cowardly commanders and were galled by the taunts of their tactless former adversaries. Those that returned to England caused violent disorder for some time.

Edward's policy was unpopular but financially sound. He knew that he could not afford to sustain a long war against France. The trade agreements with Louis were beneficial to the merchants of England and the pension allowed him to rule without parliamentary taxation for the rest of the reign. Commercial prosperity and peace were good returns for an expedition that had been scuppered through no fault of the king. The attitude of Richard and the duke of Buckingham may partly account for their readiness to make common cause in 1483. Both dukes had ancestors who had achieved renown in France. Buckingham's grandfather had done so, and Richard's great-uncle, Edward, had been killed at Agincourt. On 25 July 1475, Edward's great army had camped for two days by the field of Agincourt itself, 60 years after the famous victory won by Henry V. The memory of that great battle was more than a distant glimmer in the gloom of historical record. In Richard's retinue were men, like himself, who had direct connections with the battle through the exploits of their own kin. Thomas Pilkington's uncle and great uncle had both fought at Agincourt. The grandfather of the Harrington brothers had carried Henry V's banner at the battle. Remarkably, John Huddleston's father was there in 1415. To these men, whose families had risen to prominence through the valour of their ancestors, the exploits of King Harry were not so far distant that they failed to kindle the fire of emulation in their hearts. In Richard's case, it was not so much his great-uncle's death at Agincourt, but the memory of his father's renowned valour against the king of France that he cherished. Richard duke of York had put the French king, Charles VII, to flight in 1441 at Pontoise. This action was one of the last memorable military exploits of an Englishman in France. It was remembered with fond pride by a population that had subsequently endured a decade of bad news from France culminating in humiliating defeat. Richard and his fellowship were keen to restore an English military ascendancy. A knightly caste, these men were trained for warfare. They thrived on the shared danger and the rapid rise to fame and fortune that warfare offered. Some expiation for the damage to their hopes and pride was presented by the war with Scotland at the end of the reign, but Richard's distaste for the lack of martial enterprise shown by Edward in 1475 is revealing. He was militarily ambitious and he shared this ambition with many of his retainers.[20]

REBURIAL OF THE DUKE OF YORK

In July 1476 Edward decided to attend, rather belatedly, to the reburial of his father in the family vaults at Fotheringhay. Richard, duke of York, had been hastily buried in the Franciscan priory at Pontefract. Richard was sent to Pontefract to oversee the translation of the relics of both his father and his brother, Edmund, from their humble graves to more fitting monuments. Richard was to accompany the solemn funeral procession on its week long journey, and to act as chief mourner in the solemn obsequies that followed. As constable of England, the responsibility for managing such an important state occasion would naturally have devolved upon Richard's shoulders, but it is also possible that his prominence during the proceedings owed something to his own inclination. In what we are able to discern of the personal predilections that motivated Richard's actions, there is a consistent commonalty with those of his father. Their attitudes to France, to justice and to popular opinion, are strikingly similar. Their love of pageantry and display, chivalry and honour, appear to coincide, at least in their outward manifestations. Edward stood to gain, of course, from such a public affirmation of the nobility of his descent, but it was probably less important to him than to Richard. Edward had won his throne by right of conquest and had crushed his opponents in further battles. He was secure on the throne and had no need to shore up his credentials. If Richard were the prime motivator in the ceremony that culminated in a spectacular service at Fotheringhay church, at which 5,000 people received alms and an enormous banquet was held in the grounds of Fotheringhay Castle attended by 20,000 people, it would accord with what we know of his personality. For seven days he followed his father's hearse before being met at the gates of Fotheringhay church by the king with all the senior nobility of the realm. As the body had been prepared for the journey it had lain in state, guarded by a silver angel bearing a crown 'as a reminder that by right the duke had been king'. As the coffin was taken from Pontefract, the chariot on which it was placed was drawn by six horses covered to the ground by black trappings charged with the arms of France and England. The message was simple: here was the body of a man who had been the rightful king of England.[21]

A year later, when Richard made his grant to Queens' College Cambridge for the foundation of four fellowships and a chantry, in their prayers for the souls of his relatives and friends, Richard instructed them to include, at the head of the list of the dead, 'the right high and mighty prince of blessed memory, Richard duke of York'. Similarly the statutes for the foundation of his college at Middleham stipulate that prayers should be said for the souls of his close relatives 'and specially for the soul of my Lord and father Richard Duke of York'. Consciousness of this dynastic legacy and of belonging to the 'old royal blood of England' is a significant feature of Richard's character. His father's proclaimed values, to restore English pride abroad and justice at home, could be interpreted in a practical sense to mean enmity with France and an acknowledgement of York's right to a place in the royal council. Richard tended to follow the same line. In 1483 the possibility of his own exclusion from the inner royal circle could not be tolerated. The emphasis he continuously placed on his own noble blood may not have been entirely welcome in Edward's household. Edward's own sons could not boast a comparable pedigree to that of their uncle.[22]

WAR WITH SCOTLAND

In late 1479, when the five-year truce with Scotland arranged by the Treaty of Edinburgh in 1474 was coming to an end, tension and the renewal of cross-border raiding increased to alarming proportions. The causes of the renewal of conflict are obscure. It is possible that Louis XI was up to his old tricks, encouraging James III to cause trouble on the northern border so as to distract Edward from the alliance with Burgundy for which Margaret was lobbying, but there is no concrete evidence. It is also true that Richard, unhappy with the Edinburgh truce, would not stand idly by if raids had indeed resumed in the western March where he was warden. Certainly his tenants would have expected nothing less than a vigorous response. In early 1480 Edward demanded reparations from the Scots for breaches of the truce. The terms of the ultimatum were so severe, the surrender of Berwick and the handing over of the son of James as a hostage, that they amounted to a declaration of war. On 12 May 1480 Richard was appointed lieutenant-general with the power to call out the levies of the northern counties. The situation may have been retrieved if James had been able to control his own turbulent nobility, but in the summer of 1480 the earl of Angus led a devastating raid into the eastern march that succeeded in burning Bamborough, 20 miles inside English territory.

In November Edward declared that he would lead an army into Scotland on a punitive expedition in the spring of 1481. While he prepared for the campaign, Richard and the earl of Northumberland worked together to resist three Scottish forces sent by James III. The Scots crossed the border and caused havoc and destruction before they withdrew. Richard and Percy were hampered by the need to wait for the king, whose inexplicable delays prevented them from taking the war to the Scots before the campaigning season finished. Edward reached Nottingham in October 1481 before returning to London three weeks later. Richard spent the winter of 1481–2 besieging Berwick and attempting to contain the endemic raiding on the border. Edward may have been troubled by the threat of war with France, Louis having refused to pay the pension until he had been reassured that England was not preparing a continental alliance against him. Once the pension had been restored, Edward set off for the north once more. In April 1482 the brother of James III, the duke of Albany, agreed to stake a claim to the Scottish throne, and to pay homage to Edward and restore Berwick to him if the English army were successful. On 11 June 1482 a treaty was signed at Fotheringhay. Richard joined his brother at Fotheringhay, having successfully led a raid deep into south-west Scotland that had burned several Scottish towns. On 12 June 1482 Richard's commission as lieutenant-general of the north was renewed, and Edward promptly departed south for London. He left Richard in charge of the English army in an unusual position of authority and trust. Richard was now effectively commander-in-chief in a war against Scotland. It is not known why Edward decided to hand over his command of the expedition so precipitately, but ill-health cannot be ruled out. The king had less than a year to live and his sluggish progress throughout the campaigning season in 1481 may indicate a waning of his powers. It is also credible that the appearance of Richard, eager to go back to war and finish a task in which he and his northern affinity had so much concern, may have led him to realise that his brother was the right man for the task.[23]

Richard lost no time in exercising his command and by the middle of July 1482 had assembled an impressive force on the border of Scotland. Richard was assisted by Lord Stanley, the earl of Northumberland, the marquess of Dorset, Sir Edward Woodville and the northern baronage as his principal lieutenants. As the English approached Berwick the town surrendered, although the citadel held out until 24 August. Richard moved north towards Edinburgh to meet the Scottish army heading south. In the face of his massive force the Scottish nobility arrested their own king and withdrew the army to the east of Edinburgh. Richard entered the Scottish capital unopposed before the end of July. The situation was complicated by the defection of the duke of Albany who now renounced his claim to the Scottish throne, requiring only restoration to his lands. The Scottish nobility agreed to the surrender of Berwick and wished to negotiate a peace treaty, but Richard declared that he did not have a commission to conclude a treaty without Edward's instructions. The Scottish leaders made promises that satisfied the duke of Gloucester and he returned to Berwick to reduce the citadel and disband his army. The return of Berwick into English hands was a significant achievement in its own right, securing the eastern coast of England from Scottish naval depredations and making the border itself more secure. It was also a tremendous morale booster for the English borderers and the campaigners themselves.

Richard has been criticised for the lack of further success on this campaign but it is difficult to see what more could have been achieved. No agreement with the Scots could be guaranteed in the political turmoil into which they had been plunged. Further conquests and permanent acquisitions would have required a massive outlay of resources for an indefinite period. The chief source of the criticism is the Croyland chronicler, who complained that Berwick was too expensive to maintain under English control. There is no logic to his conclusion. He argued that the upkeep of the garrison at Berwick 'swallows up ten thousand marks' a year, and that the capture of the town was 'a trifling, I really know not whether to call it gain or loss'. He tells us that 'King Edward was vexed at this frivolous outlay of so much money'. This latter may well be true as Edward lost his French pension at the end of the year when the Burgundians concluded a treaty with France at Arras. Edward's last years are characterised by an obsession with money, and the destruction of his diplomatic hopes on the continent could not have done his health much good. The Croyland chronicler, writing after Richard's death, rarely credits Richard with success. He is not only inclined to paint him in a bad light but also displays a consistent prejudice against northerners in general. Richard's swift conclusion of the campaign, achieving a limited but significant and lasting goal, should not be underestimated. In terms of cost the outcome could not have been bettered. A garrison in Edinburgh would have given the Croyland chronicler a justifiable grievance. The obvious flaw in his argument did not prevent Charles Ross from agreeing with him, concurring that the recovery of Berwick was 'the sole positive outcome of the campaign' and that 'it proved highly expensive to maintain in English control'. The logical conclusion we must draw from these remarks is that it would have been cheaper, and therefore more successful, to have left Berwick in Scottish hands. No Englishman living north of the Humber in the 15th century would have agreed with that. It was more probably Richard's subsequent investment in the town, repairing the castle and the town walls and building 120 new houses, that so distressed the Croyland scribe.

Confirmation that Edward was far from displeased by the outcome of the campaign can be discerned in the unprecedented royal grant of January 1483 vesting in Richard the new county palatine of Cumberland and making his wardenship of the West March hereditary. In Cumberland his offices of warden and sheriff were made hereditary and his lands were increased. He also granted Richard the right to keep, and pass on to his heirs, any territory and all the rights pertaining to it, that he was able to 'get and achieve' in south-western Scotland. Edward's confidence in Richard's ability is striking. That he was pleased with his brother's efforts is further confirmed in a letter sent by Edward to Pope Sixtus IV shortly after the campaign. Richard is described as 'our most loving brother, whose success is so proven that he alone would suffice to chastise the whole kingdom of Scotland'. As for Berwick, the king explains that 'the chief advantage of the whole expedition is the reconquest of the town and castle of Berwick'. The town had been 'in the uninterrupted possession of our forefathers, whose just title having descended to us, we were bound to recover what was ours.'[24]

From Edward's point of view, Richard's power in the north was merely an extension of royal authority in a territory notoriously difficult to govern. Even if Richard were able to carve out a swathe of south-west Scotland for himself it would only alienate land from the Scottish crown and not from the English. It would place the burden of conquest and retention on Richard, rather than the king, and it might be expected to increase security and stability in the northern counties. From Richard's point of view he had acquired a northern empire under the crown. At no stage in his trajectory had his power conflicted with that of his brother, the king. His desire to ensure the administration of impartial justice in the north, his vigorous and popular campaigns against the Scots, his generosity to the city of York and his reputation as a benevolent lord, were creditable achievements by any standards. He was able to resolve the long-running Neville feud and the Percy-Neville rivalry under his own strong leadership. The northern magnates, Stanley and Percy, had worked with him and accepted his dominance in the north. To see his achievements in the north as a prelude to further advancement is to go beyond the evidence. He could look forward to many years of popular and well-supported rule over a lordship unprecedented in its scope. His loyalty to Edward had earned him substantial and well-justified rewards. Nevertheless, Richard's power had been won largely by his own efforts. He had utilised his kinship with the king to his best advantage and he had been given the rewards he merited and expected. Edward's early and unexpected death was a calamity for Richard because it opened up the possibility that his authority would not only be challenged, but might also be destroyed.

5

THE USURPATION: 1483

THE DEATH OF EDWARD IV

On 9 April 1483 Edward IV died after a short illness. Though he had time to add codicils to his will, his death at the age of 40 took everyone by surprise. Richard was in the north and the prince of Wales, now Edward V, was at Ludlow. Tensions within the polity over which Edward IV had presided now emerged and began to tear the royal council apart. Two distinct camps began to polarise in a deadly battle for control. Our knowledge of these events is chiefly derived from the Croyland Chronicle, written in 1486 by a councillor of Edward IV, and the more contemporary account of Dominic Mancini, an Italian observer in London in 1483 who wrote his account shortly afterwards. Mancini may have derived his information from an Italian-speaking scholar, Dr John Argentine, the physician of Edward V. Both sources appear to include information gleaned from eyewitnesses and both give plausible readings for the sequence of events in the summer of 1483. They differ in some important respects, however, and leave gaps in our knowledge of key episodes and the roles of certain individuals. Both are decidedly anti-Richard in their narratives, assuming that the duke intended to seize the throne at an early stage. The Croyland chronicler describes Richard as a 'ringleader' who dissembled from the start. Mancini is less reliable than Croyland but concurs with him in the view that Richard had plotted a coup and 'rushed headlong into crime' to secure the outcome. There is no northern account of one of the most dramatic episodes in English history, although Rosemary Horrox has argued that Mancini may have had an informant from among Richard's circle, and there is little evidence of the private, rather than the publicly proclaimed, motives of the protagonists. The gaps in the evidence have allowed commentators to interpret the events in widely different ways and sometimes to fill the spaces in between the facts with opinion and prejudice. Within three months of Edward IV's death, Richard had set aside his nephew, Edward V, and taken the throne himself. So extraordinary, unexpected and shocking were the events at the time that it is no wonder they continue to baffle and divide historical opinion to this day.[1]

We do not have the text of Edward IV's final will but it is clear that he intended his son, Edward, to rule after him. The question that ignites controversy and debate is why Richard ignored his brother's wishes. We can never gain a definitive answer to this question, but it is possible to examine the available evidence and, on the basis of a balance of probabilities, make suggestions about his most likely motives. There can be no doubt that Edward's death could not have come at a worse time. The eldest of his two sons was only 12 years old and too young to be expected to rule in his own right, but too old for a stable minority government to be established. His age made it likely that any interim regime would face the difficulty of managing the supreme authority in the state and then having to relinquish it before very long. This would expose the leaders to recrimination and reaction. The boy-king might be susceptible to undue influence, or might already hold his own views which it would be dangerous to ignore. An immediate division of opinion appeared and the formation of two hostile camps followed quickly. A council assembled in London, without the young king or Richard duke of Gloucester. The king, with Anthony earl Rivers, the queen's brother, and Sir Richard Grey, the queen's youngest son by her first marriage, was still preparing to leave Ludlow and head for the capital. He did not depart until 24 April. It is possible that Rivers was waiting for a substantial number of the king's retainers to muster. Richard was in York, having held his own funeral service there and sworn fealty to the new king. He left on 20 April with a retinue appropriate to the occasion, and moved slowly to Northampton.

A DIVIDED COUNCIL

It was at this time that the council met. Mancini believed that the council divided between those who believed that Richard should be regent for the new king, because that had been the will of Edward, and those who believed that he should be the leader of a regency council. He tells us that the queen's family supported the latter resolution because they were afraid that if Richard governed alone they might 'suffer death or at least be ejected from their high estate'. Mancini was of the view that there was enmity between Richard and the Woodvilles because he held them responsible for the death of his brother Clarence. There is no substantial evidence that Richard had previously shown any distaste for the Woodvilles, or blamed them for the death of Clarence, but it is clear that the Woodville party in London feared a collapse of their dominance. We know that they seized the treasure of Edward IV from the Tower of London and that Sir Edward Woodville, a younger brother of the queen, set sail with a fleet. Mancini also wrote that Hastings, the former king's chamberlain, sent letters to Richard, advising him to make all speed to London with a strong force.

HASTINGS, BUCKINGHAM AND RICHARD

William lord Hastings had shown common cause with Richard over the French campaign of 1475 and had been a strong believer in a pro-Burgundy policy thereafter. He was also engaged in a very public feud with the queen's elder son by her first marriage, Thomas marquess of Dorset. He saw Richard as his natural ally at a court in which he was surrounded by the Woodvilles. While Richard wrote a conciliatory letter to the council, proclaiming his loyalty to Edward V and his willingness to do all in his power for his sake, he nevertheless insisted that he should be the protector of the young king, according to his brother's wishes. According to Mancini a majority in the council rejected this proposal and determined on a speedy coronation, writing to Edward V to that effect. To add to the widening rift that seemed to be opening up, Richard had been in touch with Henry Stafford duke of Buckingham. Buckingham is an elusive, not to say enigmatic, figure. He was a duke descended from the fifth son of Edward III, Thomas of Woodstock, and yet had been excluded by Edward IV from any significant role in his government. From his subsequent actions we might assume that he bore a grudge against the Woodvilles, but this is by no means certain. He had married the queen's sister Katherine, by whom he had a family, and the fact that she was not present at the coronation of Richard has led some to conclude that she was estranged from Buckingham, and that he resented the marriage and wanted revenge. Mancini tells us that he had been forced to marry Katherine 'whom he scorned to wed on account of her humble origin', but there is little evidence to support the statement. Her rather shabby treatment after his execution – she was granted a meagre annuity of 200 marks – suggests that she was complicit in his rebellion. It is more likely that Buckingham's apparent detestation of the Woodvilles stemmed not from his marriage but from his inability to achieve dominance in Wales because of the Woodville control of Prince Edward. His disaffection may have led to his political demise and his exclusion from the court, but this is just as likely to have been a consequence of Edward's accurate assessment of his abilities and ambitions. He was a volatile and dangerous individual in whom Richard placed, one might say misplaced, considerable trust in the events leading up to his own coronation.

With Buckingham, Hastings and Richard forging common cause against the Woodvilles, the queen's family had every reason to be fearful. Their prominence had been secured through a single fortuitous marriage and would evaporate without continued control of the government. Attempting to prevent the duke of Gloucester from gaining control, and advocating an early coronation to secure the initiative, could be seen as natural responses to the threat they faced from a weakening of the dominance they had hitherto enjoyed for almost 20 years. They had many enemies who might be only too keen to see them fall and suffer retribution. The Croyland chronicler tells us that while the council were united in wishing to see Prince Edward 'succeed his father in all his glory', the more prudent members of the council were of the opinion that guardianship of the youthful king 'ought to be utterly forbidden to his uncles and brothers on his mother's side'. He tells us that Hastings, concerned that Rivers and Grey would appear in London with such a strong force that they would be able to dictate events, threatened to withdraw to Calais, where he was captain, unless they agreed to come with a modest escort.

Croyland adds to Mancini's evidence that Hastings had a feud with Thomas Grey by telling us that Hastings feared that if supreme power should fall into the hands of the Woodvilles 'they would exact a most signal vengeance for the injuries which had been formerly inflicted on them by that same lord'. An early coronation would serve to increase the authority of those who controlled the king, and allow them to use the instruments of state to prevent a protectorate from being established. Some members of the council voiced their concern that such matters properly concerned the duke of Gloucester and should await his arrival for a decision. At this, Mancini reported, Thomas Grey marquess of Dorset, replied, 'We are so important, that even without the king's uncle we can make and enforce these decisions.' If Dorset really did utter this remark, he had completely misunderstood and underestimated Richard duke of Gloucester. For the man who exercised the greatest lordship in the land, who was the dead king's brother and most successful military leader, and who had been entrusted with the greatest extension of royal authority ever granted by a king to a lord, for such a man to be excluded from proceedings of such importance was tantamount to treason. It was true that a regency council was not bound to adhere to the wishes of the dead king, but the council could not claim to exercise authority without the presence of the leading magnate. It was the attempt to do so that precipitated the crisis. Even if Mancini is not correct when he states that Edward IV had wanted Richard to be the regent, but instead the dying king had envisaged an immediate and complete transfer of royal authority to his son, he could never have expected decisions to be taken without consultation with the duke of Gloucester.

Although a consensus appeared to have been achieved, with the queen writing to her brother, Earl Rivers, requesting him to reduce his escort, and Richard duke of Gloucester writing respectfully to her with declarations of his dutiful obedience to Edward, her son, the atmosphere created by suspicion and the threat of a sudden loss of power was tense. The council set 4 May 1483 as the date for the coronation and urged the king to arrive by 1 May to prepare for it. The key to the preservation of the Woodville hegemony was the early arrival of Edward V.

COUP AT STONY STRATFORD

On 29 April Buckingham and Richard met at Northampton. The king was 10 miles away to the south, at Stony Stratford, where Anthony earl

Rivers left him to join the two dukes for a convivial evening. Rivers stayed in Northampton for the night, but at dawn on 30 April 1483 he was arrested by Gloucester and Buckingham who then rode to Stony Stratford and took the king's party by complete surprise, arresting Richard Grey and other members of the young king's household including his chamberlain Sir Thomas Vaughan. The dukes then paid their respects to the king with bared heads and bended knee. Richard explained, according to Mancini, that the men he had arrested had been conspiring against him. They had also ruined the health of Edward IV and were unfit to be the ministers of the new king. Richard declared that he alone, of whom the boy's father had approved, with his experience of affairs and his popularity, was the most suited to protect the young king. Mancini then records the boy's response. He told the duke of Gloucester that:

> He merely had those ministers whom his father had given him; and relying on his father's prudence, he believed that good and faithful ones had been given him. He had seen nothing evil in them and wished to keep them unless otherwise proved to be evil. As for the government of the kingdom, he had complete confidence in the peers of the realm and the queen, so that this care but little concerned his former ministers.

At this point, Mancini relates, on hearing the queen's name, Buckingham 'who loathed her race', answered 'it was not the business of women but of men to govern kingdoms, and so if he cherished any confidence in her he better relinquish it'. Steps were immediately taken to secure the Great Seal and to postpone the coronation. Both Croyland and Mancini speak of a conspiracy being suspected by Richard and weapons subsequently being displayed in carts to confirm the truth of the accusation. Whatever the motivation for the arrest of Rivers and other members of the king's entourage, an irreversible step had been taken. The king's reported response highlighted the uncertainty at the heart of any political arrangement. He had clear views of his own, and these were distinctly contrary to the attitudes of Buckingham and Gloucester. It would only be a matter of time before these views led to a weakening of the power of the dukes, and to their possible destruction. It is difficult to believe that a growing and independently-minded king would indefinitely postpone the day when the dukes were brought to account for their actions on 30 April 1483. The arrest of the king's uterine uncle and his step-brother were one thing, the insult to his mother another. It is also difficult to assess the intentions of Richard at this stage. If this was a pre-emptive strike, and it can be reasonably supposed that he had decided that possession of the king was absolutely essential, why was it accompanied by a determination to destroy Rivers, Grey and Vaughan? These men were sent to Pontefract and imprisoned while Richard sought the council's agreement to have them executed. He failed to get the requisite authority, even as protector. Only when his commands could not be challenged, on the very day that he accepted the crown, 25 June, Rivers, Grey, and Vaughan were beheaded. It is difficult to see what their offences were, unless we accept that they really were attempting to give the dukes the slip and rush on ahead to London without them. Richard seems to have believed that they were plotting to kill him. The behaviour of Rivers does not betray any hostile intentions, nor does it suggest that he had any suspicion that Richard would behave in anything but a friendly way. A poem he wrote shortly before his death speaks of 'unkindness without redress' and 'grievance with no assurance of remedy'. He seems to attribute his fall to Fortune and 'the unsteadfastness of this world'. His will, written on 23 June 1483, makes no mention of a king. He must have known by then that his young master would be replaced by Richard. He begs 'humbly my Lord of Gloucester' that his executors 'may with his pleasure fulfil this my last will'.[2]

If Rivers suspected nothing, the news of his arrest had an immediate impact on the queen, who attempted to raise support against the duke of Gloucester before fleeing to sanctuary with her other son, Richard, duke of York, and her daughters. This behaviour might be construed as confirmation that Richard was correct in discerning a plot against him, but it might also be seen as recognition that a consensus was now impossible and a power struggle inevitable. Richard had seized the initiative and he was to retain it throughout the unfolding drama. If he had attempted to gain security by taking control of the king, either because he feared for his present safety, or because he wished to prevent future threats, it must have been evident soon afterwards that he had not achieved his objective. The young Edward would not forget the violence at Stony Stratford. He was a Woodville after all. It seems likely that the meeting between Buckingham and Richard on the day before the arrest of Rivers had some bearing on the outcome. Buckingham had much to gain by a new political horizon.

PROTECTOR

On 4 May 1483 the king entered London escorted by the two dukes. He was taken to the bishop's palace at St Paul's where oaths of fealty were taken by the lords temporal and spiritual and the mayor and alderman of London. At a council meeting on 10 May Richard was made protector, parliament was summoned for 25 June and the postponed coronation of Edward V planned for 22 June. For the rest of May Richard used the protectorship to confiscate Woodville lands and to reward Buckingham with massive grants of land and power. He was made chief justice and chamberlain of both north and south Wales for life, constable and steward of all the castles and lordships belonging to the crown in Wales and the Marches, with powers of supervision over the counties of Shropshire, Herefordshire, Somerset, Dorset and Wiltshire. He was able to use these powers to raise troops and revenue for his own use. An unprecedented stream of grants over the next 10 days allowed Buckingham to acquire an enormous concentration of power in Wales, the March and three southern counties of England. There were rewards for John Howard, who was made chief steward of the duchy of Lancaster south of the Trent, and the earl of Northumberland was confirmed as warden of the East March and appointed captain of Berwick. Dispositions were made to deal with Sir Edward Woodville and his fleet in the Channel, which were fairly effective, though Edward Woodville managed to escape. In central administration, John Russell bishop of Lincoln was made chancellor in place of Thomas Rotherham archbishop of York, and Russell's place as keeper of the Privy Seal was now filled by John Gunthorpe dean of the royal household. These changes, made in the king's name, 'by the advice of our dearest uncle, duke of Gloucester, Protector of this our realm during our young age', were promotions from within Edward IV's establishment.

Apart from Buckingham, there were no spectacular beneficiaries of the protector's patronage, no major redistribution of land or offices and no attempt to undermine the royal household established by Edward IV. This may have been partly owing to the fact that there were no large-scale confiscations, apart from the Woodville lands that had gone to Buckingham, but the impression is that Richard intended to maintain the status quo as much as possible and exercise a genuine protectorate in the king's name. Thomas lord Stanley, for example, remained steward of the household. The queen was still in sanctuary with her younger children, for reasons that are not entirely clear, but Richard seems to have thought that this was the most convenient arrangement for the time being. For five weeks the government proceeded relatively smoothly. The Croyland chronicler tells us that at a council meeting to discuss removing the new king to a place 'where fewer restrictions could be imposed on him', Buckingham suggested the Tower of London, and this was carried, though there were a few objections. It is impossible to tell whether the chronicler was being ironic about 'fewer restrictions' but Buckingham's ubiquity during this period is striking.

THE EXECUTION OF HASTINGS

Throughout the period of the protectorate there remained an unresolved dilemma, hanging like an invisible cloud over all proceedings. The question concerned Gloucester's power after the coronation. His protectorate followed the specific precedent of 1422 when Humphrey duke of Gloucester had been made protector after the death of his brother, Henry V. Henry VI had been a mere baby of 2 years, but Humphrey's protectorate was deemed to have ended in 1429, when the 9-year-old Henry VI had been crowned. With the protectorate dissolved, the king was guided by a ruling council until he was declared of age in 1437, at the age of 15. If this precedent was strictly adhered to then Richard's power would last only a few weeks, until the coronation planned for 22 June, before it was replaced by a council that would rule in the king's name for three years. There is some evidence that suggests Richard intended to extend the protectorate beyond the coronation. A draft of a sermon written by Bishop Russell to be delivered at the parliament called for 25 June is still extant. In it Russell speaks of Richard retaining the office of protector:

> Till ripeness of years and personal rule be, as by God's grace they must once be, concurrent together, the power and authority of my lord protector is ... to be assented and established by this high court.

It would seem that Richard's control of the council, and his ability to gain the assent of parliament, were reasonably assured and provided a solution to the political crisis caused by the death of Edward IV. This did not resolve the real question, however. When the king had reached 'ripeness of years', possibly in less than three years, what then would become of Richard and the duke of Buckingham? Whether this consideration was entertained by Richard must remain a matter of pure speculation. If he did reflect on the future, then his conduct at Stony Stratford and the subsequent reduction in the Woodvilles' power would have left him in little doubt that he had already reached the zenith of his career. Edward V would be 15 years old on 2 November 1485. He had been well-educated, and appears to have been an intelligent and articulate youth. He would be unlikely to have forgotten about the forcible removal of his closest advisers. Sir Thomas Vaughan had been his chamberlain almost from the beginning of his life. He is recorded carrying the baby Edward, not quite 2 years old, on his first appearance at a state occasion. The young king would surely have a view about his removal, and that of Sir Richard Haute, the queen's cousin and comptroller of the prince's household, also arrested at Stony Stratford, who had been with Edward since he was 3 years old. As king he would be increasingly difficult to control, and unlikely to forgive these acts of inexplicable hostility. Every day after the coronation would bring Richard's authority a step closer to dissolution.[3]

On 13 June 1483, at a council meeting in the Tower, Hastings, Rotherham, Morton and Stanley were arrested. As the meeting started, Richard suddenly charged them with conspiring with Elizabeth Woodville to overthrow him. Armed men, Charles Pilkington and Robert Harrington among them, rushed in and seized the unsuspecting councillors. Hastings was immediately taken outside and executed, without trial. Rotherham and Morton, being prelates, were not executed but imprisoned, and Stanley, who may have received a slight wound in the commotion, was later released. Stanley, the master of political survival and adroit shifts of loyalty, emerged largely intact as usual. With old enemies in the arresting party it may have been a close shave. No doubt Stanley was able to show that his loyalty to Edward V was no greater than his loyalty to anyone else. His usefulness always outweighed his duplicity. Hastings, clearly the primary target, was not so lucky. According to the Croyland Chronicle he had 'been elated at these changes' when Gloucester and Buckingham had taken control of Edward V. He was in the habit of saying that 'nothing whatever had been done except the transferring of the government of the kingdom from two of the queen's blood to two more powerful persons of the king's'. He exulted that this had been effected 'without any slaughter, or indeed causing as much blood to be shed as would be produced by the cut of a finger'. It is ironic that the first blood to be shed would be his own. Mancini reported, 'Thus fell Hastings, killed not by those enemies he had always feared, but by a friend whom he never doubted.'

Hastings had been a popular figure and well-supported. As news of his summary execution spread throughout London there was uproar. The disturbances were only quelled when news of the arrival of the forces of Richard and Buckingham began to circulate. On 10 June Richard had sent Richard Ratcliffe to York with a letter commanding the northerners to come to his aid and assist him: 'against the queen, her blood adherents and affinity, which have intended and daily doeth intend, to murder and utterly destroy us and our cousin, the duke of Buckingham, and the old royal blood of this realm'.

When the letter was issued as a proclamation in the city of York on 19 June, Richard was described as 'Brother and Uncle of Kings, Duke of Gloucester, Protector, Defender, great Chamberlain, Constable and Admiral of England'. The proclamation commands 'all manner of men, in their best defensible array, incontinent after this proclamation made, do rise and on up to London to his highness'. They are to assist 'his highness' in subduing, correcting and punishing the queen and her adherents who are planning to murder and utterly destroy 'his royal person, his cousin the duke of Buckingham, and other of old royal blood of this realm'. The emphasis on Richard's royalty and the distinction between his old royal blood and that of the queen's, is striking. In his thinking, perhaps, the young king was part of the queen's affinity, which 'by many subtle and damnable ways' was plotting the 'disinheritance of them, and all other the inheritors and men of honour'. The proclamation also refers to the threat to 'the common weal'. The appeal to the north is couched in terms of an attack on their royal duke that would lead to the loss of their 'honours, weals and sureties'. If Richard did fall then the stable structure he had created in the north might well begin to unravel. Certainly the prominence of his northern retainers in the steps now being taken suggests that they understood this; a reduction in the duke's power would affect them all. From the little evidence we have, it appears that they had no compunction in supporting his usurpation of the throne. There was to be no northern rebellion in favour of Edward V.

Richard's father, the duke of York, had also emphasised his royal blood, and he too had made a bid for the throne in the name of 'the common weal'. It had cost him his life. By 13 June 1483 it was clear that his son was also aiming for the throne, rather more carefully and decisively.[4]

There is little evidence of a conspiracy against Richard. Mancini mentions that before the protector arrested Hastings, Rotherham and Morton 'he had sounded out their loyalty through the duke of Buckingham, and learnt that sometimes they foregathered in each other's houses'. If this accusation is true, it hardly constitutes treasonable activity, unless the duke of Buckingham construed it in that way. The removal of Hastings would certainly have been to his advantage, opening up, as it would, the possibility of extending Buckingham's lands in the Midlands. It is difficult to see what threat the Woodvilles posed to Richard at this juncture. The queen was in sanctuary, Rivers and Grey were in prison and Dorset and Edward Woodville were abroad. The only reasonable explanation for the sudden removal of Hastings is that he stood between Richard and the throne. Hastings may have become suspicious of Richard's intentions, particularly if he had heard about the commissions of array sent north and west, and may even have opened up a line of communication with the queen, but the real threat he posed was his loyalty to Edward V. Hastings had been at the centre of Edward IV's household throughout his reign, and his loyalty to Edward's son and heir was unquestionable. He had supported Richard and Buckingham to prevent the destruction he might face at the hands of the Woodvilles, but he would never support a usurpation of the throne. His swift execution was essential because of the power he commanded. If he had been able to escape to the Midlands then a civil war between Buckingham and Gloucester on the one hand, and Hastings and the Woodvilles on the other, would have been too close to call.

The methodology employed both at Stony Stratford on 30 April and the coup at the Tower on 13 June was remarkably similar. Without warning, the potential targets were isolated and seized. There was no judicial process, no collateral damage and immediate justification. If swift, they were nevertheless planned carefully. Whether the two events are related in other ways is more difficult to determine. Certainly if Richard's intention had been to seize the throne before 30 April, as the contemporary chroniclers and the early Tudor historians believed, then all his subsequent actions make sense and can be fitted into a rational framework. If, on the other hand, the coup at Stony Stratford was a precautionary measure, to ensure a succession free from Woodville influence, then the murder of Hastings marks a radical departure from the plan. There is no evidence free from prejudice and coloured by hindsight that shows that Richard intended to seize the throne before June 1483. Richard's actions up until 10 June seem to show that he expected Edward V to be crowned, but only as long as his own power and authority could be guaranteed. If this seemed to be challenged, he acted decisively to remove the threat. His concept of his own position, as protector and subject to no other person or group of persons, was certainly an elevated one. In the long term it was unsustainable. The exercise of that power on the one hand, and the prospect of relinquishing it on the other, may have created a gulf too wide to bridge. We cannot know what thoughts went through Richard's mind between the death of his brother and his decision to take the throne, but in the five weeks in which he controlled events, that decision had been taken. All his actions after the calling for assistance from the north are predicated on his accession.

PRECONTRACT AND TITLE

On 16 June the aged Thomas Bourchier archbishop of Canterbury was prevailed upon to enter the sanctuary at Westminster and to persuade the queen to surrender her son, Richard duke of York. She assented, having accepted the prelate's personal guarantee of the boy's safety. The Abbey had been surrounded by armed men and the queen may have realised that she had no choice. The coronation of her elder son could not take place without the presence of the younger, or so it was argued. As soon as the 10-year-old duke of York had joined his brother in the Tower, writs were issued cancelling the parliament planned for 25 June. It was at this time too that orders were sent north for the execution of Rivers, Grey, Vaughan and Haute. They were all beheaded on 25 June; if there were any judicial proceedings they were at best cursory. The timing of this act strongly suggests that Richard had made the decision to take the throne before the public pronouncement of the illegitimacy of Edward IV's children.

As the northern troops began to arrive, a sermon was preached at St Paul's Cross on 22 June by Dr Ralph Shaa, or Shaw, alleging that the princes were illegitimate on the grounds that Edward IV was himself illegitimate. According to a London chronicler, this sermon was not well received. He tells us that the sermon 'so discontented the greater part of that audience' that afterwards Shaw 'was little reputed or regarded'. Mancini also reported that the basis of Richard's claim was that Edward IV 'was conceived in adultery and in every way was unlike the late duke of York, whose son he was falsely said to be'. For this reason, he wrote, 'Richard, duke of Gloucester, who altogether resembled his father, was to come to the throne as his legitimate successor'. The sermon was preached in the presence of Richard and the duke of Buckingham, and its cool reception must have given them pause for thought. In an address to the mayor and aldermen of London on 24 June in the Guildhall, and again to an assembly of lords and gentry the following day, Buckingham seems to have dropped the allegation of Edward IV's bastardy and focused instead on the illegitimacy of the sons of Edward on the grounds that their father had been pre-contracted in marriage to Lady Eleanor Butler when he married Elizabeth Woodville. Although the purpose of both allegations was to declare Edward V and his brother Richard illegitimate, it was the pre-contract theory that became the official claim when Buckingham's address was converted into a petition to Richard. When this petition was itself presented to parliament in January 1484 as the *Titulus Regius*, a hint of the original claim survived in the reminder that Richard had been born in England. Bastardising Edward IV on the pretext that he had been born in France and did not look like his father did not impress the people of London and would not have been warmly received at Baynard's Castle where Richard was lodging with his mother, duchess Cecily. There is no evidence that Richard was on anything but good terms with his mother and to impugn her morality with a charge of adultery, however expedient, was an unwelcome option for them both. The pre-contract theory had greater credibility.[5]

Philippe de Commynes believed that Robert Stillington bishop of Bath and Wells was the author of the pre-contract story, and hints at a motive when he explains that the bishop had formerly been the chancellor of Edward IV 'before being dismissed and imprisoned'. Stillington had, in fact, been implicated in the treasonable activities of Clarence and had only escaped from the Tower on the payment of a hefty fine. It is possible that he bore a grudge against the old regime in general and, as an adherent of Clarence, the Woodvilles in particular. It was certainly no handicap to his career to suddenly divulge such a convenient impediment to Edward's marriage and, moreover, to disclose that he was the only witness to the pre-contract. Stillington's revelation formed the central plank on which Richard's title to the throne was formally established. A pre-contract, when alleged as an impediment to a subsequent marriage, was an actual marriage and not simply a contract to marry. Eleanor Butler, part of the Neville clan, had died in 1468 and, if she had been clandestinely married to Edward, she did not make this claim herself. Nor were Edward and Elizabeth Woodville aware of it. If they had been, there were many remedies to the defect that they would surely have deployed. In canon law, it was true, if Edward had been married to Eleanor Butler, even in secret, then the children of any subsequent marriage were illegitimate. But in English law, if the children of the subsequent union had been regarded as legitimate during the lifetime of the father, then they might continue to be regarded in law as legitimate, even if they were later found to be illegitimate. This could be confirmed in the courts, or in this case, in parliament. To declare them as illegitimate would require judgement in a church court, which would also need to have the judgement ratified in parliament. Edward and Elizabeth's marriage, even if technically invalid, would be considered to be valid unless a church court ruled against it. No case was ever brought. If it had been it would have failed because of inadequate witness evidence. Even if Edward V was indeed a bastard, this did not bar him from the throne. Elizabeth I was declared illegitimate in 1536, and this judgement was never overturned in law, but her coronation went ahead unimpeded. Only Richard's most partisan devotees would argue that the discovery of the illegitimacy of Edward V was a fortuitous coincidence rather than a convenient pretext.[6]

Buckingham, continuing to play the most prominent role in the proceedings, now took the lords and other worthies to Baynard's Castle, and presented a petition to Richard requesting him to accept the throne. The petition only survives in the *Titulus Regius* of January 1484, which may therefore be an amended version of it, but we can assume that in outline the case for Richard's title was the same. The pre-contract to 'Dame Eleanor Butler' forms only the fourth claim, but by far the strongest. The other arguments relate to the invalidity of Edward's marriage to Elizabeth Woodville. The marriage was secret, 'without the knowing and assent of the lords of this land'. It had come about through the 'sorcery and witchcraft' committed by Elizabeth Woodville and her mother, and it had been performed in secret 'and not openly in the face of the Church'. A secret marriage was still a valid one in canon law, if both parties freely consented, with or without the consent of the lords, though it could easily be dissolved later if either of the parties sued for divorce. The charge of witchcraft, by implying that one of the parties had been coerced, rather than freely assenting, was a grave one. This was the charge made against Eleanor Cobham duchess of Gloucester, in 1441. She was accused of bewitching Humphrey of Gloucester in such a way that he had been forced to marry her. She was convicted, and the marriage dissolved. Henry VIII made a similar accusation against Anne Boleyn. That too led to divorce and condemnation. Although this charge was never substantiated and no proceedings were brought against Elizabeth Woodville, it was, and was intended to be, a very serious threat. It is interesting to note that when Richard wrote to York calling for help, on 10 June, he referred to the queen and her 'subtle and damnable ways'. If he believed that she was practising witchcraft, or if he wanted others to believe it, then he may have already formulated a case for declaring her marriage invalid.[7]

TAKING THE THRONE

On 26 June Richard accepted the petition and rode to Westminster, taking his place on the marble chair representing royal authority in the court of King's Bench in Westminster Hall. He addressed the assembled lords and commons, declaring that he would take the crown upon himself in the place where the king administered the law 'because he considered it the chiefest duty of a king to minister the laws'. The *Great Chronicle of London* adds that he called before him the judges 'commanding them in right straight manner that they justly and duly should minister his law without delay or favour'. At his side was John Howard, newly created duke of Norfolk. He had been excluded from this title by Edward IV, who had reserved the lands pertaining to it to his son, Richard duke of York. The new duke of Norfolk was also made earl marshal of England, and specifically appointed steward of England in preparation for the coronation ceremonies. At the coronation on 6 July, however, it was Buckingham who held Richard's train and bore the white wand of high steward. Both these men had been excluded from the corridors of power under Edward IV. They both sought to gain by supporting the usurpation of Richard III. Without their support, and the quiescence of Stanley and Percy, the removal of Edward V would have been extremely difficult. Only Hastings and the Woodvilles, from among the nobility, could be guaranteed to support the accession of the son of Edward IV. They had been decisively forestalled by two precise attacks. In just eight weeks from the death of Edward IV, Richard had been crowned instead of Edward V.[8]

Richard's actions and his behaviour during this critical period can be fairly closely followed. His motives, on the other hand, are shrouded in mystery and controversy. What he did, by any objective assessment, was illegal and unprecedented. It may have been justified in his own mind by the potential destabilisation of the realm by minority rule. The partisan nature of a Woodville-dominated regime may have led to the renewal of civil war. Richard himself would not tolerate his own exclusion, which they might well have preferred. The flight of the queen into sanctuary with her youngest son, immediately upon hearing the news of the arrest of Rivers and Grey, suggests that she had cause to fear the ascendancy of Richard duke of Gloucester, even during a minority. If she could not hope to accommodate Richard as the protector, then trouble was inevitable. All this, however, is predicated on the assumption that Richard needed to be at the centre of the new regime. Usurpation was not the only option open to him. He could have accepted a lesser role, as leader of the council for instance, and ensured the safe transition of the throne from his brother to his nephew. He chose not to do so. If he made this decision in order to prevent civil strife, then he overlooked or underestimated the enormous damage caused by usurpation. The institution of monarchy itself is weakened, not strengthened, by usurpation. By flouting the rules of natural inheritance and succession the body politic is endangered and destabilised. Taking the throne should have been the very last resort of a lawfully-minded magnate.

It is not possible to understand Richard's behaviour in 1483 without some consideration of his own history and character. His father, whom he admired and whose memory he cherished, had also attempted to seize the throne. He failed and the attempt cost him his life. His brother had attempted to take the throne and succeeded, but was only secure after numerous battles and the deaths of thousands of men. Even after eight years of rule Edward had been unseated by Warwick and Clarence and had had to fight all over again. Richard had played a part in these events. He had experienced, in rapid succession, the enormous difference between power and oblivion. From 1471 his power had begun to flourish and grow as a consequence of his own merit and his own efforts. He had achieved an unprecedented position of trust and authority by 1483. While few would argue that he had any intention of making himself king before his brother's death, his steady accumulation of power made a period of political uncertainty particularly unwelcome to him. A diminution of his power was an unexpected possibility, but it seems to have been countenanced in the council after Edward IV's death. A threat to his authority may have been conceived as a threat to his security. Richard was not the man to stand idly by and watch his power be circumscribed, diminished or perhaps even destroyed. If he concluded that these were possible outcomes after 9 April 1483, then the swift elimination of his enemies and the final security inherent in taking the throne may have made sense to him. Whatever his motives, and these can only be a matter of speculation, his action contributed to the destruction of the Yorkist dynasty and a further erosion of the aura of sanctity attendant upon medieval monarchy. The future of monarchy was to depend on the reduction of magnate power and a consequent growth in royal power. Tudor absolutism was partly a product of Richard's usurpation of the throne.

THE PRINCES IN THE TOWER

The fate of Richard's nephews has become one of the most enduring, and certainly the most celebrated, of mysteries in English history. The two princes, Edward V and Richard duke of York, were put in the Tower, withdrawn from public view, and never seen again. The *Great Chronicle of London* recollected that 'the children of Edward IV were seen shooting and playing in the garden of the Tower at sundry times' during the mayoral year of Sir Edmund Shaw, which ended on 28 October 1483. Writing in the 1490s the chronicler was certain that 'they were rid out of this world' during Richard's reign, but could only speculate about their fate and comment that 'of the manner of their deaths were many opinions'. Dominic Mancini left London in July 1483 amid rumours of the deaths of the two boys. He tells us that they 'were withdrawn into the inner apartments of the Tower proper, and day by day began to be seen more rarely behind the bars and windows, till at length they ceased to appear altogether'. The attendants of the two princes were dismissed and the last to depart, John Argentine, the physician of Edward V, reported to Mancini 'that the young king, like a victim prepared for sacrifice, sought remission for his sins by daily confession and penance, because he believed that death was facing him'. Mancini saw 'many men burst into tears' at the mention of the young Edward V, recording the general suspicion 'that he had been done away with'. The Italian visitor admitted that, whether they had been killed or in what manner, 'so far I have not at all discovered'.[9]

George Cely, a London merchant, in a hastily written memorandum of June 1483, reported the rumour that Edward V was dead, even before Richard had been crowned. The Croyland chronicler, writing three years later in the first year of Henry VII's reign, also reported the rumour that Edward IV's sons 'had met their fate', but he too, despite the generally well-informed nature of his chronicle, could only guess that they had died 'by some unknown manner of violent destruction'. There can be no doubt that the general opinion in London was that the two princes in the Tower were doomed. The assumption was that they had probably been killed by the late summer of 1483. With no evidence for their continued existence, and no information about how they had met their fate, speculation was rife. Both the political elite and the community at large began to react in ways that suggest that they presumed the boys had been killed. John Rous, writing in 1489, was of the view that Richard killed the princes 'within about three months or a little more of Stony Stratford'. Richard did nothing to dispel or disprove this notion.[10]

Foreign observers were less circumspect. Philippe de Commynes bluntly reported that 'the duke had his two nephews murdered and himself made king'. Writing in about 1500 he was quite certain that 'King Richard had his two nephews cruelly murdered'. In January 1484 Guillaume de Rochefort, the chancellor of France, addressing the States-General assembled at Tours, declared that the sons of King Edward 'have been slaughtered with impunity, and their murderer, with the support of the people, has received the crown'. Ferdinand of Aragon and Isabella of Castille held similar views, according to a letter written in March 1486 by Mosen Diego de Valera. 'It is sufficiently well known to your royal majesty,' he wrote, 'that this Richard killed two innocent nephews of his to whom the realm belonged after his brother's life'. Jean Molinet, the Burgundian court chronicler took the same view and Caspar Weinreich, a citizen of Danzig, writing in 1483, reported as fact that 'late this summer Richard the king's brother seized power and had his brother's children killed'. Jan Allertz, the recorder of Rotterdam, noted the same in a nearly contemporary account. Back in England, but away from London, the recorder of Bristol, Robert Ricart, in an entry for the year ending 15 September 1483, noted that 'in this year the two sons of Edward were put to silence in the Tower of London'. Perhaps, away from the fevered atmosphere in the capital, objective judgements were easier to make. Nothing was done to refute or prevent these damaging assumptions spreading far and wide.[11]

Several sources implicate the duke of Buckingham in the murder of the two princes. Commynes, having stated earlier that Richard killed his nephews, later writes that Buckingham murdered them. Molinet, the Burgundian, said that people believed that Buckingham had murdered them in order to claim the throne himself. A Dutch chronicle, the *Divisie Chronicle*, written in 1500, believed that Richard had poisoned the two boys but also reported that some held the view that Buckingham had killed them. This chronicle also reported that some believed that one of the princes had been spared and 'secretly abducted from the kingdom'. This was the story repeated by Perkin Warbeck, who claimed to be the escapee, in a letter to Isabel of Castille. Earlier English sources also point the finger at Buckingham. A fragment among the Ashmolean manuscripts in the Bodleian Library reports a rumour that Richard had first taken the advice of the duke of Buckingham before killing the princes, while the historical notes of a London citizen, written in 1488, report this as fact. There is some doubt about what the London citizen meant when he wrote that King Edward IV's sons were put to death in the Tower 'be the vise' of the duke of Buckingham. He may have meant 'by the device of' or 'by the advice of': the first shifting the blame towards Buckingham, the second implicating Buckingham and Richard together. These sources all reflect the prominent role Buckingham played in the usurpation, and express the view, prevalent in many quarters, that he was the driving force behind the events of the summer of 1483. These reports can be regarded as no more than speculation. Buckingham was known to be an ambitious, bitter and unstable character; it would begin to explain the shocking and unexpected demise of the two princes if the blame for their fate was placed at Buckingham's door. There is no more reason to believe this, however, than to accept that Richard behaved in a way that nobody had anticipated and few understood. It is certainly possible that the duke of Buckingham had a hand in the deaths of the two princes but the ultimate responsibility for their fate rests with Richard. As protector, and then as king, he was the ultimate guarantor of the safety of the boys. Their security was fatally compromised by the act of usurpation. A document known as the *Anlaby Cartulary* contains an entry that gives the date for the death of Edward V as 22 June 1483. The anonymous author, writing after 1509, is generally correct in the dates he gives for other reigns but, in this case, he takes a more or less informed guess. While his choice of date may be no more than speculation, it is accurate in one sense. On 22 June 1483 sermons were preached declaring Edward illegitimate; Richard had decided to take the throne and Edward V was as good as dead. When his title to rule was removed, his future was fatally jeopardised.[12]

Thomas More, writing his *History of Richard III* in 1513, created a vivid description of the fate of the princes in which Sir James Tyrell, keen to impress Richard and feeling thwarted in his ambitions by the dominance of Ratcliffe and Catesby, devised a plan to murder the boys in their beds. Tyrell engaged the services of two strong men who, at midnight, smothered the boys with their pillows. The two brutes, Miles Forest and John Dighton, according to More, wrapped the two boys in the bedding,

> so keeping down by force the featherbed and pillows hard unto their mouths that within a while, smothered and stifled, their breath failing, they gave up to God their innocent souls into the joys of heaven, leaving to their tormentors their bodies dead in bed.

This was the story that was to stand the test of time. More admitted that he had heard many stories and was unsure of the truth, but believed his informants were sufficiently credible that 'me thinketh it were hard but it should be true'. After the murder Tyrell orders the men to bury the bodies 'at the stair foot, meetly deep in the ground, under a great heap of stones'. More's account, supposedly derived from a confession made by Tyrell before his execution in 1502, is supported by Polydore Vergil and

The *Great Chronicle of London* in so far as they mention both James Tyrell and the smothering. It was given further credibility by the discovery of two skeletons of children found 10 feet deep at the foot of a staircase leading to the chapel in the White Tower in 1674. The bones were examined in 1933 by Lawrence Tanner, archivist of Westminster Abbey, Professor William Wright, an anatomist, and George Northcroft, president of the Dental Association. They concluded that the bones could indeed be those of Edward V and his brother Richard, duke of York. The bones were reburied in their ornate urn, and returned to Henry VII's chapel in the Abbey. Unfortunately the analysis of 1933 has not impressed the modern scientific community. The skeletons might be those of girls, might not be related to each other and might be the bones of children considerably younger than Edward V and Richard of York. Furthermore, according to Thomas More the bodies were later removed from their original resting place and taken to 'a better place'. The site of the finds matched the description of the first burial place but not the second. While there is sufficient scope to allow for the possibility that the skeletons might indeed be those of the princes, they might just as well be those of two young people who died in a settlement on the site several thousand years earlier. Modern forensic techniques, radio carbon dating and DNA analysis could lead to greater knowledge but they will have to wait until the authorities at the Abbey allow the bones to be re-examined.[13]

The truth is that we do not know, and are unlikely ever to know, what happened to the princes in the Tower. The most reasonable assumption, based on the surviving evidence, is that they were killed in the late summer of 1483. It is highly unlikely that Richard had no knowledge of the deed before it was committed and more than likely that he ordered it to be done. Alive, however closely guarded, the two sons of Edward IV would always have provided a focus for discontent and rebellion. As Edward IV discovered in 1470, it was unwise to allow an ex-king to languish for too long without being put to death. Similar mystery has attached itself to the fate of Edward II after his throne was usurped in 1327, and even to Richard II, who was deposed in 1399, but, however ingenious the arguments used to posit their survival, once they had been supplanted they were almost certainly killed by their supplantors. To allow them to escape into benign retirement would have been equally dangerous, if not more so. Abroad they would not only provide opponents with a figurehead, but also attract the interest of foreign enemies and exiles. Even to have demonstrated that the boys were indeed dead, perhaps by displaying their bodies, would have been political suicide. Edward V may have been declared illegitimate but he was innocent of any crime and certainly not deserving of death. There would have been a public outcry if the bodies had been put on display. As it was, rumours of their demise led to a serious outbreak of rebellion. The only solution to a highly charged and difficult situation was the one that seems to have been adopted: the princes had to be killed, in secret, and the rumours concerning their fate allowed to circulate. Richard translated the body of Henry VI from Chertsey Abbey to Windsor in an acknowledgement of the cult that had sprung up around the tomb of one of the worst kings in English history. Henry VI was considered to be a saint because not only was he an anointed king, but he had also lived a spiritually blameless life. Even kings who had the worst of reputations were honoured in death. King John at Worcester and Edward II at Gloucester had impressive shrines. The likelihood that an innocent child would have become the focus of a cult must have been a serious consideration for Richard. By ensuring that the body was not discovered he at least prevented the whole panoply of medieval miracle-working and the veneration of holy relics from developing in the case of his nephew.

The two princes disappeared forever because their bodies, dead or alive, had to be removed from the political equation. The continuing controversy surrounding their fate is a testament to the success of the operation. The most striking feature of the contemporary sources as a whole is their lack of knowledge. The *Great Chronicle* stated that after Easter 1484 there was 'much whispering among the people that the king had put the children of King Edward to death'. The Croyland chronicler, under a marginal heading that read 'Rumours of the death of the children', was only able to report that they had met their fate 'by some unknown manner of destruction'. Foreign commentators clearly had no idea what had happened to them. Philippe de Commynes gave three different stories concerning their fate. The Dutch *Divisie* chronicle also gave numerous possibilities and Jean Molinet, while himself convinced that Richard murdered the princes, records several beliefs current at the time. Nicholas von Poppelau, a Silesian knight in the service of the Emperor Frederick III, while staying with the king in May 1484 reported that 'they say' Richard was said to have killed his nephews. 'However' von Poppelau opined, 'many people say – and I agree with them – that they are still alive and kept in a very dark cellar'. Interestingly, these grim rumours in no way diminished von Poppelau's admiration for his royal host. The mystery that amused and intrigued Richard's exotic guest in 1484 continues to excite interest to this day. There are many opinions about what happened to Richard's nephews, but the only certainty is that nobody knows.[14]

6

THE REIGN 1: BUCKINGHAM'S
REBELLION, 1483–1484

ROYAL PROGRESS

Richard began his reign with a splendid coronation in Westminster Abbey on 6 July 1483. Like his brother, Edward IV, he fully understood the importance of magnificent display. Through ceremony, ritual and pageant, monarchy could attest its ancient pedigree and its mystical power. Enveloped by the trappings of kingship and their primeval symbolism, a man might become invested with the aura of majesty that could elevate him beyond the ordinary mortal. Richard's understanding of the significance of royal behaviour and its visible manifestation in public offered his subjects the opportunity to devote their loyalty to the institution as much as to its present incumbent. The message Richard aimed to promulgate was that monarchy was safe and that strong government would follow from good kingship. It was a skilful strategy aimed at obscuring the violent overthrow of the rightful king. Unfortunately for Richard, and despite his best efforts, the innocence of the usurped king and his legitimate rights could not be so easily brushed under the carpet, however lavish and munificent that carpet might be. Richard pursued his objective by embarking on a spectacular royal progress through the heart of the kingdom, less than three weeks after his coronation.

Moving west from London towards Gloucester and then north-east via Warwick, Coventry, Leicester, Nottingham and Pontefract to York, the new king took every opportunity to distribute largesse and win support by acts of public generosity. At Oxford on 24 July he was entertained at the newly-founded Magdalen College where he listened to scholarly disputations before visiting other colleges. At Woodstock he was presented with a petition from the local people asking for a tract of land, which had been seized by Edward IV, to be disafforested and returned to them; Richard granted their request. At Gloucester the king granted the city a charter of liberties that would allow it remarkable political and commercial freedom under its own mayor and sheriffs. At the same time he declined the customary gifts they and other towns offered, declaring that he would rather have the hearts of the people than their money. As he entered Yorkshire, 70 knights and gentry from the north were summoned to meet him at Pontefract to add to the magnificence of his train. The king's secretary, John Kendall, wrote to the mayor, aldermen and sheriffs of York advising them of the king's approach and requesting them to receive him 'as honourably as your wisdoms can imagine'. Throughout the royal progress, Kendall told them, the king had been received with pageants and splendid ceremonies. He had reciprocated, Kendall wrote, by hearing the petitions of poor folk and satisfying their complaints, administering justice and punishing those who had transgressed his laws. It was at York, however, that Richard wished to make the greatest impression on the 'many southern lords and men of worship with them, which will mark greatly your receiving their graces'. In many ways Richard was coming back to his spiritual home, a place he loved and felt secure. As Kendall informed the city authorities:

> The cause I write to you now is for so much as I verily know the king's mind and entire affection that his grace beareth towards you and your worshipful city, for manifold your kind and loving deservings to his grace showed heretofore, which his grace will never forget, and intendeth therefore so to do unto you that all the kings that ever reigned upon you did never so much, doubt not hereof.[1]

Richard entered York on 29 August and spent three weeks in the city. He was splendidly received and magnificently entertained. Rich gifts were offered to him and his wife, paid for by the leading citizens, while the king processed through the streets wearing his crown. A great service of thanksgiving held in the Minster was followed on 8 September by the solemn investiture of the king's son, Edward, as prince of Wales and earl of Chester. On 17 September the king rewarded the city for its lavish hospitality by reducing the annual fee-farm, payable to the exchequer, by almost a third and appointing the mayor as the king's chief serjeant-at-arms. The mayor's salary was to be deducted from the remainder of the fee-farm, reducing the tax to less than half the sum previously paid. Local churches and religious houses received generous gifts and grants and Richard let it be known that he intended to establish a great college of a hundred priests at York Minster. Since his coronation on 6 July Richard had spent more time in York than in London. There can be no doubt that he intended to be buried in York Minster in due course, and that part of the function of the projected college was to pray for Richard's soul. His affection for the city, and their reciprocal devotion, can partly be explained by his long association with the people in his capacity as their regional lord, but powerful ties with every rank of northern society inspired a trust and loyalty that went further than mere mutual advantage. To most Richard observers it must have been clear that Richard preferred the north, its saints, landscape, customs and people, to the south. This was an unprecedented royal predilection. His father and his brother had both drawn strength from the south, and London in particular, while the lack of a strong southern connection had cost Margaret of Anjou dearly.

Richard's regime differed from that of his predecessor in other ways too. A notable absentee from the festivities in York was Thomas Rotherham, the archbishop. Such a high-profile dissenting cleric was in stark contrast to the papal endorsement afforded to Edward IV and the consequent spiritual authority this lent to his claim to legitimacy. Furthermore, the attempt by Richard to quietly remove the princes mirrored the situation at the beginning of Edward IV's first reign when an alternative king provided a focus for opponents. Edward was only really secure on the throne after the murder of Henry VI in 1471 and the displaying of the dead body in public. The lack of information about the fate of Edward V would always count against Richard and undermine the stability of his rule.

SUPPORT

Richard's magnificent tour, accompanied by demonstrations of royal liberality and justice, was designed both to display the strength of his support and to win the admiration of any doubters. His kingly attributes and the promise of security and prosperity would give the commonalty sufficient reassurance to enable them to set aside any lingering qualms about the manner of his throne-taking. There can be little doubt that Richard succeeded in this objective, at least in the short term and at least in the areas he visited. Although they are cynical about his motives, even hostile chroniclers admitted that the royal progress succeeded in its primary objective. The Great Chronicle of London observed that the king had given strict orders to the lords who had returned home after the coronation that 'they should see the countries where they dwelt well guided and that no extortions were done to his subjects'. The chronicler, having been obliged to record this inconvenient truth, added, 'And thus he taught others to exercise justice and goodness which he could not do himself.' Polydore Vergil also attributed Richard's beneficent qualities to calculation and deceit. The king, he tells us:

> began afterwards to take on hand a certain new form of life, and to give the show and countenance of a good man, whereby he might be accounted more righteous, more mild, better affected to the commonalty, and more liberal, especially to the poor.[2]

One man who accompanied Richard on the royal progress, Thomas Langton, newly consecrated bishop of St David's in Wales, had no reservations about the qualities of the new king. Writing from York in September 1483 he extolled Richard's virtues with unfeigned enthusiasm:

> He contents the people where he goes best that ever did prince, for many a poor man that has suffered wrong many days have been relieved and helped by him and his commands now in progress. And in many great cities and towns were great sums of money given him, which all he hath refused. On my troth I liked never the conditions of any prince so well as his: God hath sent him to us for the weal of us all.[3]

Langton was a northerner who had risen in Richard's service and, having been newly promoted, might be accused of partisanship. He was promoted again the following year, to the bishopric of Salisbury made vacant by the flight of Lionel Woodville, and he hints in the letter from York that he expects to receive an English see. Nevertheless the views Langton expresses are strictly private, written to his friend William

Sellyng prior of Christ Church Canterbury, and undoubtedly his genuine opinion. While the bishops of Salisbury and Ely and the archbishop of York could not be relied on, Richard had the support of Langton and also the bishops of Durham, Oxford, Lincoln and Bath and Wells.

In these first few months of the new reign Richard might well have been confident about the strength of his support at all levels. Support among the nobility was, on the face of it, impressively strong. The duke of Buckingham was the most powerful magnate in the kingdom and stood to gain from Hastings' fall. John Howard duke of Norfolk had been elevated to his dukedom by Richard. Howard's son, Thomas, was made earl of Surrey and joined the ranks of other promoted earls. William viscount Berkeley became earl of Nottingham and William Herbert was made earl of Huntingdon. The earl of Lincoln, John de la Pole, was Richard's nephew, by his sister Elizabeth, and was to become the new leader of the Council of the North. Edmund Grey, the earl of Kent, was an old man, but his heir, Edward, was promoted to the title of Viscount Lisle. Richard's lifelong friend, Viscount Lovell, became chamberlain of the royal household.

Impressive though this array of nobles might appear at first sight, it was in fact, with a few notable exceptions, rather limited in terms of wealth and following. The key men in the kingdom, upon whom Richard depended above all others, were the four dominant magnates, Buckingham, Norfolk, Northumberland and Stanley. If Richard believed that he had done enough to secure the loyalty of these men he was to be disabused with startling rapidity by the rebellion of Buckingham. The loss of Buckingham reduced Richard's support to a dangerously narrow base among the most powerful members of the nobility. Norfolk was to die in Richard's service at Bosworth but Stanley and Northumberland were sufficiently independent to take a more cautious line. In the end Richard did not have enough time to create a reliable group of magnates on whom he could depend.

BUCKINGHAM'S REBELLION

CAUSES

On his progress Richard was well aware of the rumours and the intrigue swirling about the kingdom, particularly in London and the south. He knew that reaction to the surprising events of the summer of 1483 was inevitable and he was reasonably well informed about trouble and potential trouble-makers. Nevertheless the extent and the seriousness of the rebellion that erupted in the autumn took him completely by surprise. Clearly Richard had no inkling that nearly 40 per cent of the southern gentry who had attended his coronation were about to rebel. Even less likely was the possibility that the duke of Buckingham would become involved. The duke had left the royal entourage when it had reached Gloucester at the end of July 1483, to visit his Welsh estates. He had been at Richard's side since April and there could have been no suspicion in Richard's mind that the departure of the duke was a prelude to his defection. Buckingham's motives for betraying the man he helped to take the throne are nearly impossible to ascertain. It is most likely that he was led by events, rather than taking a lead in them himself, and joined the tide of an already existing swell of insurrection. The rebellion that bears his name was not initiated by him, but having joined it he naturally became, by virtue of his rank and profile, its main figurehead.

Even before Buckingham's departure Richard had become aware of a plot against him. On 29 July he wrote from Minster Lovell to the chancellor ordering him to put on trial certain persons who 'had taken upon themselves the fact of an enterprise'. In early August Margaret Beaufort was implicated in a plot against Richard when her half-brother, John Welles, was discovered to have organized a conspiracy against the king. Welles forfeited his lands and fled abroad to join Henry Tudor in Brittany. At Leicester on 17 August Richard organised an array of Welsh troops and instructed Buckingham to lead commissions to investigate treason in London, Kent, Sussex, Surrey and other southern counties. These dispositions suggest that Richard was wary of a Tudor-sponsored rising in Wales, and at the same time placed the utmost confidence in the duke of Buckingham. By the time he left York, however, on 20 September, he may have had his suspicions. He had become aware of a plot involving Robert Morton and Lionel Woodville. Morton was Master of the Rolls but, more importantly, the nephew of John Morton bishop of Ely, who had been arrested with Hastings during Richard's coup. John Morton may well have been at the heart of a plan to overthrow Richard and have him replaced by Henry Tudor. He was later attainted for conspiring with Buckingham at Brecon Castle where he was being held in custody. As Buckingham's prisoner there he would certainly have had the opportunity, suggested by Thomas More, of persuading the duke to support a plan involving the marriage of Henry Tudor and Elizabeth of York.[4]

On 24 September Buckingham wrote to Henry Tudor informing him of the rebellion and asking for his support. Edward Hall, a Tudor writer, believed that Margaret Beaufort herself had invited the duke to join her and Elizabeth Woodville in a plot to place her son on the throne. She had already used the duke as a go-between in negotiations with Richard, in June and July, designed to allow her son to return from exile and to marry a daughter of Edward IV. One can understand why Richard might not have been very enthusiastic about this proposal: enhancing the credentials of a potential rival at such a critical juncture would not have made much political sense. Nor can there be any surprise that Margaret Beaufort may have decided to secure the interests of her son despite the lack of support from the king. If this meant overthrowing Richard and replacing him with Henry, then Lady Margaret was quite prepared to work towards that goal. With Elizabeth Woodville on board and the potential support of Thomas Stanley, Margaret's husband, the recruitment of Buckingham gave the plot a massive boost. Quite why Elizabeth Woodville would want to secure the candidature of Henry Tudor, rather than that of her own son Edward V, has invited considerable speculation. The obvious answer is that she understood by August or September 1483 that her son was dead and that her interests could be best protected through the marriage of her daughter, Elizabeth of York, and Henry Tudor. This is not the only credible explanation, however. By promising to work towards a restoration of Henry Tudor to his earldom of Richmond she may simply have been enlisting Beaufort support for her main objective: the restoration of her son, Edward V. Margaret Beaufort had reached an agreement with Edward IV in 1482 to allow Henry Tudor to return from exile and recover his earldom. The accession of Richard had jeopardised the project; Margaret may have simply been attempting to secure this limited objective rather than the accession of her son. Elizabeth Woodville's involvement in the rebellion does not necessarily prove that her son, Edward V, had already been killed.[5]

While it is not surprising that Margaret Beaufort and Elizabeth Woodville were involved in a plot to overthrow Richard III, it is more difficult to find a rational explanation for the involvement of the duke of Buckingham. There are three possible alternatives. The first is the overweening ambition that a self-obsessed descendant of Edward III may have harboured. His claim to the throne was certainly better than that of Henry Tudor. His great-grandfather, Edmund earl of Stafford, had married Anne, the only daughter of Thomas of Woodstock, the youngest son of Edward III. The violent removal of the hereditary claimant of the house of York may have led the duke to perceive that a rebellion against the usurper would clear the way for his own elevation. A second possibility is that, for any number of reasons, the duke was persuaded that supporting Henry Tudor would be to his own advantage. It is not inconceivable that Buckingham, despite his extravagant gains and unrivalled power at the heart of the new regime, believed that he had not been adequately rewarded by the new king. Another candidate with even fewer credentials than Richard might be expected to rely heavily on the duke and compensate him accordingly. The difficulty with this explanation is that Tudor's elevation could only cause problems for a powerful man like Buckingham. A nonentity wielding supreme authority was more likely to damage the interests of a potential rival like Buckingham than foster his interests. The third and most likely possibility is that the duke was driven by events rather than taking a leading role in them. If a rebellion in favour of Henry Tudor was already gaining significant momentum and Buckingham had become worried that it might have the strength to succeed, his own prospects as a pillar of the old regime would have looked fragile. This was particularly so if the duke had been involved, or had at least been complicit, in the murder of the two princes. The surge in support for the rebellion among the former household servants of Edward IV seems to have been inspired by the belief that they had been killed. The scale of the uprising may have caused the duke to seek to distance himself from any association with such a crime in order to protect himself from retribution.

A reading of the nearly contemporary account written by the Croyland chronicler indicates that the rebellion may have had two distinct phases. The first occurred almost immediately Richard had left the capital following his coronation. Its objective was to rescue the two princes from the Tower. At the same time a plot was hatched to remove the daughters of Edward IV from the sanctuary of Westminster and to convey them to safety abroad, in order that 'if any mishap should befall the said male children of the late king in the Tower, the kingdom might still, in consequence of the safety of his daughters, some day fall again into the hands of the rightful heirs'. The manifest response to this insurrection was to tighten the security around Westminster Abbey so that 'it assumed the appearance of a castle and a fortress'. No doubt security at the Tower was also increased given that fires had been started in the city to distract the guards while the rescue of the princes was attempted. If doubts had been harboured about the necessity of removing the princes from this world, the rescue attempt in late July 1483 will have focused the minds of Richard's supporters.

The next phase in the rebellion, according to the account of the Croyland chronicler, appears to have been a reaction to the failure to secure the release of the princes. We are told that this not only involved the citizens of London, but that it now also spread throughout the counties of Kent, Essex, Sussex, Hampshire, Dorset, Devon, Somerset, Wiltshire and Berkshire, 'as well as some others of the southern counties of the kingdom'. It was at this point that a public proclamation was made to the effect that Buckingham, having 'repented of his former conduct', would lead the rebellion. We are also told that it was at this time that 'a rumour was spread that the sons of King Edward had died a violent death'. Croyland adds that the leaders of the insurrection 'seeing that if they could find no one to take the lead in their designs, the ruin of all would speedily ensue, turned their thoughts to Henry, earl of Richmond'. It would seem that at this stage the rebels had abandoned any hope of restoring Edward V. A message was accordingly sent to Henry by the duke of Buckingham, acting, according to the chronicler, on the advice of John Morton bishop of Ely, who was his prisoner at Brecon. The letter sent to Henry requested him to hasten over to England as soon as he possibly could for the purpose of marrying Elizabeth of York, Edward IV's eldest daughter, and 'taking possession of the throne'.[6]

We know that Buckingham contacted Henry Tudor on 24 September. The Croyland chronicler has therefore presented the events of a period of at least seven weeks as if they form a single coherent narrative. On closer inspection it becomes apparent that Buckingham joined an already existing and very extensive rebellion. The failure to rescue the princes and the rumour of their deaths had led to a widespread movement across the whole of the south of England. Buckingham may well have been persuaded to join the revolt by John Morton, finding common cause with Margaret Beaufort, but an uprising of such proportions may have narrowed his options. He may have become convinced that the rebellion had a chance of succeeding, in which case his close association with the new regime would leave him dangerously exposed to accusations of complicity in the murder of the princes. The chronicler does not seem to know what had happened to the princes but, like most of his contemporaries, he is convinced that they have been killed. The rumour that they had died a violent death may have added impetus to the rebellion but in any case their overthrow would have provided sufficient cause for the former servants of Edward IV. It is difficult to see what Buckingham hoped to achieve by supporting a second coup, the purpose of which was to undo the first. Backing Henry Tudor had little to recommend it from the point of view of a man keen to enhance his position and his estates. He could hardly gain any more than he had done already, or be more prominent in the councils and administration of kingship. If he harboured ambitions to become king himself then the promotion of Henry Tudor would necessitate a third coup, and not even Buckingham would have been so rash as to contemplate that. The most likely explanation for his strange behaviour is that he began to fear for his own safety when he saw the strength of southern feeling against Richard. If he briefly considered making a bid for the throne in his own right he was quick to see the folly of making such an attempt. The rebellion was aimed at a Yorkist restoration of some sort, and Buckingham could not hope to command support from a political community that held him responsible in some degree for its overthrow.

Having joined the rebellion, Buckingham unwittingly caused it to collapse. The Stanleys might have had many reasons for supporting Henry Tudor, but they would not countenance an increase in Buckingham's power. His designs in north Wales already encroached on a sphere of influence in the north-west that the Stanleys believed to be their own. The downfall of Buckingham was to prove too tempting a prospect for an acquisitive family that had already shown remarkable diligence in securing and defending its interests. The calculated manoeuvrings of the Stanleys throughout the Wars of the Roses had always been based on sound intelligence and careful consideration. The uncertainty surrounding Buckingham's motives and the unlikely prospect of success against Richard and his northern adherents would have been sufficient to ensure that the Stanleys remained loyal, for the time being at least.

EXTENT

Although Buckingham was unable to attract his fellow peers into the rebellion, and while the north and the Midlands remained loyal, the events of October 1483 represent a substantial gentry rising in the southern and western counties of England, from Kent to Cornwall. The most prominent among the rebels were the former household retainers of Edward IV. Having been taken off guard and been unable to oppose the usurpation at the time, they belatedly offered whatever opposition they could now muster. In Kent, Surrey and Sussex these former household servants of Edward IV had strong connections with his royal court, and with Elizabeth Woodville and the princes, and had prominent positions in local society. They included the likes of Sir John Fogge of Ashford in Kent. He had been treasurer of the king's household during Edward IV's first reign, then a councillor in the household of Edward prince of Wales and also MP for Kent in 1478. Sir William Haute, the brother of the Sir Richard Haute who had been executed by Richard after the coup at Stony Stratford in April 1483, had also been a councillor of the young Edward prince of Wales at the same time as being sheriff of Kent. Such men were leaders of local society in the south-east where their collective authority was unchallenged by the presence of a substantial magnate power.

In the south-central counties of Berkshire, Hampshire, Wiltshire, Dorset and Somerset there were strong Woodville connections as well as the usual collection of Edward's household men. Sir John Cheyne was prominent in Wiltshire society, had been master of the king's horse in the last four years of Edward's reign and had strong links with Thomas Grey marquess of Dorset, Elizabeth Woodville's son. Sir William Stonor, a former knight of the body to Edward IV with links to the former queen, had been MP for Oxfordshire in 1478. Another prominent member of Edward's household, Sir Walter Hungerford, illustrates the reliance of the former king on the local influence of these men. They could bring royal authority directly into their communities. Sir Walter was an esquire of the body, sufficiently important to act as one of the pall-bearers at Edward's funeral. He was also MP for Wiltshire in 1478 and 1483, lieutenant of Dover and sheriff of Wiltshire 1478–9. Lionel Woodville bishop of Salisbury, the former queen's brother, was not surprisingly a member of this region's rebel fraternity.

Further west the leaders, Thomas Grey and Sir Thomas St Leger, were closely tied by family interests, as were many of the prominent rebels. St Leger, a knight of the body to Edward, had married the king's sister, Anne duchess of Exeter, and his own daughter was now contracted in marriage to the son of Thomas Grey marquess of Dorset. Here the dominant motive was self-interest, as both men stood to lose substantial estates from the Exeter inheritance if Richard remained king, but they rode the crest of a wave of local dissent among the former servants of the crown. They were joined by men like Sir Robert Willoughby, who had been sheriff of Cornwall and Devon in the latter part of Edward's reign, and Sir Thomas Arundel of Cornwall. In this region there may have been a strong imperative in local politics to support the attempt to reverse the Woodville faction's loss of influence. For the most part, however, there were as many motives for rebellion in the restless and remote south-west as there were rebels. Sir Edward Courtenay was keen to resurrect his claim to the earldom of Devon, a hope that had been extinguished by the death of his father at Tewkesbury and which was unlikely to be achieved under any Yorkist king. Henry Tudor represented his brightest hope. His kinsman, Peter Courtenay bishop of Exeter, had, by contrast, risen as a clerk in the service of Edward IV and clearly joined the revolt in sympathy for the household of his former master. How much any of these individuals were moved by the rumoured plight of the princes must remain a matter of conjecture. The loss of influence occasioned by an illegal seizure of power was a strong enough motive.[7]

RICHARD'S RESPONSE

The king moved from York on 20 September. The Croyland Chronicle tells us that he knew of the plot 'by means of spies', but Richard preferred to remain in Yorkshire nevertheless. He waited for news at Pontefract until 8 October before making his move. The rebellion began in Kent on 10 October and quickly spread as far as Wiltshire. Richard reacted swiftly and decisively. On 12 October he was at Lincoln from where he sent a letter to John Russell, the chancellor, ordering him to deliver the Great Seal to him as soon as possible. Richard understood that Russell had been ill and he urged him to send the seal and chancery officials to Lincoln immediately, if the chancellor could not come in person. The seal authenticated royal documents and was the chief instrument for controlling the machinery of government. Richard was determined to prevent it falling into the hands of the rebels:

> And whereas we by God's grace intend briefly to advance us towards our rebel and traitor the duke of Buckingham to resist and withstand his malicious purpose as lately by our letters we certified you our mind more at large. For which cause it behoveth us to have our Great Seal here.

The letter is written in the neat secretary hand of a royal clerk, who ended the official request with the formal protocol, 'Given under our Signet at our city of Lincoln, the 12th day of October'. There then follows a larger and less carefully written footnote in the king's own hand (see Plate 7). Through it we are able to hear the authentic voice of a perturbed monarch, so unexpectedly and shockingly betrayed:

> We would most gladly you came yourself if that you may, and if you may not we pray you not to fail but to accomplish in all diligence our said commandment to send our seal incontinent upon the sight hereof as we trust you with such as we trust, and the officers pertaining to attend with it, praying you to ascertain us of your news. Here, loved be God, is all well and truly determined and for to resist the malice of him that had best cause to be true, the duke of Buckingham, the most untrue creature living, whom with God's grace we shall not be long till we will be in those parts and subdue his malice. We assure you never was false traitor better provided for, as this bearer Gloucester can show.[8]

Having run out of space at the bottom of the letter at the words 'to resist the malice of him', Richard turned the letter on its side and continued in the margin. The use of the words 'trust' (twice), 'truly', 'true' and 'untrue', suggest that Richard expected loyalty as a matter of course. The duke of Buckingham 'had best cause' to be loyal, presumably because he had gained so many advantages which he would not otherwise have obtained. Buckingham, 'the most untrue creature living', had rebelled through malice. He is a false traitor, barely human, who will be subdued with the help of God's grace.

To the modern reader, aware that Richard's unlawful seizure of the throne was the greatest betrayal of trust imaginable, the expectation that his chief supporter would remain unfailingly loyal seems a touch naïve. The letter was not for public consumption and the bearer, Richard's illegitimate son John of Gloucester, would no doubt have enlarged on the sentiments it expressed. Richard had forged a career on loyalty, and valued it more highly than anything else, but he did not seem to understand the damage the usurpation had done to the concept in general and to the monarchy in particular. To depose the legitimate heir was to divest the crown of the protective mantle with which hereditary succession endowed it. Richard, as the unprotected incumbent, was exposed to the vagaries of a waning code of loyalty that he had, unwittingly, damaged beyond repair.

Richard's remark that all was 'truly determined' to resist the rebels is borne out by the speed with which he reacted once the rebels had shown their colours. He was at Grantham on 19 October from where he moved to Leicester and on to Coventry, which he reached on 24 October. Turning south-west he reached Oxford on 28 October, Salisbury on 2 November and Exeter on 8 November. Buckingham had raised his standard at Exeter on 18 October awaiting the landing of Henry Tudor. As the royal forces approached, splitting the rebels in two, Buckingham's route into Wales was blocked by a combination of betrayal and bad weather. The duke's own retainers destroyed the bridges across the rivers, while floods made it impossible to ford them. Finally, one of his servants delivered him into the king's custody at Salisbury on 1 November where Richard, refusing to allow the duke a hearing, executed him the following day. Buckingham's leadership of the rebellion had been a disaster. There was to be no serious military confrontation with the king and no significant collapse of royal support from among Buckingham's peers. Even within his own region in Wales, support for the rebellion was noticeably lacking. This may have had as much to do with conflicting local interests as with loyalty to the new regime. The Talbots and the Stanleys would only stand to lose out if the newly prominent Buckingham were to increase his power and influence even more than he had already done. The loss of the rebellion's figurehead ended any hope of its success. With Richard's swift and decisive response, combined with the scattering of Henry Tudor's fleet in a storm, the rebel leaders fled or sought pardons. Richard was back in London on 25 November, less than six weeks after the rebellion had broken out. The rebellion continued to cause difficulties into the new year, with the after-shocks of disturbances and score-settling rumbling on in Kent and the West Country, but the death of Buckingham and the failure of Tudor to make a landing had taken the heat out of it.

THE NORTHERN PLANTATIONS

While Richard had been able to deal with the rebellion effectively, its consequences were to have a profound effect on the rest of the reign. The flight of many leading officials from the south and the loss of faith in many of the remainder created a severe problem of governance across a great swathe of the kingdom. The majority of rebels had been led by the former gentry adherents of Edward IV and the loss of this constituency was of major significance. Unable to rely on the household retainers of the former king, Richard was compelled to fill vacancies with his own northern retainers. This altered the character of the regime. Richard could no longer claim to be the continuity candidate representing the status quo. Having been the most powerful and loyal of all Edward IV's servants, Richard was no longer seen as the mainstay of the house of York. In securing his rule after the rebellion, it was the sense of intrusion and change, rather than stability and normality, which communicated itself to the southern counties of England. This was a consequence of the fact that the rebellion, even if Richard had anticipated some reaction to the usurpation, turned out to be from within the very ranks Richard had believed to be trustworthy and sympathetic. The nature of the revolt came as a profound shock to the new king, as the letter written at Lincoln illustrates, and was to have far-reaching consequences. Richard now had to find a new method of exercising royal influence in the counties of southern England.

The scale of the rebellion, and the flight of many of its adherents, left a vacuum of royal influence in many areas. This needed to be filled by men whom Richard could trust. Ideally he would have liked to utilise the time-honoured system of raising influential members of the local community into royal service. In this way both the king and the localities benefited from the flow of patronage, influence and revenue. Richard, however, no longer felt able to trust the prominent members of the rebellious counties and immediately began the process known as the northern 'plantations'. The term comes from the description of the process of imposing new northern lords on southern communities given by the Croyland Chronicle. When Parliament met on 23 January 1484 an act of attainder was passed on over a hundred named rebels. The chronicler commented:

> What immense estates and patrimonies were collected into this king's treasury in consequence of this measure! All of which he distributed among his northern adherents, whom he planted in every spot throughout his dominions, to the disgrace and lasting and loudly expressed sorrow of all the people of the south, who daily longed more and more for the hoped-for return of their ancient rulers, rather than the present tyranny of these people.[9]

The Croyland chronicler shows a marked prejudice against northerners throughout his account but this is not to say that this was not a commonly held bias. The north and the south were separated by a distance that accentuated differences in wealth, culture and customs. While Croyland might well be exaggerating the 'disgrace' and 'sorrow' felt by southerners, he may also be expressing a widely held distrust of northerners by his fellow southerners. It was not, however, the alien geographical origins of the new leaders intruded into the counties of the south that was the chief object of the anguish described by the chronicler. The main concern was the loss of traditional elites and the imposition of 'the present tyranny'.

There can be no doubt that Richard did introduce a radical policy of filling southern vacancies caused by the rebellion with northerners from within his own household and affinity. Over 30 northerners were planted into southern society by the king. They took over the offices of the previous incumbents, sitting on commissions of array, commissions of the peace, acting as sheriffs, constables, receivers and escheators. Moreover, they took over the lands formerly held by the rebels and were expected to inhabit their new districts in order to perform their royal functions. What scandalised the Croyland chronicler, and local society across the south, was the disruption caused to the network of local alliances and interests built up over many years through patronage, service and reward. Local connections and status were intricately woven into a hierarchy of mutual advantage. Gentry service to the king combined with local lordship to protect communal interests. Richard's need for loyal followers in the localities caused him to override the traditional patterns of gentry service and to replace them with a direct channel of royal authority. It was not so much the change of personnel that outraged the southern communities – they had always accommodated novel political currents – it was more the speed and nature of the change. Many of the new arrivals rapidly overturned the circles of influence created by the erstwhile local gentry. They took over forfeited estates without waiting for the cumbersome processes of law to establish true title and protect the innocent. They arrived in force, ostensibly to suppress rebellion on the king's commission, and often used that force to impose themselves on the estates and the manor houses of the disaffected. There was little to stop them acquiring rather more than legality might allow. They could ride roughshod over privileges and traditions established over many generations and, to make matters worse, they were often of low-born status.

One of the most prominent of the northern intruders was Sir Richard Ratcliffe of Yorkshire, who received an extraordinary array of lands in the aftermath of the rebellion. He was given the Courtenay lands in Devon and land in Dorset, Cornwall and Wiltshire. Sir Robert Brackenbury of Durham, who became sheriff of Kent, received the lands in Kent, Surrey and Sussex forfeited by Earl Rivers and the Cheyne family. He also received lands in Buckinghamshire and Essex. Others included Sir Ralph Ashton of Lancashire, who became vice-constable of England, and John Saville, John Musgrave, Marmaduke Constable and William Mauleverer. These were mainly lesser gentry who had risen in the service of Richard in the north. Further examples are provided by Thomas Huddleston of Cumberland who became sheriff of Gloucestershire, and John Hutton of Durham who became constable of Southampton castle and a prominent landowner in Hampshire. Edward Redmane, who became sheriff of Somerset and Dorset, was no more than an esquire in Richard's service before his elevation to prominence in southern society, and the same is true of John Huddleston and Edward Frank.

There were those who were above the rank of gentry. Northern lords also suddenly found themselves in prominent positions in the south. The lords Scrope of Masham, Scrope of Bolton, Dacre, Fitzhugh, Lumley and Viscount Lovell all cashed in under the new dispensation. These were mainly lesser peers who had formed part of Richard's northern affinity when he had been duke of Gloucester, but they did not replace the lesser peerage across the south. Many of these had remained aloof during the rebellion and some, lords Dinham, Ferrers and Zouche for example, actively supported Richard. Of the hundred or so attainders in the January 1484 parliament, the vast majority were for members of the gentry. A third of these were subsequently granted pardons but hardly any were ever restored to office. Outsiders replaced Edward IV's former household knights and retainers, and the majority of these were of the same class as the men they replaced. It was not so much the status of the new men that caused offence as the fact that they were strangers, indifferent towards and ignorant of the character and personality of local history.

The Croyland chronicler's sweeping generalisation ignored a non-northern element in the plantation of new men in the south. One of the most prominent, not to say notorious, of these men was William Catesby, a lawyer and former retainer of William Hastings. His phenomenal rise – he was elected speaker in the one parliament of the reign – can only be attributed to the personal confidence the king placed in his company and counsel. His legal services had been used by both Elizabeth Woodville and William Hastings and his usefulness to Richard is indicative of the rise of a new breed of educated men, often lawyers, who were to dominate the corridors of power in the Tudor period. John Kendall was another man who profited from the plight of the rebels but cannot be described as a northerner. His sphere of influence was to be found in Leicestershire and Warwickshire. James Tyrell and Gilbert Debenham were servants of the duke of Norfolk in East Anglia and Henry Bodrugan and Morgan Kidwelly were from the West Country, where they continued to be utilised by Richard.

There were gentry in the southern counties who had not rebelled, or had quickly sued for pardons, and these were just as keen to serve in the administration of Richard III as they had been to serve Edward IV. Richard had to make use of these if at all possible, if only because the number of loyal northern retainers was always going to be too small to fill the gaps across the south. It would be a mistake to take the Croyland Chronicle at face value and to assume that Richard became totally reliant on his northern supporters. Nevertheless, there can be little doubt that Richard used as many northerners as he could, for the simple reason that he trusted them. They were also available to be deployed in the south because of the stability of the north. There had been no rebellious stirrings in Richard's extensive heartlands while Buckingham's rebellion had been raging.

CONSEQUENCES OF THE REBELLION

It is possible that Richard envisaged the policy of planting northerners in the south as a temporary security measure and that he knew in the longer term he would need to woo back the former rebels. If this was a factor in his thinking it was a fatally flawed strategy. Granting the northerners the estates of the attainted rebels had made it almost impossible to give them back to their former owners without alienating the king's most trusted supporters. The policy had effectively driven them into exile and created a dangerous nexus of opposition around Henry Tudor. The son of Margaret Beaufort, an inconsequential minor member of the Lancastrian nobility, now became the sole focus of opposition to Richard and an ever growing danger. With the support of the marquess of Dorset, the three bishops of Ely, Salisbury and Exeter and a not insubstantial group of gentry ever ready to raise tensions in their former territories, Henry Tudor had become sufficiently viable as an alternative to Richard as to become a factor in European politics. His failed attempt in 1483 had been supported by Francis II of Brittany. At Rennes Cathedral on Christmas Day 1483 Henry pledged himself to Elizabeth of York and received the homage of the English exiles. Richard could not ignore the threat brewing in Brittany but the pressure he was able to bring to bear on Francis was to lead to Tudor's flight to France and the dangerous prospect of French backing for a descent upon England.

Another consequence of Buckingham's rebellion was the manifest breach between the new regime and the old. The new king no longer trusted the old king's establishment. Instead of setting himself up as the guarantor of the maintenance of the Edwardian polity, albeit with some reforms and a few changes in personnel, Richard was forced to cut the old asunder and to attempt to create a new royal affinity. This would take time, which ultimately was not available, but Richard had few alternatives. The Edwardian household had rejected him and he now distrusted them. Richard's policy of depending primarily on men whom he knew he could trust, in order to re-establish his authority and maintain security, led to an overt discrediting of the old government and the ending of the pretence of continuity. In the aftermath of the rebellion, for example, Richard ordered the lands and goods of all the former household men and gentry in Wiltshire and Hampshire to be seized, regardless of whether there was any evidence that they had or had not joined the rebellion. All Edward's former servants were now implicated in sedition, and therefore distrusted. While there are examples of men who flourished at both courts, William Catesby being the obvious example, and there were those such as Thomas Fowler and John Sturgeon who continued in the royal household because they were useful, they are the exception rather than the rule. Richard began to distance himself from the former regime and to avoid relying on its servants. Before the rebellion, Richard had been keen to associate himself with the good reputation of the erstwhile king. It was Edward IV's record of restoring good governance that provided Richard with the basis of his justification for taking the throne. It was strong government, and the stability that came with it, that Richard claimed to be protecting in the aftermath of his brother's untimely death. He had been the principal mainstay of Edward's government and had taken pride in the benefits it had brought to the whole realm. After Buckingham's rebellion, Richard set out to denigrate the former regime and to characterise it as corrupt, licentious and immoral. Richard was no longer to be seen as the protector of Edward's good government. Edward's government had, after all, been bad. This new emphasis led in turn to a narrowing of support for Richard. The excluded felt aggrieved and unjustly treated. They sought alternatives that might lead to a restoration of their property and rights. The southern gentry were to provide a pool of discontent that the next usurper would find only too useful.

One possible further consequence of the rebellion may have been a psychological one. Having been so shockingly betrayed by his most powerful magnate supporter, Richard may have been less inclined to allow any magnate to acquire sufficient power to challenge him in the same way again. His own ducal council in the north had been nominally superseded by a council headed by his son, Edward prince of Wales. It was clearly intended to allow the king to continue to exercise his well-established control of the north through the agency of the new council operating in the name of his son. Edward died in April 1484 and a new president of the council would have to be appointed. Richard chose his nephew, John de la Pole earl of Lincoln. Any prospect of Richard's preoccupation with his royal duties allowing Henry Percy earl of Northumberland, or even Ralph Neville earl of Westmorland, to fill his shoes in the north, was removed. Richard intended the new council to act for him as a continuation of his lordship in the region. He was to be lord of the north and king of England at the same time. The earls of Northumberland and Westmorland would never be allowed to become as independently powerful as Richard had been as duke of Gloucester, or perhaps as Buckingham had been in October 1483. They may have had their own views on this apparent limitation on the growth of their power. Richard's dependence on lesser men, often men of gentry status of his own choosing, was the continuation of a trend already evident in his own exercise of lordship and also that of Edward IV, but it was accelerated by the search for trustworthy supporters after Buckingham's rebellion. The use of northern men of this type in the south may also have encouraged Richard to retain his personal interest and control of the north. To have removed so many influential members of his own lordship from the region was one thing: to have compounded this by also removing the cohesive power of his own direct control was another.

Given more time it is possible that John Howard as duke of Norfolk or Francis Lovell as the regional magnate in the Thames Valley may have developed powerful lordships over their regions, but it is unlikely. Howard was given a freer hand in East Anglia than Percy was in the north, but the situation in the east was volatile with Howard's own claim to a share in the Mowbray inheritance still causing difficulties. Although Howard was a local man with strong regional connections, a considerable number of his manors and estates had been acquired from the confiscations of Earl Rivers and John de Vere earl of Oxford. It would take a considerable length of time for the new lord to win the hearts and minds of the former retainers of these men. During Buckingham's rebellion the new duke of Norfolk had found it difficult to exercise control over his dukedom. Richard's plantation of trusted northerners was to extend into East Anglia as a consequence. Lovell's power came more from his place in Richard's confidence, and as king's chamberlain, than in any regional lordship. Stanley, a magnate with a strong local power base, was never trusted by Richard and the king was careful not to allow him to extend his regional hegemony. William Herbert earl of Huntingdon took over from Buckingham in south Wales and married Katherine, the king's illegitimate daughter, but he would not be allowed to recreate the great earldom of Pembroke held by his father. A magnate with real regional connections and power of the kind exercised by Gloucester was a thing of the past.

7

THE REIGN 2: GOVERNING THE REALM, 1483–1485

PARLIAMENT

The fruits of the new policy of distancing the Ricardian regime from the Edwardian one became evident as soon as parliament met at the end of January 1484. Its main business was to pass an act ratifying Richard's claim to the throne, known as the *Titulus Regius*, and to attaint the traitors. The *Titulus Regius* purported to reproduce the petition presented to Richard in June the previous year asking him to take the throne. It is highly unusual in that a reigning monarch sought to legitimize his rule by an act of parliament. Only a legitimate king could have the authority to call a parliament in the first place so that if Richard's title was made good by the act, parliament itself had been called illegally and the act was necessarily invalid. Such legal niceties were not debated at the time. The constitutional rules governing the exercise of power always found a way of shaping themselves to meet reality. The desperately clumsy effort to confer a semblance of legality on the usurpation amounted to the proposition that the original petition had been presented 'by the three estates out of parliament' and now parliament had met it was able, by the authority of those same estates, to make the petition 'ratified, enrolled, recorded, approved and authorised'. The primary function of the *Titulus Regius* was, in fact, to set out Richard's justification for taking the throne for the purposes of propaganda. The incorporated petition, if that is indeed what it is, asserts that the whole stability, prosperity and tranquillity of the realm had been subverted by the counsels of insolent, vicious and indolent persons who, by their adulation and flattery, and led by 'sensuality and concupiscence', had reduced the realm to 'extreme misery and desolation'. The process of corruption had begun with Edward's 'ungracious pretensed marriage' to Elizabeth Woodville 'late naming herself and many years heretofore Queen of England'. Law and justice had been subverted, oppressions and extortions multiplied 'by the destruction of the noble blood of this land'. Edward's marriage was invalid because he had been pre-contracted to marry Eleanor Butler, and therefore the princes were bastards. Richard's credentials are then established, one of them being that he had 'been born within this land' and therefore was 'more naturally inclined to the prosperity and common weal of the same'. This may well be a remnant of the original petition; it makes absolutely no sense in 1484. In the summer of 1483 there were two strands to the attack on Edward IV's heirs. One was to proclaim that they were bastards because Edward's marriage had been invalid. The other was to claim that Edward himself was a bastard, and not the true son of Richard, duke of York. This claim rested on the presumption that Edward's birth at Rouen was suspicious. Dominic Mancini believed that both accusations had been preached in June 1483. The *Titulus Regius* does not go this far, leaving only a faint hint of impropriety in the suggestion that Edward was not English because he was born abroad. This is hardly relevant to Richard's claim to the throne. Richard may have claimed to be more English than Edward IV but he could not claim to be more English than Edward V. It would be reasonable to assume that the original petition, drawn up in such haste and confusion, would have been 'tidied up' for incorporation into the act of parliament. If we are to admit this possibility, then we have to admit that it may well have been altered significantly between June 1483 and January 1484. Richard's vitriolic attack on the corruption of the previous regime and the damage this allegedly caused to the peace of the realm would have been a fantastic claim in June 1483. It only makes sense in the context of the aftermath of Buckingham's rebellion.

The *Titulus Regius* is as much a manifesto denigrating the previous government as a formal representation of a legal title to the throne. It represents Richard's change of heart after the defection of Buckingham and the former household of Edward IV. The petition refers to Richard's wisdom, prudence, justice and 'princely courage'. It is his 'excellent virtue' in contrast to the vice of his predecessor that causes the people to beg him to take the throne. Parliament is described as a 'court' with the power to decree that Richard is 'very and undoubted king'. Not only is Richard king by blood and inheritance, but also by 'lawful election', consecration and coronation. By being forced to accept that he can no longer rely on the loyalty of the Edwardian household Richard found a new justification for taking the throne. A lawfully constituted body had asked him to correct the wrongs of the previous administration.[1]

Richard's parliament abolished the much-hated benevolences, the arbitrary tax levied by Edward IV. This lost revenue for the king and he found it necessary to extract loans from his subjects later, but there was a fundamental difference between a benevolence and a loan. A benevolence placed no obligation on the king whereas a loan might be repaid at some time in the future. The abolition of benevolences was a populist measure, and might be viewed within the context of the need for support, but it was also the remedy of what had been considered to be royal injustice.

LAW

As duke of Gloucester, Richard had built up a reputation for the impartial administration of justice promoted by his ducal council. The peace and stability of the region owed as much to this aspect of 'good lordship' as to Richard's power to enforce his will. This concern was reflected in the articles by which the new council was to be governed. The first of these enjoined the councillors to act impartially at all times. They are not to be swayed by 'favour, affection, hate or meed'. They are to speak in the council only as 'the king's laws and good conscience shall require' and they are to 'be indifferent and no wise partial'.[2]

When Thomas Langton bishop of St David's noted that Richard 'contents the people where he goes best that ever did prince', he reflected the euphoria of his own promotion and the conciliatory attitude of a new king in need of support, but also a concern for the rights of poor people consistent with other evidence. Langton noted approvingly that 'many a poor man that hath suffered wrong many days have been relieved and helped by him and his commands in his progress'.[3]

In the aftermath of Buckingham's rebellion, Richard issued a proclamation in Kent condemning the rebels, concluding:

> And over this the king's highness is fully determined to see due administration of justice throughout this his realm to be had, and to perform, punish and subdue all extortions and oppressions in the same. And for that cause will that at his coming now into this his said county of Kent, that every person dwelling within the same that find him aggrieved, oppressed or unlawfully wronged, do make a bill of his complaint and put it to his highness, and he shall be heard and without delay have such convenient remedy as shall accord with his laws. For his grace is utterly determined all his true subjects shall live in rest and quiet and peaceably enjoy their lands, livelihoods and goods according to the laws of this land which they be naturally born to inherit.[4]

It was at the same time, December 1483, when disorder provoked by rebellion had disturbed communities over a wide area, that Richard appointed John Harrington, a clerk of the council, to hear the petitions of poor people. Harrington was granted an annuity of £20 'for his good service before the lords and others of the council and elsewhere and especially in the custody, registration and expedition of bills, requests and supplications of poor persons'. The delegation of a clerk of the council to attend to the petitions of poor men has been seen by some historians as a step towards the establishment of a court of poor requests.[5]

There can be little doubt that Richard's concern for the welfare of the poor was genuine and sincere. Of course, there was a propaganda element in his proclamations to that effect as there was also a degree of self-interest. Injustice and disorder had a major debilitating effect on the ability of the king to administer the realm effectively and, if it became endemic, on his capacity to remain secure on the throne. It could be argued that he showed scant regard for justice in the cases of Hastings, Rivers and others, not to mention the case of Edward V, but, having 'secured the throne and removed potential threats, what he offered was justice for the common man. There is also an irony in the fact that the usurpation, and the rebellion that followed, were major causes of violent disorder and rampant criminality. Indeed, his confiscation of rebel estates without waiting for the passing of acts of attainder was itself illegal and an abuse of due process. It was clearly Richard's intention, however, to extend the security he had achieved in the north to the whole realm, in the long term. The dichotomy between *Real Politik* and justice does not seem to have troubled him.[6]

Other measures enacted in the parliament of 1484 attempted to introduce changes in legal processes to improve the administration of justice at local level. Changes in land law allowed the beneficiary of land to be regarded in law as the owner. This might have significant implications in cases where the legal title was obscure and maliciously challenged even though an award had been made in the past. Another clause forbade the imposition of conveyances in the sale of land. These had been hidden charges imposed after the sale and regarded as secret fines. Another measure established property qualifications for jurors in an attempt to improve the quality of serving men. These qualifications only applied to the 'sheriff's tourn', but these courts had been a significant concern in localities where the sheriff had packed the jury with low-born cronies. Similarly there were measures restricting the jurisdiction of 'piepowder' courts. These courts had exercised summary jurisdiction over markets and fairs and had exposed the traders to the bullying tactics of corrupt officials. An important act allowed bail to suspected felons, protecting them from imprisonment before trail. This prevented the sheriff and bailiffs in the localities from bringing malicious prosecutions in order to confiscate the property of the accused. There were further measures designed to protect the English cloth trade and to give advantages to English merchants over their foreign rivals. Whatever the motivation behind these conciliatory measures, they were economically, commercially and legally sensible. They reveal the growing importance of a class of educated lawyers and merchants.[7]

FINANCE

The parliament of 1484 made the customary grants of indirect taxation to the new king, but he did not ask for a subsidy, which would have necessitated direct taxation. With the abolishing of benevolences, the king was dependent on his extensive landed interests and on effective management of the crown lands. If any extraordinary expenditure was required, for war with Scotland for instance, or to resist foreign invasion, or occasioned by the need to suppress rebellion, it would rapidly deplete the royal coffers. It was too politically risky to ask parliament for a subsidy, even though Richard was in need of extra resources to pay for the cost of mopping up the recent rebellion.

Richard took care to maximise the revenue from the crown estates by more effective management and control, and ensured that the revenue thus generated came directly to him for his immediate use. The inhabitants of land owned by the crown, and these included those within the extensive territories belonging to the duchy of Lancaster, were to pay their rents directly to crown officials. Royal rights within these lands were reviewed, investigated and exploited. The officials themselves were to take oaths of allegiance to the king, along with all the inhabitants, and to be accountable to their superiors. There was to be no extortion for private gain. With these measures Richard continued the policy of his brother, Edward IV. It was his predecessor's system of bringing these revenues directly into the royal household, the chamber, rather than through the cumbersome machinery of the exchequer, that became one of the lasting administrative reforms of the Yorkist period. Edward had introduced the system used on his estates within the earldom of March, and on other private estates, to the crown lands. These had traditionally been subject to the exchequer fee-farming system, which had been far less efficient and not nearly as profitable. Edward's use of professional officers such as receivers, surveyors and auditors also had their counterparts within the duchy of Lancaster. Effectively, duchy methods were adopted across the crown lands. The system had fallen into abeyance when Edward died, but Richard was aware of its value and revived it. He had experience of its use and value through his role as chief steward of the duchy of Lancaster. He went further than his brother in extending the reach of the financial administrators of the chamber by removing more payments from the competence of the exchequer in favour of his own officials. He took a great interest in the quality and training of the auditors and receivers working on the crown's behalf and replaced stewards with men learned in law, requiring full and regular accounts.[8]

Much of this reforming zeal was driven by necessity. The war with Scotland at the end of Edward's reign had drained the royal reserves. Despite better management and accountability within the crown lands, Richard still faced severe financial difficulties. In March 1485 he appointed commissioners to investigate the king's feudal rights in the south-west. This was the beginning of a process that was to reap great benefits in the Tudor period, but it was too slow a process to bring relief to Richard. By the end of the reign the king was in serious financial straits. The cost of suppressing the rebellion of 1483 was still being met at the same time as a war with Scotland broke out, in the summer of 1484. To compound these difficulties, the threat of an invasion by Henry Tudor, now with French backing, necessitated heavy expenditure. Although peace with Scotland freed Richard to concentrate on the threat from Tudor, the expenses created by the need for vigilance were great. Castles and ports needed to be garrisoned and supplied with arms, ammunition and victuals, while a fleet had to be provisioned and maintained for an indefinite period. Finally, in the spring of 1485, Richard was forced to raise a loan. It was intended to be short term, repayment was due in 1487, and had the advantage of targeting those able to pay, unlike general taxation from a parliamentary subsidy, but there was likely to be a political cost at a time of increased tension. Richard had not succeeded in living off his own resources, and further financial reform would be necessary to make the crown consistently solvent, but he had taken Edward's reforms forward and provided a foundation on which the Tudors could build.

FOREIGN RELATIONS

Richard III inherited a difficult set of foreign relations from Edward IV. In 1480 Edward had revived English claims over Scotland. Peace with France had made a successful campaign against Scotland, and the recapture of Berwick, an achievable objective. The problem was that French and Scottish amity was bound to be aroused by such a policy. Louis XI of France may have made peace with England but he was an opportunist, always alert to promote a revival of French fortunes and conscious of the need to reduce English support for his enemies. English friendship with Burgundy and Brittany posed a threat to France, and the English garrison at Calais was a constant reminder of the grandeur of English claims to French territory. The key factor in European politics at this time, perhaps invisible to Richard, was the growing strength of France. Edward IV had been obliged to recognise that Burgundy was no longer the force it had been. Brittany could not possibly hold out for ever as a dukedom independent of France, without substantial backing from allies. Edward had also realised that England alone could not attack

France. When, shortly after his coronation, Richard was visited by an ambassador from Isabella of Castille offering an alliance and urging a joint attack on France, he could not possibly have acceded at that stage of his reign. Nevertheless the fleeting prospect of such a venture probably represented the last hope of seriously threatening France.

A problem Richard brought to the diplomatic arena was his known proclivities. He had successfully waged war against the Scots in 1482 and would no doubt do so again if material advantages could be gained. His dislike of France was also well attested. He had refused to attend the peace negotiations at Picquigny in 1475 and had supplied the largest of Edward's military contingents for the invasion. These were the traditional, if somewhat predictable, prejudices of Richard's forebears; the new king gave no reason to doubt that he would continue to harbour them. In the end it was to be French support for Henry Tudor that brought about Richard's demise. A policy of friendship towards Scotland as a precursor to diplomatic overtures to France might have prevented this. It was not to be. It was not possible for Richard to so distance himself from his inherited attitudes or to see the situation in northern Europe with such detachment.

In August 1483 there must have been real hope that a new era in Anglo-French relations was opening up. Louis XI had died and was succeeded by his young and sickly son, Charles VIII. Francis II of Brittany was harbouring Henry Tudor and the English exiles but there was every prospect that Francis might be induced to act as Henry's keeper rather than his supporter. What ensued, however, was open warfare on the seas between Brittany and England, which inevitably led to the involvement of French ships. France and Brittany had common cause against the English and an alliance between the two, in the Treaty of Arras in December 1483, allowed Francis to strengthen his hand. With French help he could retaliate against English shipping and use Henry Tudor as a useful bargaining chip.

As it happened, internal divisions wracked all the protagonists in northern Europe at this time and made establishing relations of any kind difficult. In 1484 Richard's plans for Scotland had to be altered for a number of reasons. In February he appeared to have every intention of following up his recent successes against the Scots and summoned his forces to array at Newcastle by the end of May. The king set out from London and reached Nottingham in March. It was here that he was stunned by the news of his son's death at Middleham Castle on 9 April. He remained at Nottingham with Queen Anne until 27 April 1484. The loss of his heir, the prince of Wales, was a devastating blow to the king and queen. The Croyland Chronicle noted 'You might have seen the father and mother almost out of their minds for a long time when faced with sudden grief'.[9]

The death of his son Edward had serious implications for the king. Henry Tudor's credentials could only be enhanced by the sudden loss of Richard's heir. The king had to take the threat from Tudor more seriously. This consideration, and the grief he had experienced, may explain Richard's slow progress north. He spent the next three months on a tour of Yorkshire and Durham. He visited his castles at Middleham and Sheriff Hutton and attended the funeral of his son. On 22 July, Alexander duke of Albany, who was the English-sponsored claimant to the Scottish throne, brother of James III of Scotland, was defeated with the earl of Douglas at Lochmaben. Richard cancelled the Newcastle muster and on 14 September at Nottingham concluded a three-year peace treaty with James III. Richard stayed at Nottingham until November before returning to Westminster for Christmas.

Richard needed to persuade the duke of Brittany to hand over Henry Tudor, but this was all but impossible in the tortuous political conditions prevailing in the dukedom. Francis was old and ill. Real power was wielded by Pierre Landais, the treasurer. He was so unpopular that many Breton nobles had joined a significant faction opposing him. Although Landais was in favour of an alliance with England, and was prepared to attack and arrest the English exiles gathered around Henry Tudor, he needed English military support. To protect himself from the rebellious Breton nobility, Landais had made overtures to the duke of Orleans in France. The duke was a rival to Charles VIII, his cousin, who was being governed by the regent, Anne of Beaujeu. Orleans envisaged an alliance between Brittany, Burgundy and England that would support his efforts to oust the young Charles VIII and become king of France himself. This scheme would have suited Richard perfectly and was also supported by Maximilian of Austria the duke of Burgundy. With the Scottish war concluded for the time being, the delicate shifting balance of power in both France and Brittany opened up the very real prospect of the arrest of Tudor. In September 1484 Landais was in a position to act against the English exiles, but needed a guarantee of English military assistance in case the alliance with Orleans provoked a French attack on Brittany. Richard would have to commit himself to war with Charles VIII, or at least to the defence of Brittany against him. The king of England did go so far as to agree to send a company of archers, but just as Landais was about to pounce, Henry Tudor was warned and fled to France. His escape was the worst possible outcome for Richard. In France Tudor was far more dangerous. Richard's support for Charles VIII's opponents, his continued attacks on French shipping and his well-known chauvinism against France in general, allowed the French to see their backing of Tudor as a convenient way of threatening Richard III and retaliating against his hostility.

Events continued to conspire against Richard. A rebellion mounted against Charles VIII by the duke of Orleans in March 1485 failed. French military resources, raised to resist Orleans, were now available for the interesting project of assisting Henry Tudor to invade England. If he succeeded the French would have managed to replace the hostile Richard III with the grateful Henry Tudor. In Brittany, Landais was also defeated, in June 1485, and shortly afterwards executed. The French no longer faced a threat from Brittany and could support Henry Tudor with far more than he would ever have been able to get from Brittany. Indeed there was a powerful faction in France keen to teach the English a lesson and strike a blow against the power that continued to claim French sovereignty. The leader of this party, Philippe de Crevecoeur the Seignuer d'Esquerdes, known to the English as 'Cordes', was able to supply Tudor with 1,500 professional and well-equipped soldiers from his base at Pont de l'Arche in the Seine valley. They were to be led by Philibert de Chandee, an experienced captain who was to be created earl of Bath by Henry Tudor for his role at the battle of Bosworth. Henry also received a substantial loan of 40,000 livres, and all the necessary shipping. A combination of bad luck, misjudgement and poor understanding of the realities behind the murky and confusing political changes taking place across the Channel, had created a highly dangerous threat to Richard's kingship.[10]

THE KING IN PERSON

Richard's reign was too short to provide a significant measure of his qualities as a king. Much of his public behaviour was defined by the needs imposed upon him by the usurpation. Security was the primary and most pressing need, combined with consolidation of his position and establishing a viable government. Given time it is possible that he would have made a good king, even a great one, but the manner of his taking the throne would inevitably bring problems and preoccupy him until such time as he was firmly accepted and established. He was, in many ways, in the same situation faced by Henry IV after the usurpation of 1399 and the death of Richard II. Henry IV's kingship survived because he was able to defeat his opponents at the battle of Shrewsbury in 1403. If Richard had won at the battle of Bosworth in 1485, there is reason to believe that a successful Ricardian regime might eventually have been established. As it is we have to view his acts through the prism of necessity and reaction, scarcely able to extrapolate from them a picture of the real man.

An example of this is provided by his treatment of the Woodvilles. Elizabeth and her daughters were persuaded to leave the sanctuary of Westminster Abbey on 1 March 1484. The former queen was given sureties for her safety and that of her daughters. Richard agreed to treat them as his kinswomen, to pay an annual pension to Elizabeth and to find suitable gentlemen to marry the daughters. At the Christmas celebrations at the end of 1484 they were feted by the king. Elizabeth of York dressed in the same apparel as Queen Anne and danced with Richard. The Croyland chronicler was scandalised by these events, or purported to be, and hinted darkly that the death of Queen Anne, on 9 March 1485, was anticipated by Richard and that he intended to marry his niece in her stead. He reported that Richard Ratcliffe and William Catesby were delegated by the council to warn Richard to abandon this project or face a rebellion. Richard was forced to declare publicly that he had no intention of marrying Elizabeth of York. It is possible that Richard's attempts to demonstrate a healing of his rift with Elizabeth Woodville, and her support for his kingship, backfired and was misinterpreted. The death of Anne was grist to the mill for Tudor historians who were able to see a calculation and a pattern in these events that may not have been there. After Anne's death, however, the possibility of marrying his niece may well have entered Richard's mind, if only to pre-empt the growing threat of Henry Tudor. Tudor's projected marriage to the daughter of Edward IV was a serious political threat to Richard.[11]

Similarly, Richard's reverence for the memory of Henry VI has suffered the same fate. In August 1484 Richard staged an elaborate ceremony in which the body of the Lancastrian king was taken from Chertsey Abbey and reburied in St George's chapel, Windsor. Rather than attempting to suppress the cult of Henry VI, as his brother had done, Richard III promoted it and placed his tomb beside that of his brother. He began to patronise Henry VI's foundation at King's College Cambridge, again in stark contrast to the behaviour of Edward IV. The cult of Henry VI was a popular one, but Richard's adoption of it is open to speculation. With his death at Bosworth it is possible to view his association with Henry VI as another cynical ploy to garner popularity and to undermine Henry Tudor's hopes. If the Lancastrian legacy was safe in Richard's hands and proper respect was paid to their saint, then there was no need to support another Lancastrian. Henry V had behaved in a similar fashion shortly after his own coronation. He had translated the relics of Richard II and brought them into Westminster Abbey, in stark contrast to his own father's treatment of them. Because Henry V was such a successful king, nobody later accused him of attempting to shore up the shaky credentials of an illegal regime by honouring his opponents' martyr. All Richard III's acts are open to interpretation and misunderstanding because there was no future context to provide a pattern of consistent and logical behaviour.

Richard did, in fact, show a real and genuine interest in Queens' College Cambridge, as well as King's. His interest in Cambridge had begun when he was duke of Gloucester and he took the opportunity, once he became king, to lavish Queens' with land and money. In his short reign Richard took sufficient interest in Cambridge, and his projected foundations at Middleham, York and Barnard's Castle, to demonstrate an awareness of his spiritual needs and an appreciation of scholarship. His private chaplain, John Docket, was a humanist scholar who had not only studied at Eton and King's College Cambridge, but also in Padua and Bologna.[12]

In May 1484 a Silesian knight in the service of the Hapsburg Emperor Frederick III, and on a tour of Europe, visited Richard III at Pontefract and left an account of his meeting. Richard was inquisitive and as they dined he asked Nicholas von Poppelau about the empire and its lands and people. The king was so interested in the knight's replies that 'he hardly touched his food'. When he asked the visitor about the Turks, von Poppelau recounted the recent victory of the king of Hungary over them, to which Richard replied:

> I would like my kingdom and land to lie where the land and kingdom of the king of Hungary lies, on the Turkish frontier itself. Then I would certainly, with my own people alone, without the help of other kings, princes or lords, properly drive away not only the Turks, but all my enemies and opponents.

The traveller commented, 'O dear God, what a great-hearted lord I recognised in the king.' He enjoyed Richard's hospitality for eight days before taking his leave. Richard gave him a collar of gold as a gift and letters of safe-conduct. Von Poppelau noted that Richard was said to have killed his nephews 'so that not they, but he was crowned', and also commented, 'However, many people say – and I agree with them – that they are still alive and kept in a very dark cellar'.[13]

Von Poppelau's account chimes with what we know about Richard from other sources. His patronage of All Hallows, Barking, the supposed resting place of the heart of the great crusading hero, Richard the Lionheart, sits well with Von Poppelau's tale. Similarly, Richard's patronage of the crusading knights of the Order of St John, at their headquarters at Clerkenwell, demonstrated a dedication to the crusading ideal. His outburst before von Poppelau may reflect the genuine sentiments of a beleaguered and frustrated king. The admiration for his father and the devotion to his father's memory as demonstrated by the reburial at Fotheringhay in 1476, his hunger for glory in France in 1475 and his own record as a soldier, all suggest a man conscious of his warrior heritage and keen to emulate the deeds of his forebears.[14]

Perhaps the French were right to distrust him. Richard was in many ways the product of a medieval world in which enmity for France and a desire to fight the Turks were defining characteristics of English knights. In the end he was unable to free himself from the shackles of his throne-taking. Von Poppelau mentions the princes in a cheerful and gossipy way. Speculation about their fate seems to have had no impact on his admiration for the king. No doubt the politics of Renaissance Europe with which he was familiar had inured him to such scandals, but in England the speculation was corrosive. Before Richard could lead armies against France or against the Turks, he would have to fight a minor Lancastrian Welshman called Henry Tudor, and he would have to fight him on English soil.

All that remains of Fotheringhay Castle, Richard's birthplace, with the church, where his father is buried, in the background.

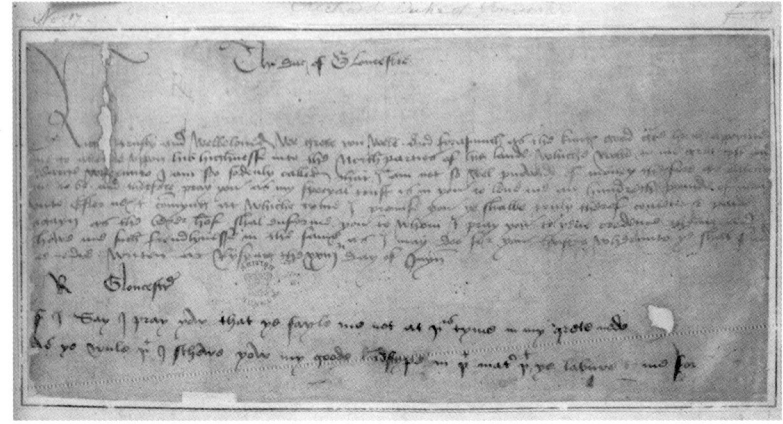

Richard's first letter, dated June 1469.

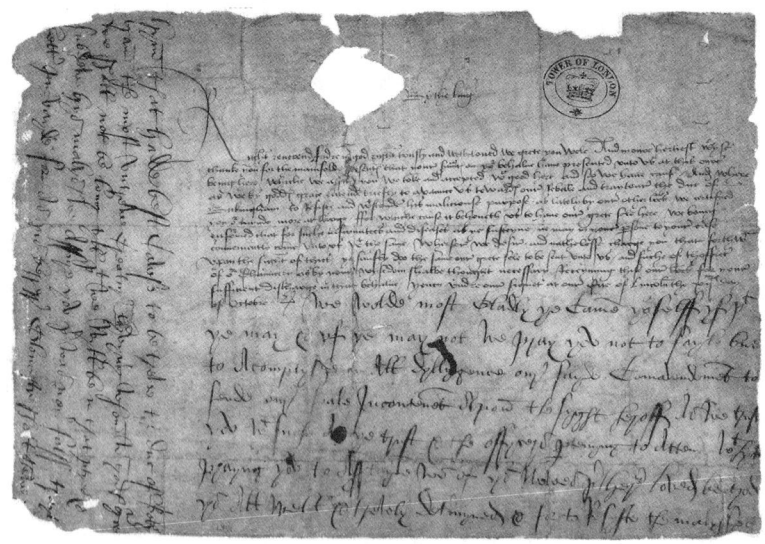

Richard's letter 12 October 1483 requesting the Great Seal. This has a postscript in Richard's own hand referring to the treachery of the duke of Buckingham.

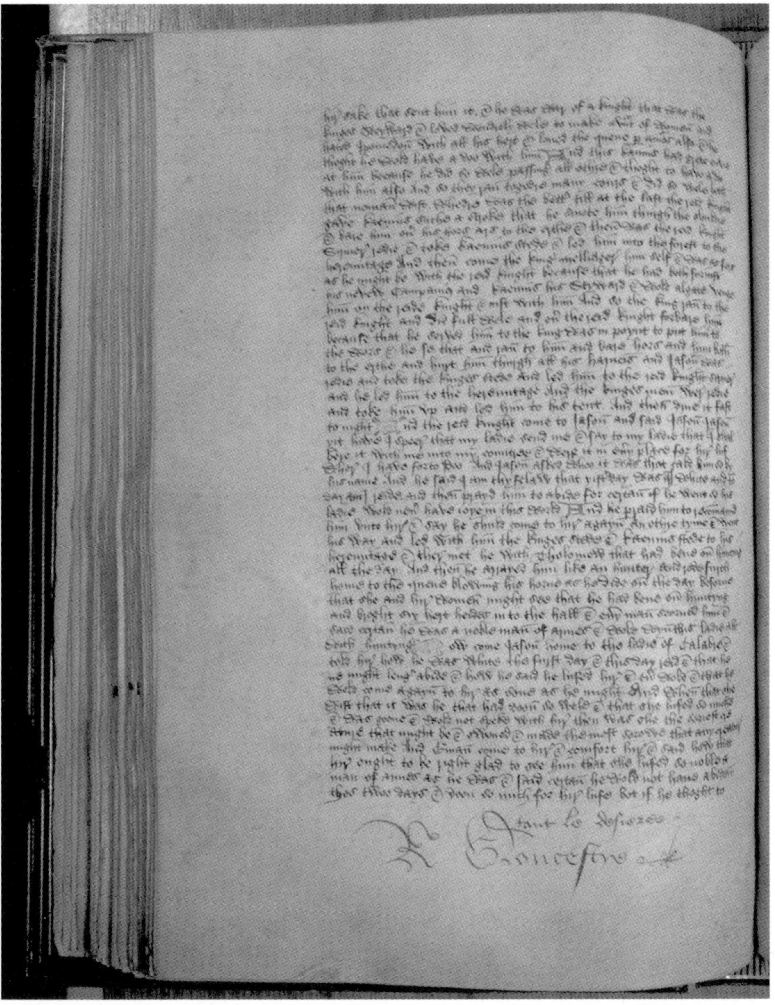

Richard's teenage signature and motto *Tant le desieree* ('I have desired it so much') on his copy of the romance *Ipomedon*, the story of the perfect knight.

An illustration of Jean de Waurin presenting his *Chroniques* to Edward IV with Richard second left (the earliest likeness), French School.

Richard III, English School.

All that remains of the Great Hall at Middleham Castle in Wensleydale, on the first floor, where Richard would have conducted much of his business as Lord of the North.

RICARDVS · III · ANG · REX ·

Richard III, by an unknown artist.

Statue of Richard III in Castle Gardens, Leicester, by James Butler MBE RA.

At some point during the reign a prayer was composed for Richard and inserted into his book of hours. These hand-crafted and beautifully illustrated devotional books were popular among the aristocracy and provide an indication of the inner life and religious tastes of their owners. The prayer gives a distinct impression of having been composed for a man experiencing some kind of mental torment:

> Most merciful Lord Jesus Christ, very God, who was sent from the throne of Almighty God into the world to deliver the sinful from their transgressions, comfort the afflicted, ransom the captives, set free those in prison, bring together those who were scattered, lead travellers back to their native land, minister to the contrite in heart, comfort the sad, and to console those in grief and distress, deign to release me from the affliction, temptation, grief, sickness, necessity and danger in which I stand, and give me counsel.

The prayer, which rambles on at considerable length, seems to emphasise the need of the supplicant for forgiveness and protection from his enemies. 'Lord', he begs, 'Deign to make and keep concord between me and my enemies.' He continues:

> Deign to assuage, turn aside, destroy and bring to nothing the hatred they bear towards me, even as you extinguished the hatred and anger that Esau had for his brother Jacob. Stretch out your arm to me and spread your grace over me, and deign to deliver me from all the perplexities and sorrows in which I find myself ...

There are then given a series of examples of the men who had been rescued from similar predicaments by the mercy of God. Again these include Jacob being rescued from the wrath of Esau. This is a particularly interesting reference in the context of Richard's predicament. Jacob had, of course, stolen the birthright of Esau. We know God forgave Jacob and enabled him to found a famous dynasty. Presumably God allowed the usurpation of Esau because Jacob was a more suitable progenitor of the Chosen People. It would be speculating beyond the exegesis the text will bear to suggest that these words speak to us from Richard's conscience and contain the hint of his justification for seizing the throne. What is clear, however, is that the prayer is full of references to rebellion and the king's enemies, and is pervaded by a sense of foreboding and fear:

> Therefore, Lord Jesus Christ, son of the living God, deign to free me, thy
> servant King Richard, from every tribulation, sorrow and trouble in which I am
> placed and from all the plots of my enemies ...[15]

A similar pessimism accompanies many of the royal proclamations,
particularly towards the end of the reign. On 19 April 1485 the king
wrote a letter to the council of York explaining the measures he wanted
implemented for the suppression of sedition. The problem seems to be
centred on London but, the king informs them, is widespread:

> Trusty and well beloved we greet you well. (know that) ... diverse and
> seditious and evil disposed persons both in our city of London and
> elsewhere within this our realm, enforce themselves daily to sow seed of
> noise and slander against our person and against many of the lords and
> estates of our land to abuse the multitude of our subjects and avert their
> minds from us if they could ... some by setting up of bills, some by
> messages and sending forth of false and abominable language and lies,
> some by bold and presumptuous open speech and communication one
> with other ...

The remedies to be employed appear quite draconian. He instructs the
mayor, all other officers, servants and 'faithful subjects wherever they
be', to arrest anyone:

> speaking of us or any other lord or estate of this our land otherwise than is
> according to honour, truth and the peace and restfulness of this our realm, or
> telling tales and tidings whereby the people might be stirred to commotion
> and unlawful assemblies.

Those who offend in the manner described are to be 'taken and
punished according to his deserts'. The impossibility of stemming
what appears to be a tide of discontent by deploying these heavy-
handed tactics is illustrated at the end of the letter where the authorities
are advised that:

> whoever first find any seditious bill set up in any place (is to) take it down and
> without reading or showing the same to any other person bring it forthwith to
> us or some of the lords or other of the council.[16]

We can only presume that the king expected the finder to know, without reading any of its contents, that anything stuck up in a public place with writing on it was likely to be a seditious bill. Whether a climate of fear and suspicion covered the realm at this point is open to question, but it certainly affected the king.

One of Richard's mottoes, *In Loyalte me lie*, or 'loyalty binds me', can be found in Richard's own handwriting with his signature in a document dating from the beginning of the reign, and in a charter making a grant to the Wax Chandlers of London in 1484. The powerful sentiment evoked by the motto reveals a dichotomy at the heart of the mystery surrounding Richard's personality. He valued loyalty highly and rewarded it generously. His own life before the usurpation was, in many ways, an exemplification of devoted and faithful service. The honour and respect with which he treated the memory of his father was manifest throughout his life, not only in the indentures for his foundations at Queens' College Cambridge in 1477 and Middleham in 1488 and in the great ceremony of reburial at Fotheringhay in 1476, but also in the values Richard espoused. Richard duke of York seems to have believed, and his son appears to have understood this, that strong government gave to all subjects the best hope of prosperity and justice. The duke had claimed to be fighting for the 'common weal' and was prepared to overthrow a king who had become surrounded by a faction. York's authority came not only from his royal blood but also from his successful prosecution of the war with France. To the young Richard his father may have appeared to be the epitome of honour and justice. Richard's service to Edward IV cannot be faulted for effective and devoted prosecution of the royal will. His lordship in the north became a model of impartial and stable rule. The virtues of honour, trust and justice seemed to be the motivating factors in his behaviour. And yet, in 1483, he committed the most profoundly shocking act of betrayal. It seems impossible to reconcile these two aspects of his life: the faithful loyalty to Edward on the one hand, and the ruthless destruction of Edward's sons on the other. The truth may be that Richard himself found it impossible to reconcile these two aspects of his personality. The lack of decisive action had ruined his father's hopes and cost him his life. Only the triumphs of Edward had rescued the house of York. If he believed that strong government was dangerously threatened by the accession of Edward V, or that justice and security might be undermined, perhaps he decided to avoid his father's mistake and act swiftly, before his enemies could ruin him. Whatever he thought, and, of course, we will never actually know, it is possible to detect in his later behaviour and pronouncements the workings of an anxious mind, uneasy with itself.[17]

THE END OF THE REIGN: BOSWORTH FIELD

When William Collingbourne, a former household servant of Edward's, pinned his famous verse onto St Paul's Cathedral door in July 1484 unrest was rife. His clever jibe, 'The Cat, the Rat and Lovell our Dog rule all England under the Hog', was an indictment calculated to resonate with malcontents. The Cat was Catesby, the Rat was Ratcliffe and, with Lovell, they were accused of ruling over England under Richard, whose emblem was the white boar, or hog. There is evidence to support his claim. When Anne Neville died in March 1485 and Richard contemplated marrying his niece, Elizabeth, it was Catesby and Ratcliffe who warned him of the damage this proposal would cause among his northern supporters. The Croyland chronicler added to his account that it was Ratcliffe and Catesby who told Richard to his face that he had to denounce the idea, because it was these men 'to whose opinions the king hardly ever dared offer any opposition'. The chronicler, hostile to Richard, was in all probability merely giving voice to a popular sentiment, in the same way that Collingbourne was confident of catching the public mood. The men Richard chose to trust and reward were the focus of popular discontent and there was little that Richard could do about it.[18]

Collingbourne was more than a scurrilous political satirist. His lampoon was intended to be the start of a major uprising in London that would see Henry Tudor land on the south coast and oust Richard. He was in contact with the growing number of rebels with Tudor in Brittany. He is typical of the former servants of Edward IV, and also of the disaffected gentry in Wiltshire treated so harshly after Buckingham's rebellion, who could not be reconciled to Richard's rule. Richard had issued pardons to 28 rebels and made overtures to opponents when he could, but a pardon was not a restoration of property and title. This would need to be earned in royal service, and for many it was easier to seek an overthrow of the king than to have to work to secure his favour.

Richard's known distrust of rebels did not endear him to the disaffected. He only restored the lands of six rebels after the acts of attainder. Collingbourne was hung, drawn and quartered for his efforts, but his treasonable activity demonstrated that the perpetual unrest in the West Country had spread to London, Essex and East Anglia: all regions with connections to the discontented in Brittany. Men like William Stonor, John Fortescue, William Berkeley and William Brandon were pardoned rebels whose loyalty to Edward IV united them in opposition to Richard III. Their links extended to the garrison at Calais, where rebellion led to the defection of some of the garrison in January 1485. The lieutenant of Hammes, James Blount, had released the earl of Oxford and joined Henry Tudor. With Oxford on the loose his supporters in Essex and Suffolk were encouraged to consider the possibility of a restoration of their fortunes under Tudor's banner. Richard's failure to secure the loyalty of Edward's former household servants had caused him to rely on men from his northern affinity, but this had only exacerbated the problem.[19]

By the summer of 1485 Richard was well prepared to face Henry Tudor, and no doubt keen to do so. Trial by battle would not only confer God's judgement on Richard's kingship, but also rid him of a troublesome enemy. Commissions of array had put the county levies on standby at an hour's notice. The south coast was well defended. If Tudor should penetrate the defences, Richard's experience in battle against an untried adventurer would surely settle matters swiftly and decisively. Richard left London on 11 May, arriving at Nottingham on 9 June ready to respond to an expected landing, wherever it might be. He took with him George lord Strange, the eldest son of Thomas lord Stanley, as a hostage for the good behaviour of his father. Finally on 7 August Henry landed at Milford Haven. Richard summoned the earl of Northumberland, the duke of Norfolk, Thomas lord Stanley and knights and esquires from various parts of the kingdom. Stanley made his excuses, professing to be suffering from the 'sweating sickness'. Although Richard was in no doubt that he could not trust the Stanleys, Henry could not be sure of their commitment either. They would do what they had done as long ago as 1459 at Blore Heath and wait upon events.

Richard moved from Nottingham to Leicester shortly after 16 August. Tudor was moving slowly south-eastwards through Shropshire in the direction of London. It is possible that he had contact with William Stanley at this stage, although by no means certain. Tudor's unopposed movements through Cheshire, Stanley country, arouse suspicion. On 21 August Richard moved from Leicester to intercept the invader, and Tudor turned to meet him. The two armies met at a place called Redemoor, near Market Bosworth, on 22 August 1485. Much of our understanding of what happened at one of the most decisive battles ever fought on English soil is nothing more than speculation. The Croyland Chronicle devotes but a few lines to it, Polydore Vergil was writing 20 years later and was not even in England at the time, and the 'Ballad of Bosworth Field' based on a contemporary account contains obvious errors and very little description of the course of the battle. In 2009 modern archaeology at last yielded results and helped to locate the battlefield, enabling us to confirm the use of artillery and Burgundian weaponry. There was far more evidence of the use of hackbuts, or handguns, than had previously been suspected, but their significance still requires interpretation. We know for certain that the battle was fought two miles to the south-west of Ambion Hill, the previous putative location, but still within reach of the Bosworth Battlefield Heritage Centre established by Leicestershire County Council. It was fought on marshy ground between Fenn Lanes and Upton Lane a mile west of Stoke Golding, between Fenny Drayton and Dadlington. The marsh may have had a significant impact on the outcome of the battle.[20]

The duke of Norfolk, in charge of Richard's vanguard, engaged the earl of Oxford on the marshy ground at the bottom of a slope. In this hard, hand-to-hand fighting, Oxford's superior weaponry and tactics overwhelmed the duke and he was killed. His son, Thomas Howard earl of Surrey, does not seem to have taken the fighting much further and he may have decided that the cause was lost. When Richard became aware of the difficulties being experienced by Norfolk he still had opportunities to turn the tide and win the battle. Being informed of a movement by Henry Tudor towards the Stanleys, he reacted immediately and decisively. Tudor was either attempting to communicate with the Stanleys, and perhaps join them, or had inadvertently been exposed by the movement of the vanguards as they attempted to avoid the marshy ground. Either way, an opportunity to attack Tudor directly and to bring the battle to a successful conclusion seemed to present itself. Richard, wearing a golden ring around his helmet and with banners flying, led a charge of his mounted household troops towards his enemy. Several hundred of his most loyal and trusted men followed the king in the last charge of knights in English history. Richard was also the last English king to lead his troops into battle. If his aim had been to prevent Tudor reaching the Stanleys and finding security with them, he only succeeded in charging across the forces of Sir William Stanley and providing his enemies with a golden opportunity. William Stanley intervened decisively to save Tudor and cut down Richard's forces from behind. Unhorsed, Richard was eventually surrounded within yards of his objective. He was hacked down as he fought bravely to the end, shouting 'Treason! Treason!'

Northumberland's forces were not engaged at all and drifted northwards as the drama unfolded. Thomas Stanley joined his stepson, now king of England, to receive the title he had been denied for so long: he became earl of Derby. Richard's body was stripped naked, flung across a horse and taken to Leicester where it was unceremoniously buried at Greyfriars. Croyland, rarely complimentary towards Richard, noted that he 'fell in the field like a brave and most valiant prince'. Rous, the Warwickshire antiquarian, while depicting Richard as 'a wretched creature', admitted that 'he defended himself as a noble knight with great courage to his last breath'. Polydore Vergil, possibly using eyewitness accounts, recorded that 'king Richard alone was killed fighting manfully in the thickest press of his enemies'.[21]

It is not easy to make sense of Bosworth. Richard should have won the battle. He had superior numbers and enough experience of warfare to outwit Henry Tudor on the battlefield. He probably had the use of the Burgundian artillery he had been purchasing from Flanders and producing at the Tower. What he did not have were French troops. The presence of these trained professionals, possibly with the deadly pikes that had turned the tide in favour of the French in the Hundred Years War, may have been sufficient to defeat the English county levies. They seemed to have granted an unexpected air of invincibility to the earl of Oxford. In all his previous battles he had been defeated and reduced to ignominious flight. He was to perform further sterling feats of generalship for Henry Tudor at Stoke in 1487. It is possible that the weaponry and battle tactics that had eventually driven the English out of French lands had been deployed on English soil with equally devastating results. It is also clear that many of Richard's forces were not engaged at Bosworth. This may have been because of the difficulties posed by the terrain and the confusion of the melee, or it may have been caused by a lack of enthusiasm on the part of some of Richard's supporters. It is unlikely, however, that disloyalty on a large scale was a major cause of the defeat. Even disaffected knights would find it difficult to see the advantages to be gained by risking so much on such a slight and little known figure as Henry Tudor. A few disaffected nobles were quite a different matter. Northumberland and Stanley had sufficient cause to betray Richard.

The likelihood is that the surprisingly effective troops deployed in Tudor's service made the choices stark and simple at an early stage of the fight. Apart from the heroic service offered by his household retainers, the underlying assumption that commitment to the king could be taken for granted had been damaged by the usurpation of 1483. Richard had tried to paint Henry Tudor as a foreigner ready to sell his soul to the French. On the battlefield Englishmen confronted Englishmen. There were certainly significant foreign elements, Scots as well as French, and these may have been decisive, but for many Englishmen this battle must have seemed like a return to the days of civil war. It was always best to end up on the winning side, or at least survive and hope to make do afterwards. There was an element of that heroic past Richard may have nostalgically wished to recreate, certainly in his own conduct on the battlefield, but it was overwhelmed by superior technology and self-serving pragmatism.

8

THE REIGN 3:
THE POLITICS OF KINGSHIP

CHANGING POWER STRUCTURES

It used to be believed that the civil wars in England in the 15th century were a consequence of the insatiable ambitions of 'over-mighty subjects'. Their ability to cause havoc, the narrative ran, was exacerbated by a gradual corruption of the feudal system that enabled them to raise their own armies of indentured retainers. Under the malevolent influence of 'bastard feudalism' men were willing to serve a lord for hard cash rather than unpaid loyalty. As the traditional bonds of service and protection gave way to self-interest and monetary reward, so social cohesion suffered and greed and ambition thrived. This was the view developed by 19th century historians that continued to prevail well into the 20th century. It was the great medievalist K. B. McFarlane who pointed out that the chief cause of the Wars of the Roses was not 'over-mighty subjects' but an 'under-mighty king'. He also showed that the term 'bastard feudalism', first coined by Charles Plummer in 1885 as a term of abuse, could be applied to the more flexible forms of service that bound men together at a time when the tenurial relationship associated with land was no longer adequate. 'Bastard feudalism' was a practical way of filling the void in contractual obligations created by the changing nature of society, particularly in the 14th and 15th centuries. With the lords requiring different kinds of service, not just military service, and the need for protection and patronage being felt by an increasingly influential class of gentry, 'bastard feudalism' allowed for some cohesion and stability. This system worked well under strong royal government, and only became a force for division and lawlessness under a weak king.[1]

It was Sir John Fortescue, a 15th century jurist and a Lancastrian protagonist during the Wars of the Roses, who first coined the term 'over-mighty subjects'. He had in mind the Yorkist lords, the earl of Warwick and the duke of York, who had challenged the authority of the king and led their troops against him. In the same way, it might be argued, Richard duke of Gloucester was, like his noble kinsmen, no more than a nobleman whose ambition got the better of him. Fortescue saw royal authority as the only legitimate authority in the realm; any challenge to it from the nobility was a breach of faith. This was a truism of medieval political thought. Fortescue was merely stating the obvious in his assessment of the unimpeachable nature of royal authority and the dangers inherent in refusing to obey its will. Very few 15th century noblemen would have disagreed with him. The problem, however, was not so much the challenge to legitimate authority as the calamitous consequences of weak and ineffectual kingship. What the 15th century is really about, in political terms, is the implosion of royal authority under Henry VI and its restoration by subsequent monarchs. In this overall scheme Richard III has his place. His brother had strengthened royal rule and restored much of its power. Richard's usurpation of the throne at least had the merit of preventing weak leadership from once again undermining royal authority. The weakness at the heart of Richard's regime was his own lack of legitimacy. Henry Tudor was able to claim greater legitimacy, through victory in battle and marriage to Elizabeth of York, and continue to strengthen the centre at the expense of the nobility. Monarchy was changing, but the overwhelming desire of the political community for legitimate and strong royal government is as much a legacy of Richard's reign as that of his predecessors.

Of course, the duke of York's rebellion against Henry VI was quite different from Warwick's rebellion against Edward IV. York's need for protection against the misuse of royal power has a certain degree of legitimacy that is wholly absent in the later case of Warwick. Similarly, Richard's seizure of the throne in 1483, while appearing to protect his own position from the threat of misrule, and to allow royal power to be exercised strongly rather than weakly, was pre-emptive not reactive. It therefore lacked the legitimacy of his father's actions. What the later two attacks on royal power, those of Warwick and Richard, share with each other is the attempt to control royal power rather than restore it. The duke of York aimed to establish firm royal government after years of incompetence. Warwick and Richard wanted to take control of an already resurgent monarchy. Both of their attempts can be seen in an even wider context. With the strengthening of royal authority in the reign of Edward IV came an inexorable decline in magnate power. The king could trump a magnate, however mighty he might be. Edward's triumph over Warwick, close fought though it was initially, provided the backdrop to Richard's usurpation in 1483. As duke of Gloucester he could not assume that his power would be secure under Edward V, or so he may have argued. He had used his brother's royal power to gain an ascendancy over other magnates in the north. What if this power was now used against him by his nephew?

THE NOBILITY

The nobility, the titled elite of the realm, formed an important element in the political community. It is too simplistic to see them as militating against royal power and imposing their authority over those of lesser rank. Above them was royal power and below them the remainder of the political classes, known as the gentry. The gentry, formed of knights, esquires, 'gentlemen' and burgesses, were a populous and increasingly important class, both in the localities and within the royal household. Their immediate overlords in the regions were the nobility. It was through the nobility, and not despite them, that royal power was, in general, made effective in the shires. The nobility, in other words, played an important role as intermediaries between the king and his lesser subjects. Their lordship over lands and men could make royal government reach into local communities, while the security and patronage they offered allowed lesser landowners to participate in a wider sphere and with greater scope.[2]

The nobility consisted of the 70 or 80 men and their families with at least the title of lord. Political power was determined by land ownership because of the control over tenants that came with it. The greater nobility, those with the greatest landholdings, amounted to only about 20 families in the later 15th century. These tended to be from among the dukes and earls, but not necessarily so. There were five ranks of the nobility. The most senior were the dukes, usually numbering only three or four who were close to the royal family and might be part of it. Next came the marquesses, sitting between the dukes and the earls. This rank was something of an oddity among the English aristocracy and they tended to be rare. There were about 15 earls, though their number could be as few as 10 and as many as 20. They were often heads of powerful regional lordships based on ancient centres of power with long-standing family interests and connections. An earl might be the son of a duke and would often have royal blood in his veins and dynastic connections with the reigning monarch. Below the earls in rank were the viscounts who had risen above the heads of 'mere' lords through exceptional service or favour. Ordinary lords, numbering between 40 and 50, formed the largest group of the nobility and contained many newly promoted to the ranks of the peerage. Any lord might be described as a baron and all, though usually only the most powerful, might be called a magnate. What united all lords in a single generic group was the privilege they all possessed of having the right to receive a personal writ of summons to parliament and to sit in the House of Lords. Unusually, in a wider European context, this amounted to the only legal privilege the English nobility enjoyed. As members of the peerage they had the right to be tried only by their fellow peers in the House of Lords, but they were expected to pay tax and perform military service. They were expected to furnish troops at their own expense, lend money to the king if required to do so and keep law and order in their communities. In England rank did not spare you from financial or military burdens as it did, for instance, in France. This gave the English nobility an important stake in the political community centred on the king. His dependency on them allowed him to distribute royal authority widely and to spread the responsibility and cost of governance. It also made them a powerful group with a legitimate concern for the conduct of national affairs.[3]

The power and influence exercised by the nobility had both a political and a social dimension. Nobles were lords over both land and men. For their part they lived as members of an elite warrior class, a martial caste engaged in a world of chivalric behaviour that had more to do with hunting, jousting and fighting than with courtesy and civility. The many tenants in a lord's large landed estates were expected to serve him as part of their tenurial obligations. These might be members of the minor aristocracy as well as the gentry. His estates would include the numerous manors and all the Hundreds spread throughout the counties. He would exercise a legal jurisdiction through the manorial courts and the Hundred courts, which not only determined the rents and services due to him but had a jurisdiction over every aspect of a tenant's life. The lords' power, symbolised in the great castles that dominated the landscape, was ultimately based on the value of the rents they could raise from their tenants. An earl, on average, could command an income of £1,000 per annum. A greater lord might be able to raise as much as £6,000, as did the duke of York, or even more: Warwick was worth £7,000 per annum in the 1460s. The king would expect to raise between £15,000 and £20,000 from his landed estates, and this would be supplemented by parliamentary grants of taxation, customs dues, the profits of justice and other royal prerogatives, but his annual income only matched that of the great magnates combined.

The king's needs could only be met if he could utilise magnate power and allow it to do his work in the localities. The nobility would expect to have an influence over the appointment of justices of the peace in their counties and the stewards of the royal manors in their neighbourhoods. Military posts such as constables and commissioners of array, as well as sheriffs and bailiffs, would usually form the backbone of a lord's territorial influence. Along with his tenants and officers he would include in his following his personal servants and retainers: those contracted to serve him for a fee. All would expect reciprocal protection and the benefits of the lord's patronage and influence, but he would also include in his 'affinity' a less well-defined group of 'well-wishers' and sympathisers. These men, rather like the retainers, might be independent landholders who were not forced to support the lord but had chosen to do so for the benefits they might achieve. A successful magnate, one who had ready access to royal influence or connections with the king's ministers, might attract the support of able and ambitious clients. The lord's authority was, therefore, partly economic – tenants owed rents and services in order to retain their land – and partly legal: the courts and royal offices at the lord's disposal made him the inescapable arbiter of justice in the region. It was also, essentially, social and deeply rooted in the culture and customs of medieval society. Deference to one's social superiors was a religious as well as a cultural obligation.[4]

It was the political dimension to noble power that made them such important players during the turbulence of the 15th century. The king could not rule alone. It was from among the nobility that he chose his counsellors and ministers and from whose ranks he filled the great offices of state. In essence, however, his power depended on his ability to enforce his will. Royal law guaranteed all land ownership, including that of the barons, and provided an overarching security to all landholders, but it operated through regional hierarchies. For the king to enforce his commands he needed to be able to bring overwhelming force to bear against those who chose to resist him. It was the nobility, the leading landowners, who could raise men quickly and effectively to subordinate individuals and communities to the rule of law. The king would hope not to need to use such drastic measures, but the ability to do so, and the threat of severe reprisals against insubordination, was vital to the stability of every community. This use of power, however, always depended on the cooperation of the greatest landowners. The nobility could raise men from among their tenants for the use of the king, but the men so raised owed allegiance to their immediate lord. The force he was able to command was necessary for the king to perform his public role, but it was a private force under the control of a lord. In times of peace and prosperity, usually guaranteed by strong kingship, the system generally tended to provide cohesion and stability. In times of uncertainty and weakness at the centre, these forces might be used for the magnate's personal objectives, and these might not coincide with those of the king.[5]

When Richard III took the throne in 1483, the tension between public and private power that had exploded into violence during the reigns of Henry VI and Edward IV had not diminished. The system in which royal rule depended on noble power had imploded into civil war and weakened both the monarchy and the nobility. Eighty per cent of the nobility had fought in the Wars of the Roses between 1455 and 1471. Of the 70 noble participants in the two main periods of fighting, 1459–1464 and 1469–1471, 31 had been killed and 20 executed. One outcome of these periods of war was a reduction in the numbers and regional hegemonies of the greater lords, accompanied by a corresponding weakening of their power and effectiveness in the regions. Royal authority had emerged the victor in one sense – the king was still more powerful than any combination of magnates – but he had been weakened by the reduction of noble power. He had a narrower base of support and a gap in the effectiveness of the royal writ in certain regions. The events of 1483, both the seizure of the throne and Buckingham's rebellion, had exacerbated these defects and exposed the fault-lines in the structure holding royal and noble power together. Edward IV had, of necessity, attempted to create a new nobility to replace the loss of so many regional lords. This had fundamentally changed the nature of noble power, at least among the new creations. They were more dependent on royal favour than the ancestral families had been, and at the same time they were less reliant on their local communities. Royal favour, usually in the form of an annuity, replaced dependence on rents and services from the new lord's estates. In such cases loyalty to the king superseded local commitments and regional sentiments, at least until the new lord had established himself in the area. In Edward IV's case, men such as William lord Hastings had developed a regional affinity, but they had had time to do so. In Richard's case, the nobility he created did not have the time to do this and ultimately, as in the case of the duke of Norfolk, failed to harness the strength of the regions for the benefit of the king.

Edward IV had summoned 41 lords to his first parliament in 1461, a not inconsiderable number and on a par with the number summoned by Henry VI in the early 1450s, but seven had been promoted for the occasion and six more were added afterwards. He created eight new earls in the first decade of his reign. Nevertheless, the remainder of his reign saw a noticeable decline in the number of lords. A combination of death in battle, rebellion followed by execution, and a lack of male heirs meant that at Richard's parliament in January 1484 only 26 peers were summoned. The reduction in the numbers of the nobility and the need to maximise royal authority in regions in which the king already had control, or access to methods of control, had caused Edward IV to look progressively to men beyond the senior nobility to perform local functions for the king. He increasingly used the men he knew, who served him in the royal household, and promoted them to offices in regions where he had an existing network of control. These areas were those consisting of his own estates from his inherited lands and those, such as the duchy of Lancaster estates, which adhered to the crown and were inherited by the reigning monarch. Edward had expanded this field of opportunity, ripe for the advancement of able and ambitious members of the gentry or the lesser baronage, by examining and exploiting his royal rights in such regions. He nevertheless continued to depend on a diminished number of magnates. Hastings and the Woodvilles, particularly Dorset and Rivers, had filled gaps in their number but Edward had been forced to depend on existing noble hegemonies, such as those of the Percys and the Stanleys, more heavily than he may have wished. In particular he had created a massive regional lordship for Richard duke of Gloucester from among the wreckage of the Neville power-nexus. This meant that when Richard became king and continued the process of binding his lordship to his kingship, in the same way that Edward had used both the earldom of March and the dukedom of York as his personal patrimonies, the base of regional lordships grew even narrower. Richard intended to continue to control his northern estates as if he were still duke of Gloucester. The king would become the lord of his former tenants and retainers, rather than risk the creation of a potential rival. At the same time, while noble power was being further eroded in this way, those regional hegemonies that remained were too entrenched and cohesive to be outmanoeuvred by the new dispensation. If Richard's reign saw a continuation of the diminution of noble power, and turned out to be an important step in dislocating localities from their regional lordships and expanding royal control, it also provided an illustration of the dangers of such a policy and the strength of loyalties that had remained entrenched in many local communities. Richard was reluctant to create new peers, in a way that none of his predecessors had been, perhaps overly cautious about the quality and loyalty of the candidates available.[6]

THE GREAT NOBLES UNDER RICHARD

Henry Percy the fourth earl of Northumberland had cooperated with Richard reasonably well during the latter stages of Edward IV's reign. He had accepted a somewhat subordinate role in the north to that of the royal duke, but had maintained his rights and authority over the Percy heartlands. He had been sufficiently confident of gaining from his working relationship with Richard in the north to back the usurpation. Richard's intention to remain the *de facto* lord of the north while also being king may have been a blow to the hopes of the earl of Northumberland. The duke of Gloucester's council now became a royal council headed by the king's son, Prince Edward. It also performed the function of the prince's household, very much in the way Edward IV's son had become established in Wales. The council moved from Middleham and Sheriff Hutton to Sandal, within the former duchy of York rather than a Neville stronghold, perhaps to prepare the way for a more expanded role for the council as the prince grew older. There were to be two centres of royal control in England, one in Westminster and one in Yorkshire. Prince Edward died on 9 April 1484, throwing not only the Yorkist succession into doubt but also the role of the prince's council. Richard's solution, to appoint his nephew John de la Pole earl of Lincoln as the head of the Council of the North, must have been a further blow to Henry Percy's ambitions. Lincoln's seat was to be within the royal household at Sandal, further emphasising the fact that he acted on the king's behalf rather than as an independent magnate. Richard's preference, which was to be continued by Henry Tudor, was to prevent royal authority being utilised by an independent magnate. Richard's own exercise of power in the north had been precisely the type of lordship he now seemed keen to prevent. His authority had been underpinned by his kinship with the king, Edward IV: the stability and unity of objective this had brought could only be maintained by another kinsman. Henry Percy received some compensation in the form of the title 'warden general of the Scottish March', but in practice Richard continued to appoint his own deputies in the western March while Percy retained control over the middle and eastern Marches. Percy's disaffection may have manifested in his lack of commitment at Bosworth, though we may never know whether his lack of engagement in the battle was simply the result of the rapidly shifting nature of the encounter. If he harboured a grudge against Richard and expected the new dispensation to improve his prospects, he must have been greatly disappointed. Independent magnates were a thing of the past and Henry Tudor was as disinclined as Richard was to allow them to flourish again. Percy's imprisonment after Bosworth suggests that his motives at the battle may not have been to betray Richard but rather to avoid taking unnecessary risks. Whatever the case, his restoration by Tudor brought him few advantages. The earl was to lose his life in a tax revolt in Yorkshire in 1489 in which he was lynched by the men of York, perhaps in reprisal for his lack of support for Richard at Bosworth.[7]

Ralph Neville, another northern magnate, inherited his uncle's earldom of Westmorland in November 1484. Like Henry Percy he too had cooperated with Richard during the coup of 1483 and acted against the rebels later in that year. He was also rewarded for his loyalty, but with lands in the south rather than in the north. He also had to come to terms with the fact that under Richard III his power in the north would be circumscribed. None of Richard's lordships would be granted to noble intermediaries. Ralph's ancestral seat at Raby remained in Richard's possession, and his heir was, perhaps somewhat pointedly, a ward of court. He seemed intent on subsuming his ducal authority in that of the crown.[8]

One magnate created and empowered by Richard III was John Howard duke of Norfolk. From the very beginning of the reign Howard was given a collection of lordships that had formerly been a royal connection. The Mowbray lands, which had been given to Edward IV's second son Richard duke of York, the lands of Earl Rivers and the de Vere lands in East Anglia, which had been granted to Richard himself when duke of Gloucester, were placed under the administration of the new duke of Norfolk. He was made chief steward of the duchy of Lancaster in the south while his son, Thomas Howard earl of Surrey, was made steward of the duchy of Lancaster in Norfolk. This was certainly a case of the king attempting to establish a regional lordship in order to create a loyal presence in an area where Yorkist influence needed to be extended. John Howard remained faithful to his benefactor but did not have the time to establish himself in his dukedom. He was unable to control the region during Buckingham's rebellion and Richard resorted to intruding his own men into the important offices in the county. The sheriffs, justices and escheators within the new dukedom were appointed from among Richard's own servants. At Bosworth the duke of Norfolk died in Richard's service, faithful even unto death, but his demise demonstrated the weaknesses inherent in imposing new magnates on regions of doubtful loyalty. At Bosworth many of Norfolk's men will have found themselves face-to-face with the retainers of the earl of Oxford, fighting for Henry Tudor. Oxford, an inveterate Lancastrian and veteran of the battle of Barnet, may have presented something of a dilemma for some of Norfolk's men from the former de Vere estates in Suffolk. John de Vere the 13th earl of Oxford had connections in that region going back centuries. Thomas Howard does not appear to have resisted Oxford for very long after his father had been killed, and while this may have been the most pragmatic approach at the time, he may also have realised that the men under his command were not as single-minded as the king had hoped they would be.[9]

Another magnate who remained faithful to Richard, fighting two years after Bosworth at the battle of Stoke in 1487, was his life-long friend Francis viscount Lovell. Lovell already had significant interests in the Thames Valley and Richard began to build on these almost immediately. Already the king's chamberlain, Lovell was made constable of Wallingford in August 1483 and, after Buckingham's rebellion, was given much forfeited land in Oxfordshire and Berkshire and all the offices pertaining to them. Rather like Norfolk, however, he was unable to control his local associates during the rebellion. Gentry families, such as the Stonors and the Norreys, joined the rebellion despite family connections with Lovell himself. The viscount's influence in the area had waned and his efforts to revive it were not sufficient to overcome the loyalty of Edward IV's former household servants. Given time it is possible that Lovell may have developed a regional affinity in the mould of that of William lord Hastings and there can be little doubt that Richard wanted this to happen.

The king's efforts to establish new regional hegemonies under Lovell and Norfolk show that Richard III was not pursuing a wantonly anti-magnate agenda. The net reduction in noble power under his government was not a matter of policy, but rather of expedience. Richard's main objective, throughout the short reign, was security. He certainly distrusted independent noble power but he was happy to use it when he could. Given time, the nobles he trusted may have become important. The earl of Shrewsbury falls into this category, as do both Thomas lord Maltravers, the heir to the elderly earl of Arundel, and John de la Pole, the earl of Lincoln. William viscount Berkeley was made earl of Nottingham, but appears to have been of little account in national affairs. The immediate need to restore royal authority after Buckingham's rebellion led Richard to turn to his most trusted servants, and these were largely men from within his own household. If Richard had reigned for longer a new aristocracy may have emerged, rather than the systematic erosion of their power that occurred under the Tudors.[10]

The nobleman with the firmest regional base during Richard's reign was Thomas lord Stanley. He was also the most untrustworthy and the most independent among the greater magnates. Richard had clashed with him as duke of Gloucester and had given his unwavering support to Stanley's enemies in east Lancashire. These powerful gentry families, the Harringtons, the Huddlestons and the Pilkingtons in particular, were now at the heart of royal government. Stanley and Richard had reached a *modus vivendi* under Edward IV, serving together, for instance, on the Scottish campaign at the end of the reign, but it had taken considerable effort on Edward's part to achieve this working relationship. During the usurpation Stanley had been arrested with Hastings, and although released it must have been evident to him that his marriage to Margaret Beaufort would continue to place him under suspicion. From 1459 onwards Stanley and his brother Sir William had increased their grip on the north-west throughout the vicissitudes of civil war. Richard's Lancashire followers, perpetually resisting Stanley aggrandisement in the county, might now expect to be able to use royal authority to effect a readjustment to the balance of power in their region. Edward IV had recognised the strength of Stanley's hegemony and had resisted calls for it to be reduced. Stanley could muster 5,000 tenants and retainers whose primary loyalty was to their ancestral lord. Edward was too much of a pragmatist, and perhaps more able and willing to rise above faction than Richard, to contemplate challenging such an important regional bloc. Any tension between Richard and Stanley was temporarily forgotten during Buckingham's rebellion. Both the Stanleys supported the king rather than Buckingham, perhaps wary of an extension of Buckingham's power in north Wales. Richard rewarded them with generous grants of land. William received land along the Welsh March valued at £600 and Thomas was granted lands valued at about £700. William was also made chief justice of north Wales and constable of Caernarvon. Thomas was also rewarded with important offices, succeeding Buckingham as constable of England and being made a knight of the Garter. He later became steward of the household, a post he had held under Edward IV. His eldest son, George lord Strange, joined his father as a member of the king's council and his other sons, Edward and James, received advancement and rewards. Nevertheless, there was no extension of Stanley power in Lancashire. Richard kept his own offices in the region, particularly the one that Stanley probably coveted the most: the chief stewardship of the duchy of Lancaster in the north.[11]

It is with Thomas lord Stanley that the growing tensions between regional magnate power and that of the new class of royal servants, usually men of gentry status with roles in the royal household and strong local ties and influence, can most clearly be seen. Richard had supported James Harrington in his feud with Stanley over the estates and castle of Hornby. Edward IV had settled the dispute in Stanley's favour and allowed him to take possession of an important stronghold in the north-east of Lancashire. It was a significant acquisition for Stanley, completing the jigsaw of his regional dominance, now stretching from north Wales through Cheshire and up through Lancashire, and also allowing him to control the routes through the county towards Cumberland and Westmorland and across the Pennines into Yorkshire. Any change in the settlement forced upon the Harringtons would be a serious threat to Stanley. On 16 February 1485 Richard made James Harrington chief forester of Bowland. This was a post that had been held by Richard himself with Harrington as his deputy. By promoting Harrington in this way, even though the practicalities would have made little difference to the *status quo*, Richard was, wittingly or otherwise, sending very unwelcome signals to Stanley. The forest of Bowland stretched across the north-east of Lancashire as far as Hornby. Stanley must have been concerned that Richard might be contemplating revisiting the Hornby dispute with a view to satisfying James Harrington, now described as 'our knight of the body'.[12]

There is some evidence that he was. After the battle of Bosworth, in which James and Robert Harrington almost certainly died, Elizabeth Beaumont wrote to the parson of Slaydburn asking about her title to the property at Hornby. She was formerly Elizabeth Harrington, who had been the co-heiress with her sister Anne when their father, John Harrington, had died at the battle of Wakefield in 1460. If, as the Stanleys had tried to prove, she and her sister were the true heirs of the estate, and not her uncles James and Robert, then she was now the owner of Hornby, since her sister Anne had died without issue. After Edward IV had made his award of Hornby to Thomas lord Stanley, the magnate had given the property to his second son, Edward. He, in turn, had married Anne Harrington. Not only had Edward Stanley held on to the castle after the death of his wife but, according to Elizabeth, he had poisoned the only male heir who might challenge him, John Harrington the son of James. Because Edward Stanley now held Hornby by a grant of forfeiture from James Harrington which he was careful to secure after the battle of Bosworth, all Elizabeth would have to do was show that James had not been the lawful owner. The parson replied to her letter telling her 'it was so laboured that king Richard commanded a note to be drawn and caused the chancellor of the duchy of Lancaster to examine the true valour of all the manors and livelihoods the which your father was lawfully possessed and died seised of'. This would have been of great concern to the Stanleys. If Richard had pursued this matter it would surely have ended with the Harringtons regaining Hornby, but the parson had to inform her that 'King Richard never made award betwixt you and your uncles'. Perhaps he simply ran out of time. The threat to the Stanleys, however, may have confirmed their worst fears about Richard. His character may not have allowed him to go as far as Edward IV had gone in placating former enemies. A king needed to rise above faction and regional disputes, but the strength of Richard's loyalty to lesser men may have made this impossible.[13]

The Stanleys' relationship with all the monarchs they 'served' was always semi-detached. Dynastic disputes were a danger and might necessitate taking sides and risking battle, but their primary concern was always to retain their regional lordship and to strengthen and augment it if they could. They ruled their territories with little interference from central authority, providing the king with money and troops if need be but always seeking to protect their patrimony and increase their power. Richard was unable to check their influence in the short time he reigned, and his inability to do so may have contributed to his defeat at Bosworth. Thomas lord Stanley did not engage his forces at the battle, while William, ever the more impetuous of the two, opted for Henry Tudor. The lesson, however, was not lost on Tudor. Regional power of the kind enjoyed by the Stanleys, that could ultimately make and unmake kings, was already an anachronism in Richard's reign. He had failed in his efforts to subordinate magnate power under the crown, but it was only a matter of time before it was achieved by his successors.

An example of the way in which Richard may have been able to build up a group of loyal magnates in time is provided by William Herbert earl of Huntingdon. He was made chief justice of south Wales in place of Buckingham, and married to the king's illegitimate daughter, Katherine, with a dowry of 1,000 marks a year. A significant revival of his family's interests and fortunes in Wales beckoned, only to be cut short by Richard's death at Bosworth. With the earls of Lincoln and Huntingdon, Richard may have vested hopes of building strong regional magnates to support his rule. The same may be said of George Talbot earl of Shrewsbury. He was the great-grandson of the John Talbot killed in the battle of Castillon in 1453, who had been the last of the great English commanders in France. George's grandfather had been killed fighting for the Lancastrians at Northampton and his uncle, Sir Gilbert Talbot, was quick to join Henry Tudor before the battle of Bosworth, but there is no evidence that George, only 15 years of age at the beginning of Richard's reign, would not have become a valuable member of the group of magnates Richard may have favoured. Of the remaining titled nobility, Edmund Grey earl of Kent, John duke of Suffolk and William Fitzalan earl of Arundel, were aged and ineffective, while Edward Grey viscount Lisle, was, like the earl of Nottingham, politically inactive.

THE LESSER NOBILITY

Among the lords who did not possess a title, Richard was considerably more successful in creating a notable group of loyal supporters. There were northerners prominent among these, such as John lord Scrope of Bolton, Richard lord FitzHugh, John lord Zouche and Humphrey lord Dacre of Gilsland, but no more than the percentage of territory they ruled might recommend. They, like all the lords in Richard's reign, were well rewarded by the king. Lord Dacre was appointed lieutenant of the West March towards Scotland, for example, allowing him to build up considerable power in the region, to the discomfort of Ralph Neville earl of Westmorland. Unlike the disparity that was to develop between the number of Richard's northern gentry supporters and those in the south, many of the lords who had been in the service of Edward IV exhibited fewer qualms about transferring their allegiance to the new king. Walter Devereux lord Ferrers, John Sutton lord Dudley, John Brook lord Cobham, Henry lord Grey of Codnor and John lord Audley, who became treasurer of the exchequer, fall into this category. There were those who had little time to make much impression but seemed to have been trusted by Richard, such as Thomas lord Lumley, Ralph lord Greystoke and John lord Grey of Powys. Lords Lumley and Greystoke had been in Richard's service when he had been duke of Gloucester and were part of his northern connection, but lord Grey had married a sister of the first William Herbert and had considerable interests in Wales. Even those with very close ties, and corresponding loyalties, to Edward IV's government, were invited to continue to work for Richard's regime. Richard Hastings lord Willoughby and Wells, brother of the executed William, was allowed to continue unmolested on his own estates. Among these lords, however, the outcome was less successful, perhaps because their support was lukewarm or simply because Richard could not bring himself to trust them. John Blount lord Mountjoy and John lord Dinham were both moved sideways and found their commands at Calais and its fortifications being superseded by the command given to Richard's illegitimate son, John of Gloucester. Lord Dinham had been generously rewarded for his services and had been made chief steward of the duchy of Cornwall but, as he began to lose favour, he lost this post to the ever-acquisitive Sir James Tyrrel. These lesser lords, on the whole, formed a considerable group of aristocratic supporters willing to work with and for the new regime. As Lord Dinham discovered, however, some of the more ambitious members of the up-and-coming gentry class had altogether more to gain and less to lose than the lesser nobility.

THE GENTRY

The term 'gentry' is a very loose, vague and unsatisfactory one that medieval historians use to describe a large and varied group, numbering perhaps 7,000 in the 15th century, who stood in the social hierarchy between the nobility and the labourers. At either end of the spectrum there was considerable overlap in terms of wealth and influence but, on the whole, the gentry as a class included all those in possession of freehold land worth £10 or those with an income of at least £5 per annum. They might be townsmen, lawyers or university graduates, rather than county landowners, and they would often perform some public office in the context of justice and administration. In the following century a more clearly defined group emerged based on the right to exhibit a coat of arms, but in the 15th century the term usually referred to knights, esquires and 'gentlemen'.

Fluidity was the key: a mere 'gentleman' might aspire to become an esquire or a knight while a knight could hope to be elevated to the peerage. It is this mobility that becomes increasingly evident during the 15th century, often associated with the growing demand for legal professionals and efficient estate managers. A man might rise through education and intelligence rather more quickly in the later 15th century than through military prowess and distinguished conduct on the battlefield. There were greater opportunities for talented lawyers, for instance, in a world growing more complex, more litigious and more determined to exploit the profits of landownership, than for soldiers whose services were becoming circumscribed and anachronistic. The ending of the Hundred Years War and the corresponding reduction of opportunities to shine in the noble arts of war had hastened this process, while the Wars of the Roses had increased opportunities for the emerging professional class of lawyers and administrators. The shifting fortunes of the houses of York and Lancaster had provided a substantial crop of attainders, confiscations and legal disputes. There were countless demands for the services of escheators, stewards, feofees, commissioners of the peace and officials engaged in commissions of judicial inquiry.[14]

It is not a coincidence that some of the most notable examples of the emergence of what might be called the class of 'super gentry' occurred during the reign of Richard III. The progress of trained lawyers in social and political advancement had been accelerating throughout the 15th century. The Paston family is just one of many examples of the ability of attorneys and searjents-at-law to rise in the service of both the nobility and the crown. It was the political dimension, their use to the crown in sensitive and often contentious work, which was to be exploited so notably by Richard. Men such as Sir Richard Ratcliffe, Sir William Hussey, Sir James Tyrell and Sir Thomas Montgomery became more significant in the king's counsels and on his commissions – and wealthier as a consequence – than many of the lesser nobility. These types of men, the 'super-gentry', who were to become a feature of the Tudor period, first emerge as a significant group in the reign of Richard. There are many possible explanations for this. Richard's experience as a duke, with extensive regional jurisdiction and commitments, had brought him into contact with these men and taught him how effective and useful they could be. It was also a consequence of the usurpation and the aftermath of Buckingham's rebellion that had increased the scale and importance of the work such men performed. A reduction in the numbers of the nobility combined with the need for loyal, compliant and trusted officials also improved the market for these effective individuals. But there may also be a case for suggesting that Richard had a preference for employing and promoting such men. Many of those he used on his most confidential assignments and commissions, such as John Kendall, Richard and Edward Redmane and William Catesby, were not even knights. Their low rank seemed no bar to their extensive briefs and no hindrance to the trust the king reposed in them, and may have been an advantage. Confidentiality and unquestioning obedience may have been the qualities the king most valued at a time when loyalty must have seemed at a premium.

WILLIAM CATESBY

William Catesby provides the archetypal example of the new political force members of his class represented. The first thing to note about his rise, which typifies the group, is that his 'humble' origins were not quite as lowly as might be supposed. He was not a noble, certainly, and did not have an aristocratic ancestry, but he was born into the fringes of the nobility with strong regional connections and influence. His father had been sheriff of the county of Northamptonshire five times. Also named William, he had had a distinguished record of service on commissions of the peace in Northamptonshire and Warwickshire and in royal service in the king's household. William senior was appointed esquire of the body to Henry VI and knighted for his service. He may have had a more glittering career himself had he not consistently backed the wrong horse during the tumult of the Wars of the Roses. He supported Margaret of Anjou against the duke of York and then against his son Edward IV, backed Warwick during his rebellion against Edward and fled to Scotland with Henry VI after the aborted Readeption. He received pardons after each of his apparent defections, but his career no doubt suffered. His son may have learnt something about the political machinations that so embroiled his father, and perhaps learnt to keep ahead of the game and not to be too scrupulous about where and how to deploy his talents.

William Catesby II's marriage in 1471 to Margaret reminds us of just how close the upper gentry came to rubbing shoulders with the nobility. His wife was the daughter of William lord Zouche and Elizabeth, who happened to be the half-sister of Margaret Beaufort. Catesby studied to become an attorney and serjeant-at-law at the Inns of Court, in the Inner Temple. He must have showed considerable promise because the records show him conducting lectures himself. Promotion to significant appointments followed, demonstrating how useful such men were

'6, we find him steward
working in the service
Buckingham. He was
er lordship of Newport.
urchier the archbishop
management, in the
ather died in 1479 he
nsiderable, and again
ere by no means low-
Northamptonshire and
nties as well.[15]

s acting as one of the
d had been appointed
by Edward IV, first as an apprentice-at-law for the duchy of Lancaster and then, in a rapid promotion, to the chancellorship of the duchy. As a retainer of both Hastings and Buckingham he was ideally placed to profit from their support for Richard III in the crisis following Edward IV's death. In May 1483, for instance, he was appointed by Edward V to be chancellor of the earldom of March, reporting to the duke of Buckingham, and at the same time he became justice of the peace for Northamptonshire. Within a year of Edward IV's death William Catesby had managed to acquire over 40 more manors, many from confiscations following attainders, and had the control of a further 46. He had become a very wealthy man. His real importance, however, lies in his role as councillor to Richard III, and in particular in the role he played in the events of June 1483. Unfortunately it is almost impossible to discern precisely what that role was. What is certain is that he profited in the service of Buckingham and Hastings, possibly acting as an intermediary for Richard, and that he also profited spectacularly from the fall of both. The trust Richard subsequently reposed in Catesby suggests that the lawyer played some important role in the shaping of Richard's decisions and actions in the summer of 1483. The most likely point at which Catesby proved his worth was during the arrest and execution of Hastings. Richard could not proceed to depose Edward V without the support of Hastings. At some time before 13 June 1483 he must have ascertained that Hastings would not accept the removal of the young king, his master's son. Mancini believed that Buckingham was given the responsibility for sounding out the loyalty of Hastings, but More gave

the role to Catesby. More's account makes some sense of the sudden arrest of Hastings and his summary execution, which lends it a certain credibility. He says that Hastings was so 'fast' against the proposal to oust his royal master that he spoke 'terrible words' and Catesby did not dare to speak about it any more. There may be truth in both accounts, with Buckingham being given the commission and delegating it to the man who was well known to both himself and Hastings. Whatever happened, a grateful king was quick to reward Catesby for whatever service he had performed. Within a matter of just a few weeks he had been promoted to chancellor of the exchequer and 'chamberlain of the receipt', in Hastings' stead. He had an important role at the coronation, bearing the mantle and 'cap of estate', and was appointed an esquire of the body and a member of the king's council. After Buckingham's fall he profited again, gaining 17 manors from his erstwhile employer's demise and 16 from other attainders after the rebellion.[16]

Catesby's rise was spectacular and unprecedented. Without receiving a title, a feature of Richard's promotion of the upper gentry, he now began to play a significant role as a confidant and trusted agent of the king. Being without a peerage he had the advantage of being able to drive the king's business in the House of Commons and was elected Speaker in the Parliament of January 1484. He was sent to Brittany in September 1484, presumably with the intention of escorting Henry Tudor back to England, although Tudor was warned and managed to escape to France. Catesby was clearly the man to know: all ranks sought his services and patronage. Francis viscount Lovell granted him the six manors in Northamptonshire that had formerly belonged to Thomas Grey marquess of Dorset, explaining that it was, 'for the singular love he bears him'. Even Thomas lord Stanley granted him an annuity of 5 marks, in December 1483, and the manor of Kimbolton in Huntingdonshire forfeited by Buckingham, 'for goodwill and counsel'. In the end their connection was not strong enough to save Catesby's life after Bosworth. He was executed three days after the battle, having made a will in which he revealed that he had expected to have been spared by the intercession of the Stanleys. 'My lords Stanley, Strange and all that blood', he wrote, 'Help and pray for my soul for ye have not for my body as I trusted in you.' Quite how Catesby believed that Stanley would have been able to get him off the hook is difficult to imagine. At least the Stanleys had helped to secure Henry Tudor's victory. The tongues of angels would hardly have been sufficient to persuade Henry that Catesby was not one of the closest and most ingenious of Richard's servants, who had not only fought against Henry's men at Bosworth but also nearly arrested him in Brittany. Given Catesby's own poor record of intercession for Buckingham and Hastings, it could be argued that he was trapped in the same web he had helped to weave.[17]

RICHARD RATCLIFFE

While William Catesby was somewhat unusual in that he was relatively unknown to Richard before Edward IV's death and did not form part of his northern affinity, Richard Ratcliffe was typical of the men who would dominate the court after Richard III's accession. He was the younger son of a lesser gentry family from Cumberland whose only recommendation was that he impressed the duke of Gloucester in some unspecified way. He had connections with Henry Percy through his father and brother, who were retained by the earl, but a profitable marriage to Agnes, the daughter of Henry lord Scrope of Bolton, was almost certainly the consequence of Richard duke of Gloucester's support. With the marriage came land in Richmondshire and promotion to significant offices. He became constable of Barnard Castle, a member of the ducal council and was created a knight banneret by Richard on the Scottish campaign. There can be little doubt that in Richard Ratcliffe we have the archetype of those men most admired by Richard III. All we really know about him, however, is that he came from the north, was an able soldier and placed all his hopes and aspirations in the service of Richard. His advice was clearly valued, but also Ratcliffe and his type seemed to have given Richard the companionship and support he most needed. It would be mere speculation to imagine that Ratcliffe was the stereotypical blunt, plain-speaking northerner that Richard found easy to mix with, but Ratcliffe and his associates in Richard's northern affinity were certainly unsophisticated, in the southern courtly sense, and more accustomed to hard riding and military activity in the border region against fierce Scottish raiders than their counterparts in the south.[18]

Rather in the manner of Catesby, it was during the usurpation that Ratcliffe was trusted and proved his worth. When Richard wrote letters north on 10 and 11 June 1483, asking urgently for his northern retainers to muster immediately to come to his aid, it was Ratcliffe who bore the letters north and organised the army that assembled at Pontefract two weeks later. The despatches describe him as 'our trusty servant'. The army arrived in London after Richard had taken the throne and been declared king, but its approach was common knowledge and, in Mancini's view, provided sufficient threat to ensure there was no resistance in the capital. While gathering the army at Pontefract, Ratcliffe carried out another important commission, which involved the executions of Rivers, Grey, Vaughan and Haute. The lack of judicial process, and the brutal speed of this act, untrammelled by considerations of mercy, humanity or legal protocol, provides a stark contrast to the more subtle machinations taking place at Baynard's Castle or the Guildhall in London at the same time. There was certainly a 'no nonsense' approach adopted at Pontefract. Men like Ratcliffe seemed willing to do whatever was necessary to promote the interests of their lord, and to do it swiftly and effectively.[19]

In the same way that Catesby received massive rewards early in the new reign, so Ratcliffe benefited from grants after Buckingham's rebellion that were spectacular. The lands of the Courtenay earls of Devon, with additional lands in Cornwall and Wiltshire, amounting to an annual income of £666, represented royal generosity on a lavish scale. A baron was defined in Edward IV's *Black Book of the Household*, compiled in 1472, as a man possessing an income of £500 per annum. Ratcliffe's income and influence outstripped those of most lords and, with a total income of over £1,000 a year, he ranked with the earls in terms of wealth.[20]

He was one of the seven knights of the Garter created by Richard during his brief reign, three of the others also being northern knights. When lord Dacre died in May 1485 it was Ratcliffe who took over the command of the western March and it was he who was appointed permanent sheriff of Westmorland and steward of Wakefield. All this demonstrates his importance as one of Richard's main agents in the north. The estates in the south-west were purely gifts, rather than an attempt to create a new regional lordship. As with Catesby and other members of the gentry elevated to national importance by Richard, such as Sir Robert Brackenbury and Sir James Tyrell, there were no titles conferred upon them. As Edward had done before him, Richard would have been expected to reward those who had served him well before and during his accession, but the scale of the rewards and the number of members of a relatively low rank in society were unusual.[21]

Apart from any other consideration, promoting these men to the peerage may have reduced their sphere of action rather than increasing it. They were not lords and therefore not attached to any specific locality. They were, first and foremost, members of the king's retinue and engaged exclusively on his business. They rubbed shoulders easily with the lords on the king's council, such as Lovell, Dinham and Zouche, while possessing the confidence and independence that came with the trust and protection of the king. It was a situation that in more ways than one may have owed something to the king's character. Richard liked these men and therefore felt more secure in their company, but he also needed them because he could trust so few. After the shock of Buckingham's rebellion and the defection of so many of the Edwardian household, the security and authority experienced at court in the last years of Edward's reign had been shattered. Richard was never able to recreate the central stability that was essential for the effective governance of the realm. The anxiety and underlying tension of the reign never subsided. The death of the king's son in April 1484 increased the uncertainty and narrowed Richard's options still further.

9

POSTHUMOUS REPUTATION

SHAKESPEARE'S RICHARD

As he faced Henry Tudor in battle in the late summer of 1485, Richard could not have imagined that his main claim to fame would be to be immortalised by the world's greatest playwright as the most hideous, tyrannical monster ever to seize the English throne. No one who was present at the battle of Bosworth would have recognised the picture of unmitigated evil painted by Shakespeare. They would certainly not have understood how a king with a distinguished military record and proven ability in battle could possibly be portrayed as the loser of a duel against Henry Tudor. Witnesses that day in the late summer of 1485 would have seen the awesome spectacle of the last charge of knights in English history led by the king himself. If he had managed to engage Henry Tudor in single combat there would have been little doubt about the speedy outcome. They would have been in no doubt that the Richard III who cries out in Shakespeare's play, 'A horse! A horse! My kingdom for a horse!' was purely fictional. They would have seen the real king lead the mounted knights of the royal household in an audacious attack on the retinue and bodyguard of Henry Tudor. If they had had a bird's eye view of the bloody and ferocious fighting that erupted when the king's troops smashed into Tudor's men-at-arms, they would have seen the king fighting furiously within feet of his objective until he was hacked down from behind. Just before his brutal demise he realised that he had been betrayed by the forces of William Stanley and shouted in horror and amazement, 'Treason! Treason!'

Everyone knew at the time that Richard had died fighting bravely. How, just over a century later, he could be so traduced on the Elizabethan stage is part of the continuing fascination of Richard III. Even today the picture most people have of Richard III is the one lodged so decisively in the collective memory by Shakespeare. That picture has few redeeming features. Every act of his crooked life was calculated to bring him the power he craved. He murdered Henry VI and his son, he murdered his nephews and he even murdered his wife. For many, even some historians, this portrait remains the interpretation of choice. Shakespeare was, after all, reasonably accurate in other historical plays and allowed his creative genius to fashion some brilliant character studies of other monarchs. Why, they ask, should we be so ready to discard his Richard III? Even if the substance of his story derives ultimately from the study of Richard penned by Sir Thomas More, this is no reason to disbelieve it. Thomas More the chancellor of England was a man of probity and veracity who died a martyr rather than break an oath. Are we to say he was a liar? Sir Winston Churchill accepted their version in his *History of the English Speaking People*. With the weight of the reputations of three of the greatest Englishmen behind it, it is not surprising that it is the grotesque caricature of cowardly evil that is still commonly evoked when Richard III is mentioned today. He is the king with the hunchback who murdered the little Princes in the Tower.

The truth is that when Richard was killed at Bosworth it was not only his body that took a battering. Dying with his loyal friends, but betrayed by his more powerful enemies, Richard's reputation died with him. Stripped on the battlefield and flung over a horse to be taken to Leicester for public display, Richard's bloody, mud-spattered body, shattered and broken, cold and lifeless, carried his hopes and ideals into oblivion. Not only had his kingship come to an untimely end and his dynasty been destroyed, but his reputation also was about to disintegrate and decompose. His Tudor successors presided over the ignominious destruction of Richard's character and the infamous demonization of his life. Their task was made simpler by the fact that no contemporary chronicle had much good to say about him. Even if the later Tudor historians were to make the miraculous effort to be impartial and objective, the material they had to hand in the written records of the day would have led them to draw unfavourable conclusions about Richard. Foreign observers and English writers alike, all seemed to dislike him and to be suspicious of him. Those who have attempted to rehabilitate Richard and to separate the facts from the myth have always been hampered by this inconvenient stumbling-block. All the primary narrative sources give the Tudor story-tellers their ammunition. To reach a balanced view of Richard's life it is not good enough merely to accuse the Tudors of fabrication and dissembling. Contemporary observers and chroniclers have to be examined and considered carefully before we can dismiss any evidence under the familiar charge of propaganda.

Richard's fate on the battlefield not only cost him his reputation but it also exposed the manner in which he took the throne to the glare of history. If Richard had defeated Henry Tudor at Bosworth, and few would have bet against it in 1485, a successful period of stability, prosperity or military glory might have allowed the usurpation to acquire a vindication of sorts. There was certainly no possibility of that after Richard's early demise. Death at Bosworth ensured that Richard's life would always be controversial and surrounded by questions, riddles and mysteries.

CONSTRUCTION OF A LEGEND

The historiography of Richard III usually begins with Shakespeare because his Richard is far more familiar to the general population than the real historical Richard will ever be. The serious historian of Richard always finds it necessary to deconstruct the powerful image of the evil tyrant that Shakespeare made synonymous with his name. Filling the rather awkward vacuum left by exposing the myth has not been easy. Historians have largely fallen into two camps: those willing to absolve Richard of many or all of the crimes for which he was condemned by Shakespeare, and those willing to recreate the image of the wicked and ambitious uncle by using more certain evidence. In both cases the spectre of Shakespeare's monster looms in the background, powerful, inescapable and lingering in the collective consciousness. The play has created a polarisation of views quite unique in English history. Historians argue about how bad King John was, but not whether he was good or bad. Similarly Ethelred the Unready may have faced calamitous difficulties beyond his control but his ineptitude is rarely questioned. No one seriously suggests that Edward II was a saint, or that James II was good for England. They were all, more or less, bad kings. Perhaps only Charles I has come close to inspiring the same degree of emotional controversy and intense debate as Richard III. In Charles' case it is possible to argue that he was a good man and a bad king. While this will not satisfy his ardent supporters, it is a compromise quite beyond the reach of the historian studying Richard III. Richard is more likely to be described as a bad man and a good king, but the short duration of his kingship will always ensure that in such an interpretation the badness dominates the narrative.

It is the very genius of the Shakespearian model that prevents our culture from relinquishing it. Shakespeare's Richard is three-dimensional, complex, evil but plausible, entertaining but believable. For many, the fact that Richard did indeed usurp the throne, cast aside his nephews and lose the crown in battle a little while later is good enough reason for thinking the worst. If Shakespeare has exaggerated for dramatic effect, that is to be expected. The picture he creates, they argue, must be true in its essentials, as it is with his other historical plays. This is still the prevailing attitude among the majority of casual historians. Deconstructing the Shakespearian myth is a relatively easy task; replacing it with a consistent historical reality will be an altogether more difficult process.

If Richard's last words in Shakespeare's play are instantly recognisable to many, his opening words are equally famous. When he ambles on to the stage alone and deformed, he tells his audience:

> Now is the winter of our discontent
> Made glorious summer by this son of York.

The 'son of York' is his brother, Edward IV. Richard, Shakespeare would have his audience believe, is unhappy about the peace and prosperity that the reign of his brother has brought. His bodily deformities reflect the twisted soul within and he longs for trouble and strife:

> Why, I in this weak piping time of peace
> Have no delight to pass away the time,
> Unless to spy my shadow in the sun
> And descant on mine own deformity.

To the historian these words are laced with both intended and unintended irony. The pun on the word 'son' in the opening lines and also the subsequent reference to his shadow 'in the sun' are both subtle devices to bring to mind the heraldic emblem of the Yorkist dynasty, the sun in splendour. The unintended irony lies in the fact that of all the duke of York's sons it was Richard who most cherished that emblem and the heritage that it represented. For the real Richard to have spoken disparagingly, with a jeer, about either his brother Edward, or his father the duke of York, would have been completely out of character, at least while Edward was king. Shakespeare's Richard, however, is 'determined to prove a villain' and is 'subtle false and treacherous'. His evil personality dominates the action, mesmerises the audience and fascinates every generation treated to a new production.

Although the vitality and sinister appeal of Shakespeare's depiction of Richard III has done much to ensure his posthumous notoriety, the great playwright cannot be accused of inventing the character he so vividly brought to life. Shakespeare did not create the story: he simply followed the account set out in the chronicle of Raphael Holinshed. Shakespeare was faithful to his source and the historical tradition Holinshed represented. He had no cause to doubt its essential veracity. Holinshed had himself lifted much of his information from an already existing framework studiedly hostile to Richard. This 'Tudor tradition' was largely the creation of Edward Hall and his literary predecessors, Thomas More and Polydore Vergil.[1]

Polydore Vergil of Urbino in Italy came to England in 1502, at which point he was already a scholar and humanist with an international reputation. Although his *English History* (*Anglica Historia*) was not published until 1534, well into the reign of Henry VIII, it had been finished, to all intents and purposes, by 1513. He came to England on official business, collecting papal taxes on behalf of his patron, Cardinal Castelli. This gave him free access to the Tudor court where Castelli was a familiar figure. Vergil wanted to be seen as an impartial historian whose work had literary merit and would stand the test of time, but the mere fact that it was directly commissioned by Henry VII and dedicated to his successor, Henry VIII, demonstrates its partiality. Vergil saw kings as suffering the retribution of the divine Creator, for their own sins and for those of their dynastic predecessors. Richard III was the last in the line of sinful monarchs paying the price for the usurpation of

Henry IV back in 1399. His own sin, killing his nephew, paid the price for Edward IV's sin in executing the unfortunate Henry VI. Henry Tudor's victory at Bosworth Field brought the whole cataclysmic cycle to an end. Richard III was killed to redeem the blood of his nephew, Edward V, and the new Tudor king's marriage to Elizabeth of York, the daughter of Edward IV, restored the universal harmony and allowed a new age to dawn in which the wounds of civil strife could be healed. If Polydore Vergil had written his version of events today it would have been castigated by his contemporary professionals and shunted into the graveyard of publishers' remainders. He might, however, have developed a successful career as an historical novelist. His era and his Renaissance education valued literary merit and moral interpretation more highly than concrete facts.

There can be no doubt that Vergil's *English History* is well written. Nor can its historical merits be overlooked. Vergil seems to have consulted people who were familiar with the events he described, and some may even have been eye-witnesses. He evidently consulted contemporary chronicles and, while favouring the Tudors throughout, he prided himself in an independence of mind. These circumstances may account for the enduring lure of his interpretation of events. He believed that Richard was filled with a burning ambition to seize the throne as soon as his brother died. His 'covetousness of reigning' and his 'ardent desire of sovereignty' led to deceit and criminality. His nephews were put to death on Richard's orders: the lieutenant of the Tower, Robert Brackenbury, hesitating to do the deed, James Tyrell was sent to kill them instead. Richard then allowed rumours of their fate to circulate in order to undermine any attempt to restore Edward V to the throne. This policy, Vergil tells us, backfired because of the horror and disgust it aroused. The king therefore employed a new tactic of currying favour with the people by reforming both his rule and his private life. This version of events allowed Vergil to accuse Richard of murdering his nephews at the same time as accounting for the fact that he appeared to be a good man and a good king. Guilt and the threat of insurrection converted him.[2]

There are clearly insights embedded in the narrative that are derived from courtiers who knew Richard. The king is described as a worried man prone to introspection with a habit of chewing his lower lip. This had a disconcerting effect on Vergil's witnesses, and they may well have reported this characteristic accurately. It is what Vergil does with their evidence that shapes the legend. In his typically moralistic fashion Vergil supposes that it is his own 'craft and deceit' that cause Richard anxiety so that his 'cruel nature' was wont to 'rage against itself'. For the most part Vergil is relentless in depicting Richard as the villain of the piece. His desire for the throne did not change a previously blameless character into a murdering devil; he had already demonstrated his capacity for evil in a number of ways. Vergil hints that Richard was responsible for murdering the blameless 'holy' Henry VI. He is one of those who killed Edward prince of Wales, the son of Henry VI. He causes his wife, Ann Neville, to die from either sorrow or poison after being rejected for being unfruitful. And as a manifestation of the deformity within, Richard has a withered arm. In other words, much of the Shakespearian villain was created by the pen of Vergil. Although Richard fought bravely at Bosworth, his 'tyranny and cruelty' were finally punished as God gave victory to Henry Tudor.

Vergil did not invent this picture of Richard. Much of its substance – the deformity out of which Shakespeare created the hunchback, the murder of Henry VI, the responsibility for the murders of the princes and the poisoning of Richard's wife – was in circulation quite soon after Richard's death. An insight into the process by which the legend was constructed can be seen in the work of two writers who wrote accounts of Richard both before and after he was killed. John Rous, a Warwickshire chantry priest and collector of historical tit-bits, wrote an illustrated *History of the Earls of Warwick* in two versions, one in English and one in Latin. After the battle of Bosworth he altered the Latin version to eradicate from it any mention of Richard III's good qualities. He was unable, however, to recover his English version, which has fortuitously survived. Written while Richard was king it describes him as:

A mighty prince and especiall good lord ... in his realm full commendably punishing offenders of the laws, especially oppressors of the Commons, and cherishing those that were virtuous, by the which discreet guiding he got great thanks and love of all his subjects great and poor.[3]

In his *History of the Kings of England*, written shortly before his death in 1491, Rous attempted to ingratiate himself with the new king and decided that Richard was not a good king after all. In fact he was no less than the Antichrist, emerging from an unnatural sojourn of two years in his mother's womb with teeth and hair down to his shoulders. This was the man who murdered Henry VI, poisoned his wife, and ascended the throne of slaughtered children. Of course a man like Rous, whose failure to destroy his earlier work has cruelly exposed him as an obsequious, sycophantic fraud, might well have written up Richard's qualities also. When Richard was king it was in Rous's interests to describe him in glowing terms. The interesting evidence can be found in the qualities of Richard that Rous does not bother to conceal in the later *History*. He is quite happy to mention Richard's generous patronage of religious houses, Cambridge colleges and chantry foundations. He faithfully reports Richard's refusal to accept money from London, Gloucester and Worcester, 'affirming that he would rather have their love than their treasure', and, in common with all chroniclers, he commends Richard's bravery at the battle of Bosworth. Perhaps Henry VII himself had made it clear what information he had about Richard, and what he was prepared to accept. The foundations, and other recipients of Richard's bounty, retained an affection for his memory that could not be so easily abolished.[4]

Another writer, the Italian poet Pietro Carmeliano, found himself in the same trap as Rous. During Richard's reign he wrote a poem dedicated to Sir Robert Brackenbury with a preface in honour of the king. Richard was described as a paragon of virtue. His piety, justice and prudence were so manifest and outstanding that no one could be reckoned above him 'throughout the world'. Carmeliano was quite beside himself in his admiration for the king:

> If we look for truth of soul, for wisdom, for loftiness of mind with modesty, who stands before our King Richard? What Emperor or Prince can be compared with him in good works, or in munificence?

Employed as a secretary to Henry VII, it became obvious to Carmeliano that his previous portrait of the late, great Richard would need some slight modification. With the same rigorous adherence to historical principles followed by Rous, Richard is suddenly transformed into a villainous murderer.

Advancement, reward and royal gratitude were the chief objectives of these egregious hacks and historical veracity an unfortunate casualty. Another sycophantic courtier keen to please his master's ear was Bernard

André, the blind poet laureate who was also Henry VII's official historiographer. His work is similar in tone and content to that of Rous and Carmeliano but is of greater interest for two reasons: his version is the one most likely to represent the view Henry Tudor himself wished to project and, as with Rous, there are certain crimes of which Richard is not accused. The angelic Henry has been sent by God to rid the earth of the diabolical Richard, but André does not accuse Richard of killing Edward prince of Wales, the son of Henry VI, and nor does he accuse him of murdering his wife, Ann Neville, or his brother Clarence. These were becoming stock charges against Richard and their omission is a little surprising. It would seem that accusing him of committing too many crimes might have its drawbacks.[5]

Polydore Vergil's account is a composite of these versions with other material and his own subtle additions. His contemporary, Sir Thomas More, borrowed from Vergil to write his *History of King Richard III*, and follows him in creating an ugly man whose outer physical deformities reveal his arrogance of heart and hateful cruelty. More's *History* has far less to commend it than Vergil's but his great reputation as chancellor of England under Henry VIII and his courageous death by execution after his refusal to break an oath, ensured that his version of Richard III's reign would far exceed Vergil's in influence. More was undoubtedly a great man, demonstrating immense integrity and fortitude, but he was not an historian. Modern commentators have tended to dismiss the work as a humanistic literary treatise against tyranny. There is an unfortunate irony in this interpretation that would not have been lost on More: his vilification of Richard as the archetypal cruel tyrant failed to save him from the crushing disapproval of a real tyrant, the Tudor one – Henry VIII. All the old *canards* are rehearsed in his work: the murder of Henry VI, implication in the death of Clarence, plotting to steal the throne long before Edward IV's death, and so on. Evil ambition drives him on and his vicious nature makes him malicious and misanthropic.[6]

The real damage to Richard's reputation caused by Thomas More lay not so much in the relentless and unmitigated portrayal of Richard as a demonic figure, but in the weight More's own saintly reputation threw behind it. What is also true is that More himself knew some of the protagonists in the Richard story, men like Dr John Morton, Henry VII's chancellor and chief fixer. This lent an additional credibility to his account. More's *History* embellishes Vergil's account with details invented by More himself, and it carefully removes any redeeming qualities that Vergil may have allowed in Richard. This process of denigration was completed by Edward Hall in 1548, with the publication of his *Union of the Two Illustre Families of Lancaster and York*.

Hall brings the story of Richard bang up to date by making Henry VIII the hero. Borrowing heavily from both More and Vergil, he takes every opportunity to demonstrate Richard's wickedness and to make gratuitous additions to their accounts in order to condemn every thought and act of the evil tyrant. Half of the book is devoted to the praise of 'The Triumphal Reign of Henry VIII'. Again the work falls into the category of moralistic literature rather than history. If More had believed that Richard had been plotting to steal the throne long before his brother's death, Hall opts for the Vergil version in which Edward's death kindles a lust for power in Richard that corrupts him. This allows Hall to draw the moral more readily. If Richard had been evil from the start, as in More's story, then the downfall of the tyrant would be merely the operation of divine justice. To have been twisted by ambition when faced with an alluring opportunity is to fall from grace. The story now takes on a tragic poignancy with good Protestant lessons for us all: temptation should be resisted and virtue preferred. With the publication of Hall's *Union*, the Tudor picture of Richard is complete. All it now needed was for Shakespeare to dramatise it and the infamy of Richard was assured.

DECONSTRUCTING THE LEGEND

It was perhaps inevitable that Shakespeare's hugely entertaining caricature of the real Richard would provoke concern among those interested in historical truth. Shortly after Shakespeare's death, Sir George Buck, master of the revels to James I, began the process of revision by producing *The History of King Richard III* in 1619. Buck went mad shortly after writing this work, and died in 1622 without publishing it. It was eventually published by his great-nephew in a somewhat distorted version, 27 years later, in 1646. Buck had access to some primary sources and used his amateur knowledge of antiquarian methodology to marshal a defence of Richard. As with subsequent attempts to deconstruct the Tudor legend, Buck had motives that were both personal and contemporary. He believed that his ancestors had served the Howards in their capacities as members of the Yorkist household. He was not only descended, therefore, from a Yorkist retainer, but also had no cause to fear the Tudors. His patron, James I, was indeed descended from Henry Tudor but did not share his ancestor's need to shore up his dynastic credentials. The time had come to unveil the real Richard, freed from the political, and slightly pathological, necessity to distort the truth. Ironically, it was precisely at this time, when conditions were so favourable for a fresh look at the Richard story, that Shakespeare's masterpiece was working its greatest magic.

A battle for Richard's reputation began, and has continued to this day. Partly as a result of the ineptitude of his early defenders and, to be more charitable, partly because of the paucity of the redeeming evidence they needed, there was always an opportunity for Richard's detractors to strike back. Revisionists also had a new phenomenon to contend with. Shakespeare's monster had become part of the culture; it was a national treasure that could not be lightly disregarded. Furthermore, the moral lessons the Tudor historians had been so keen to draw from the story of Richard's life amounted to a creed. These lessons were part of the code of inherited values one generation was obliged to pass on to the next. To unravel the tale of the wicked uncle who murdered his nephews because they stood between him and his overweening ambition, was to commit the sin of condoning immoral behaviour. It seemed more important to teach the lessons than to fiddle about with the facts. One could be altogether too rational. Buck's counter-doctrine, which asserted that Richard could only be held to account for treating his enemies too leniently, for not killing more of them, and for underestimating Tudor's forces at Bosworth, was seen by many as heresy.

Alongside Buck's attempts to take a fresh look at Richard, the great and the good continued to weigh in with their largely hostile views. Sir Walter Raleigh in *The History of the World*, published in 1614, opined that Richard III was 'the greatest monster in mischief of all that forewent him', and Sir Francis Bacon, philosopher and lord chancellor, while more temperate, largely accepted Thomas More as fact. In his *History of the Reign of King Henry the Seventh*, published in 1621, Bacon had Richard brave and honourable on the outside but cunning and wicked within. As with many of these post-Shakespearian versions of Richard, the writers were not only constrained by the political climate of their own day, but often by their own circumstances. Bacon, for instance, had been imprisoned in the Tower on charges of bribery and corruption when he wrote his *History*, and part of the purpose of its publication was to ingratiate himself with James I. The tactic paid off: a month after the king read the manuscript, Bacon was issued with a general pardon. Bacon did allow Richard the virtues of military prowess, law-making and care for 'the ease and solace of the common people' but these good qualities were outweighed by his cruelty and vices.

The slowly shifting historical landscape had opened up opportunities for others to build on George Buck's work. The Protestant Reformation had encountered a backlash in the Stuart period and an opening for those keen to promote the virtues of the Yorkists as the last dynasty faithful to the old Anglo-Catholic tradition. The moment lapsed, however, and the strength of the Tudor view enabled it to draw on the literary talents of each subsequent generation. National identity, perceived to have been strengthened and defended by the Tudors, provided the new context. Any attempt at revision was now not so much heretical as unpatriotic. It was, consequently, not for 150 years after Buck's pioneering work that another serious effort was made to revise the Richard story.

In 1768 Horace Walpole published his *Historic Doubts on the Life and Reign of King Richard the Third*. Horace was the youngest son of Sir Robert Walpole, prime minister during the reigns of George I and George II. His father's immense wealth and influence enabled the son to pursue his manifold literary interests. He may have been but an amateur historian but he hated prejudice and injustice. He had demonstrated his dislike of partisan intolerance by defending the doomed Admiral Byng who was court-martialled and shot after the loss of Minorca to the French in 1756. Walpole was convinced that Byng was innocent of the charges of cowardice laid against him and that he was being used as a scapegoat for the incompetence of the government. He was able to call an emergency debate in the House of Commons and speak on Byng's behalf, though to no avail: the unfortunate admiral was shot by firing squad. Walpole showed that the picture of Richard III handed down by previous generations was 'transmitted to us by ignorance and misrepresentation'. It was manifestly 'formed by prejudice and invention'. His main concern was not to vindicate Richard, but to show that there was scant evidence for many of the crimes he was supposed to have committed, and also that some of them would not have been in his own interests. Reason and logic were Walpole's weapons in the Age of Reason. He consciously denigrated the chroniclers of the period because they were Catholic monks, deliberately distorting the record to perpetuate untruth and propaganda as, he believed, they had always done.

Walpole's *Historic Doubts* was greatly indebted to the work of Buck and largely concerned with exposing More and Bacon to the forensic examination they deserved. In Walpole's view, chancellors should not dabble in history. There are many defects in Walpole's own work. He believed, for instance, that Edward V had attended Richard's coronation and that it had been Richard's intention to abdicate in his nephew's favour in due course. Nevertheless his defence of Richard raised serious questions about the Tudor version. *Historic Doubts* was so popular that it was reprinted almost immediately. Reviving Buck's crusade, Walpole provided a boost to Ricardians and a platform from which future work was launched. As with Buck's work, however, the solecisms and inaccuracies, the special pleading that took distorted evidence, exposed its fallacies and then promptly bent it in another direction, all provided anti-Ricardians with the ammunition they needed to maintain the traditional line. Two camps were emerging, with much vitriol separating them and little common ground on which to have a rational discourse.[7]

Both sides of the divide now attracted influential support. Convinced by Walpole's defence, John Wesley, the founder of Methodism, wrote *A Concise History of England* in which he expressed his doubts about the Tudor legend. Jane Austen did the same in *The History of England* in 1791. On the other hand, David Hume, the Scottish philosopher, and Edward Gibbon, the renowned historian, were not convinced by Walpole's arguments. What students of Richard needed was a more scientific approach to the evidence and a more professional attitude to the subject. To supply these needs the 19th century arrived and with it a gradual shift towards a focus on the evidence rather than the myth. Unfortunately, each major contributor to the debate continued the established tradition of leaning so heavily in one particular direction that an equal and opposite reaction from proponents of a contrary view was inevitable.

NINETEENTH-CENTURY RIVAL FACTIONS

The battle began with John Lingard's *A History of England*, published in 1819. Lingard was a Roman Catholic priest whose main motive was to rehabilitate Sir Thomas More, the Catholic martyr, as a man of truth. On the grounds that Thomas More could not possibly have lied, the distorted monster that he had helped to create continued to enliven the pages of history. Lingard ensured that More's view was perpetuated among intellectuals, just as Shakespeare's play continued to obscure historical reality at a more popular level. Pope Pius VII, not otherwise noted for his discerning views on the Yorkist kings, rewarded Lingard with a doctorate for his laudably pious interpretation of English history. In the same way that Walpole's *Historic Doubts* had aroused the ire of the literary journals and antiquarian societies of his time, Lingard's partisan approach was soon challenged by those who did not share his religious convictions. The task was most notably performed by a man known as Sharon Turner, a Quaker, who published the *History of England during the Middle Ages* in 1823. Turner's study was a pioneering work in many ways, not least his determination to be truly impartial and his reliance on a sound historical methodology. Using previously unused sources, Turner produced an astute character study of Richard which, while eschewing the fabrications of the Tudor writers, was by no means a vindication of the king.

Turner's aim, as he put it, was 'to reduce the obloquy under which Richard III has laboured, to its just proportion; and to distinguish how much of his exaggerated crimes is fairly imputable to himself, and how much to his age and party'. He was aware that 'prejudice, injustice and inaccuracy' had disfigured the reputation of Richard and that the only way to discover the truth about him was a dispassionate and scientific look at the evidence. Turner succeeded in revealing an unvarnished version of Richard III who was just and brave, but also a man of his times. He was a member of the selfish and ambitious European aristocracy and, when presented with the opportunity to seize the throne, he took it in the same way that any of his aristocratic contemporaries would have done. His bravery was physical only, not moral, and when faced with a threat to himself he resorted to criminal violence. Pious, intelligent and a reasonably good king, he nevertheless allowed ambition to overcome his conscience and became the villainous murderer of his nephews. This view of Richard is one still shared by many historians to this day and certainly goes some way towards unravelling the mystery that still surrounds him. The question Turner sought to answer was how a virtuous nobleman could suddenly be transformed into power-hungry murderer. While presenting himself as a moderate revisionist, Turner arrived at a solution that was quite close to the one propounded by Poldore Vergil 300 years before. Richard had been corrupted by ambition. Turner was more sympathetic towards Richard because he saw him as no different from any other 15th century prince, while for Vergil he was an evil maverick.[8]

Twenty years later, with a wealth of new documentary evidence being assembled, calendared, transcribed and published, another bold attempt was made to shift the historical consensus on Richard away from the still powerful grip of the traditional view. The work was undertaken by Caroline Halsted, wife of the rector of Middleham, who published a two-volume biography, *Richard III as Duke of Gloucester and King of England*, in 1844. Middleham was Richard's spiritual home and, in such close proximity to the awesome beauty of the castle's colossal remains on the edge of the Yorkshire Dales, it was perhaps inevitable that Halsted fell in love with the subject of her research. Conscientious and scholarly, diligent and thorough, she pared away the Tudor accretions, inventions and fantasies, and unveiled a shining paragon of medieval virtue: cultivated, merciful, just and wise. Her avowed aim was to 'untangle the web of falsehood and deceit' and to confront and weaken Shakespeare's influence on Richard's reputation. The 'mighty dramatist' had been 'misled by corrupt authorities' and national pride and affection for his plays had strengthened the distortions until they had become almost impregnable. She would not shrink from revealing the truth even though Shakespeare's towering reputation bore down upon it. To impugn the statements of the Bard might be viewed as sacrilege, but the time had come to do away with superstition and falsehood. Lies and myths had assumed the mantle of truth simply by being 'oft-repeated'. The time had come for 'truth and justice' to 'prevail over prejudice'.[9]

So ardent was Halsted, and so determined in her mission to correct so many centuries of injustice to Richard's memory, that the figure that emerged would not have been out of place in a stained-glass window wearing a halo. Halsted had herself been wary of falling into this trap and had done her best to avoid it, but in the verdict of the weighty professional historians about to wade into the arena, she had signally failed. She came very close to acknowledging a misdeed, possibly a grave misjudgement that will forever lie at the heart of the mystery of Richard's character, but could not quite bring herself to grasp the manifold thorny issues it raised. For just one week in his life, she courageously acknowledged, in the middle of June 1483, under intolerable pressure, Richard was driven to do something he perhaps shouldn't have done:

> In an evil hour [she conceded, he] yielded to the worldliness of a corrupt age and a pernicious education; and by this dereliction of moral and religious duty he cast from him the glory of being held up to the admiration of posterity as an example of rigid virtue and self-denial.

As a result of this mistake he was instead 'chronicled as an usurper and the slave of his ungovernable ambition'. In other words the fault was not his but a combination of the barbaric age in which he lived and the dreadful education he was forced to endure. He could not possibly be blamed for behaving in the way he did because, like the rest of us, he could not escape his conditioning. The tragedy was that such a good man should have been forced into this situation to the great detriment of his own reputation. This view, still very strong among Ricardians, conveniently ignores another tragedy that occurred contemporaneously. In fact, by this interpretation Edward V's demise so completely ruined Richard's fame that the 12-year-old boy becomes the instrument of Richard's ruin, rather than the other way round. For Ricardians generally, Edward V is an inconvenience at best, but certainly an irritating impediment in the struggle to free Richard from the shackles of his detractors.[10]

For Halsted the choice facing Richard was not whether or not to allow the alluring glint of the crown to wreck his judgement and fuel his latent ambition, but rather whether he should seize the throne to save himself and the nation, and in so doing court condemnation, or go against his instincts and surrender his hopes instead, in order to reap the reward of a good name in posterity. This argument at least has the merit of moving the debate on and introducing plausible alternatives to the picture of an ambitious man whose cruelty and determination damned both himself and his entire dynasty. But Halsted also, unwittingly, damaged Richard's cause by attempting to remove the element of culpability in the usurpation of the throne. Her unstinting praise for Richard's virtues, and her corresponding unwillingness to countenance any grievous fault in him, led her to deny the very fact that there had been a usurpation at all. Edward V, having been declared illegitimate by Parliament, was not the rightful king and could not therefore be the subject of a usurpation. This argument in turn exposed Halsted to an inevitable backlash from an increasingly sonorous group of professional Victorian historians. It was all too easy, despite her meticulous research and wealth of material, to brand her work as blindly partisan and in need of a corrective dose of realism.

It was in 1878 that James Gairdner, a respected historian who had spent most of his life working in the Public Record Office, published his *Life and Reign of Richard III*. This work, as prejudiced against Richard as Halsted was for him, became accepted as the definitive biography of Richard for the next seven decades. The reason for its general acceptance as a work of authority was Gairdner's evident breadth of learning and his meticulous research. He was the 15th-century specialist at the Public Record Office and could write with a clarity and conviction that was not easy to question. He was sufficiently conscious of historical principles to understand the need to appear impartial, and he therefore condemned Richard as 'headstrong' and 'reckless', rather than as scheming and duplicitous, but he detested the inadequacies of the revisionists. He had converted to Catholicism and with it had adopted a deeply held conviction in the value of tradition and received wisdom. Despite his eminent credentials and scholarly methodology he was determined to rehabilitate both Thomas More and William Shakespeare as valid historical sources. He conceded that More's portrait of Richard was 'highly coloured' and 'perhaps not without a little exaggeration' but was, nevertheless, 'true in the main'. Shakespeare also used 'colouring' as the demands of his art required, but his 'judgement on any point it is certainly impossible to ignore'.

Gairdner acknowledged that Richard had been punctilious in following the correct procedures when he took the throne, to the extent that 'in point of form, one might almost look upon it as a constitutional election', but it was, in fact, a usurpation secured after a reign of terror in London. The nation 'tacitly concurred' until the news of the murders of the princes got about, after which there was horror and amazement. Gairdner's strange reliance on the veracity of the historical tales in More and Shakespeare was based on a strongly held belief that scepticism was more likely to lead to error than to truth. If the historian was sceptical about all traditional time-honoured interpretations handed down to him, he would have to rewrite the whole of history. This would leave the present dislocated from the past with the moral harmony between the two broken. It may be that 'isolated facts' needed correction but the fidelity of the general picture of Richard's character and motives, as handed down by tradition, could not be challenged. Richard was 'indeed cruel and unnatural beyond the ordinary measure even of those violent and ferocious times'.[11]

Gairdner's great achievement was to reconcile the detailed knowledge he had derived from a close scrutiny of every scrap of evidence, with a blind adherence to the Tudor distortion of that evidence. The result was a peculiar blend of judicious scholarship and pervasive prejudice. Every motive of Richard was seen as malign, and every act the product of a defective character. Shakespeare and Sir Thomas More had said that Richard was bad; it was more important to avoid impugning their veracity than to rehabilitate Richard. This synthesis of fact and legend had such alluring appeal in the Victorian and Edwardian eras that it was readily adopted by the most influential historians. The works of J. R. Green, Bishop William Stubbs, James Ramsey and Charles Oman were all influenced by the work of Gairdner, and were all hostile to Richard. It was not that they were reluctant to admit that he had the qualities of bravery, piety and even generosity, but they saw them as corrupted by his cunning, unscrupulous, ruthless, pitiless cruelty. In 1878, the same year that saw the publication of both Gairdner's work and William Stubbs' *Constitutional History of England*, Sir John Everett Millais painted one of the most famous pictures of the two princes in the Tower. The innocent-looking golden-haired boys, holding hands, their faces shining with threatened purity, are surrounded by darkness and clothed in black. Richard III had become the archetypal wicked uncle whose tyrannical reign shed such a favourable light on the constitutional monarchy of Great Britain with its perfect model of childcare in the Victorian nursery.[12]

An orthodoxy had become established, and to set oneself against it was to make a perverse attack on civilisation itself. One man who was brave enough to challenge the formidable weight attached to the revival of the Tudor version of Richard was Sir Clements Markham. In 1891 he published an article in *English Historical Review* that set out to prove Gairdner wrong and to place the blame for the death of the princes on Henry VII. Gairdner defended himself in the same publication and went on to reiterate his views in even stronger terms in a revised edition of his *Life,* published in 1898. Markham rose to the challenge by publishing his own book in 1906, *Richard III: His Life and Character*. This turned out to be one of the most comprehensive vindications of Richard ever written, exonerating him from all the crimes he was said to have committed and setting out to demonstrate that he was one of the best kings of England there had ever been. He was a courageous and brilliant military leader, popular throughout the country, with great administrative ability, judicious diplomatic skills deployed successfully in foreign policy, and a solicitous care for the welfare of his people. There was not a shred of real evidence against him. Markham felt that the time had come to rescue the real Richard from 'the accumulated garbage and filth of centuries of calumny'.

Markham was not a trained historian, but an eminent geographer. His enthusiastic determination to champion his god-like hero merely contributed to the hostile entrenchment of the historical establishment against an impossibly romanticised view of Richard. Gairdner's blind faith in the Tudor's monster now had its counterpart in Markham's hagiography. A seemingly unbridgeable gulf had opened up between academic historians and the more amateur variety. By reacting so unequivocally to Gairdner's stance, Markham ended up damaging Richard's cause. The author could be derided for his incredulity and partisan lack of professionalism, while the work of Gairdner, by contrast, was temperate and factual. Although Markham followed in the wake of eminent brave souls, such as Buck, Walpole and Halsted, who had begun charting a path out of the mythology of the Tudor era, he only succeeded in creating a counter-mythology. What was worse, academic historians now felt obliged to eschew the excesses of the pro-Richard camp in the interests of objective historical realism.[13]

Both Gairdner and Markham did their causes few favours. Gairdner showed that a thorough and professional study of the evidence was no guarantee of impartiality or of good judgement. Markham exposed the cause of the revisionists to the accusation of romantic amateurism. This is somewhat ironic in that Markham had read far more history and done far more research than many of his professional counterparts. He had even written a book on the history of England when he was just 10 years old. Joining the Royal Navy at 14 he travelled the world before his 18th birthday and developed a passion for travel, exploration and, above all, championing the under-dog. He supported the Tahitians in their struggle for independence from the French and railed against injustice in the navy. He became fascinated by the geography and history of Peru and managed to transplant the quinine plant from South America to India, with profound consequences for the battle against malaria in the East. He promoted Arctic expeditions and joined the Indian army in the Abyssinian war as a naturalist and historian. His achievements were prodigious: he became president of the Royal Geographical Society, a fellow of the Royal Society of Antiquaries and a fellow of the Royal Society. He founded schools of geography at both Oxford and Cambridge and published at least 14 substantial history books, including a history of the Incas, a biography of Lord Halifax, a history of Peru and a biography of Christopher Columbus. A truly remarkable man, Sir Clements Markham entered the lists on behalf of Richard III because he scented a deep-seated prejudice and an injustice that had to be exposed and uprooted. He relished the challenge and, after working on his book for nine years, he was determined not to be cowed by the self-proclaimed arbiters of historical authority. Richard was a victim of calumny and Markham would champion his cause.

POST-WAR BATTLES

The work of both Gairdner and Markham prolonged the feud between the rival factions on either side of the Richard III debate. The heated arguments of such influential figures significantly reduced the possibility of a balanced view emerging. As the world became engulfed by the carnage of two World Wars, the need to rehabilitate Richard and to rewrite traditional English history seemed an unnecessary indulgence. It was not until after the Second World War that the issue received serious attention again. When post-war writers turned their attention to the subject they showed that the gulf and the ancient hostility between the two factions had not subsided at all. The enemies emerged from their corners as implacably committed to their causes as they had ever been. Shakespeare and More were enjoying national revivals and their Richards were rekindled in the popular imagination. More had suffered at the hands of a tyrant and his Richard was also a tyrant. The 20th century had produced a prodigious crop of tyrants and More's stand against Henry VIII chimed with the zeitgeist. While he had become 'the Man for All Seasons', his views on Richard III had become perennial. Shakespeare had been utilised to boost national morale during the war, with Lawrence Olivier's screen version of

Henry V reminding the beleaguered British population about their previous triumphs against the odds. Once again the stories a nation had cherished for so long, and which seemed to provide comfort on the painful march to victory, pervaded the classrooms and nurseries of England. Once again those who set out to challenge the received orthodoxy were deemed to be unpatriotic.

An additional dimension can be detected in the anti-Richard prejudice being reiterated for the common good at about this time. Both Halsted and Markham had had strong northern connections, and antipathy towards their views was naturally stronger in the south of England than it was in the north. Richard was, in their view, a 'northern king', in that his time from ducal adolescence to kingship had largely been spent in Yorkshire, and it was always in that county that he derived his greatest support.

The patriotic fervour created by the need to fight the Second World War, combined with this cultural division, produced an all too predictable retrenchment in the historical perception of Richard. The most celebrated of the exponents of the war-time orthodoxy was Arthur Bryant. In his *History of Britain and the British People*, first published in 1942, Richard's physical characteristics are again distorted to suit the needs of the dastardly cunning he hides within. He becomes 'small, introverted, secretive and austere'. His popularity and power are naturally in the 'wild' north, 'whose warlike folk he had won over by his firm, but just rule. Like them, he was reputed to be ruthless', and had killed Henry VI with his own bare hands. No doubt anyone coming from that part of the world would willingly have done the same: 'Backed by an armed force from the wild north, he was crowned king.' It is no surprise to find that Bryant accepted More's account of the murder of the princes, and much else, verbatim. The demonised Richard, as we have already noted, is always allowed certain qualities, virtues that any savage tyrant might possess, such as bravery, cleverness and decisiveness. His virtues are, of course, put to the wrong use, and all decent people are offended. Bryant tells us that:

> this otherwise able and astute king committed, not only a shocking crime, but a major political blunder. For though, after thirty years of spasmodic civil wars, Englishmen had grown accustomed to their rulers slaughtering one another, the murder of innocent children was something they could not stomach.

Those wild northerners were obviously not real Englishmen.

Henry Tudor, once again, became the avenging angel in this dramatic moral tale of evil versus good. When, in August 1485, 'the long awaited Henry of Richmond landed in Wales with a tiny force', he was naturally 'enthusiastically reinforced'. One common feature of the traditional story, now retold for the purposes of edifying a beleaguered generation, was naming the saviour 'Henry of Richmond'. The wild barbaric northerner met his match when faced with the moral indignation of true Englishmen. The fact that Henry had never been to Richmond in his life, nor England come to that, was neither here nor there. The reason Richard lost the battle of Bosworth Field and 'fighting desperately, met his death', was because half his troops stood idly by or changed sides. They and their leaders 'refused to fight for a man they believed had murdered a helpless child, his own liege lord and brother's heir, whom he had sworn to protect'. Richard's bravery, which no contemporary chronicler denied, has become mere 'desperation'. When the nation is engaged in a bitter struggle for survival against the Nazi war-machine, bravery is a virtue only the righteous should possess.[14]

In 1956, the man who had done more than most to steer Britain to victory, Sir Winston Churchill, published his *History of the English-Speaking Peoples*. His Richard III is a mirror image of Bryant's, with a few Churchillian embellishments. Churchill was aware that Ricardians had been hard at work since the war, attempting to undermine the traditional view. He took a hefty swipe at them by remarking that 'as soon as the Tudor dynasty was laid to rest defenders of Richard fell to work, and they have been increasingly busy ever since'. We must have no truck with them, Churchill explains, because whatever arguments they advance, 'More's tale ... has priority'. He offers no explanation for this judgement: it is just so. More has received the endorsement of the greatest living Englishman. Again there is a noticeable north-south divide in Churchill's account. Richard intimidates London with his 'northern bands', and after the usurpation 'throughout the Home Counties feeling already ran high against him'. How much ingrained anti-northern prejudice is contained in those two words 'Home Counties'? Richard could never be at 'Home' in them, of course, in the way that true Englishmen were. He was 'ruthless' and 'perfidious', and, the most damning verdict of them all, like 'a modern dictator'. It was for this reason that Richard should 'never be forgotten or forgiven'. Churchill, the man who vanquished Hitler, had made it clear where he stood on the Richard III front.

Churchill's assistants included some well-informed historians who supplied him with enough credible data about Richard to allow a balanced picture to emerge. Instead, the finished product appears to be hopelessly schizophrenic. He 'proceeded in the new year to inaugurate a series of enlightened reforms in every sphere of government', but this was merely to 'placate his sullen subjects' when they could not be 'overawed by strength'. The measures adopted by Richard's only Parliament are listed, which is unusual in accounts hostile to the king. They include reviving the power of Parliament itself, protecting commerce and a land law regulating trusts. Churchill concedes that 'magnanimity was shown to fallen opponents, and petitioners in distress were treated with kindness'. The problem for Richard was that he was guilty of a heinous crime: the murder of his nephews. He was therefore a bad man. The moral issue overrode all other considerations. For Churchill, and most of his audience, it was not possible for a bad man to be a good king. Hitler had reduced German unemployment, built the autobahns, produced the Volkswagens, galvanised German industry and technology, and, temporarily, restored German pride. His evil crimes against humanity had brought the world to war and led to his inevitable destruction. Here, writ large, was an example of the biblical maxim 'by their fruits shall ye know them'. Bad trees cannot bring forth good fruit. So it was for Richard. He was a great patron of learning and endowed religious houses:

> But all counted for nothing. The hatred which Richard's crime had aroused against him throughout the land remained sullen and quenchless, and no benefits bestowed, no sagacious measures adopted, no administrative successes achieved, could avail the guilty monarch.

Following More's account of the bad dreams with which the guilty monarch was plagued, Churchill explains: 'Even Richard's own soul revolted against him.'

Once more retribution is personified in a semi-divine presence as 'all hopes in England were now turned towards Richmond'. It was, of course, a national duty to rebel and so, 'as the months passed many prominent Englishmen, both Yorkist and Lancastrian, withdrew themselves from

Richard's baleful presence'. Henry Tudor, always referred to as 'Richmond', comes to 'unite all England'. The saviour destroyed the tyrant who, at the last, was 'surrounded by hatred and distrust'. Good triumphed over evil, as it always surely will. Whether this story is strictly factual or not doesn't really matter because the moral purpose of the tale transcends other objectives. The subliminal message is that Englishmen will not tolerate evil leaders: they are not duped by them and they are sensible enough to get rid of them before they create havoc.[15]

Churchill's name and reputation ensured that the traditional Tudor view of Richard would continue to thrive five centuries after the battle of Bosworth. He was, however, writing at a time of considerable social upheaval and, in many ways, attempting to prevent a new tide of disdain from sweeping away traditional values. If Churchill and Bryant represented an 'Establishment' view of history, there were plenty of post-war writers willing to challenge it. The two most successful were surprising candidates for the role of historical revisionist. In 1951 Josephine Tey published a fictional detective story, *The Daughter of Time*, in which Detective Inspector Grant of the Yard, forced to spend time in hospital, sets out to bring modern police detective skills to the murder mystery at the heart of the Richard story. In the end he is drawn to conclude that Richard was innocent of the charges brought against him and that the real culprit was Henry Tudor. This was Markham's view brought to a new audience, and it proved an instant hit. The novel became an immediate best-seller and established itself as a turning-point in the historiography of Richard III. Josephine Tey's Richard was exonerated and redeemed by a combination of factors. The author cleverly combined a seemingly innocent impartiality with the plausibly scientific approach of a detective using criminal profiling techniques. Meeting the public's taste for both detective stories and historical revisionism, *The Daughter of Time* reached a wide audience and spawned a generation of Richard III fans.

Tey's book was popular and influential, but it wasn't history. It merely whetted the appetite and aroused the curiosity of the reading public. In 1955 a new, one might almost say revolutionary, biography of Richard III appeared. It was written by Paul Murray Kendall, an American professor of English literature, and was the answer to all the prayers of the growing number of Ricardians. Murray Kendall's *Richard III* was a thorough and thoughtful piece of historical writing, combining careful use of original sources with a brilliant narrative flair. It was the first significant biography of the king since Gairdner over 50 years earlier, and it was the most realistically sympathetic ever to be attempted. Kendall's Richard was merciful, generous and just. He had a northern honesty and plainness that set him at odds against the treachery and sophistication of the court. This Richard III represented the lost cause of justice and virtue in an age of corruption and vice. Kendall's book could not be as easily dismissed as Richard's rather quirky defenders had been in the past. Buck, Walpole, Halsted and Markham had provided rather easy targets for academic historians. Kendall was an altogether more serious proposition. He had certainly strayed outside his academic speciality and had an irritating habit of supplying gaps in the narrative sources with imaginative flights of speculative fancy, but there was a coherence to his characterisation that provided a credible alternative to hostile commentaries. Richard may have been responsible for his nephews' deaths, though the evidence is not at all conclusive, but his motive was to save good government. Kendall's Richard panics a little when his enemies close in around him and one unfortunate consequence may have been the disappearance of the princes. No matter: he was a good man, brave, honourable, isolated and desperate. In an age of ruthlessness he too could be ruthless, though the body-count after the usurpation was remarkably low. If he had a fault it was that he wasn't ruthless enough.

While the public enjoyed Kendall's book, there were rumblings of discontent among the academic fraternity. In 1966 the simmering outrage of one professional historian, A. L. Rowse, boiled over in his *Bosworth Field and the Wars of the Roses*. This was positively vitriolic in its determination to blow away the fragrant breeze of favourable revisionism with an icy blast of Tudor tradition mixed in with a Churchillian dose of anti-tyrant propaganda. The post-war vision of Richard as Hitler received the endorsement of an academic historian. Unfortunately for Rowse, his almost hysterical desire to retain the Shakespearian monster did more damage to his own reputation than it did to Richard's. The world had moved on and the old view of Richard was certainly not good enough for a more enlightened age. Exactly what that view was, or would be, had not yet been resolved. Once again a division opened up between defenders and detractors. Both now had considerable ammunition to fight a protracted campaign.

THE LATE 20TH CENTURY DEBATE

If anything, although their tone tended to be more moderate and their erudition gave plausibility to their case, late 20th century academic historians were more hostile towards Richard than a neutral might have expected. J. R. Lander, for example, wrote in 1980 that 'towards the end of his life, Richard had become in the highest degree schizophrenic, a criminal self-righteously invoking the protection of the Almighty'. The old north-south divide is strongly present in Lander's *The Wars of the Roses*, published in 1990, with the south representing civilisation and the north barbarism. Richard, of course, had managed to garner support in the north. Therefore York, 'where his lavish lordship and patronage had made him popular with certain of the city cliques, received him with loud acclaim but in the home counties and in the south the murmurs of discontent grew louder'. The clue to Lander's perspective lies in his acceptance of More's verdict. It is scarcely credible that More's account of Richard's usurpation and character would continue to hold sway so long after it was constructed, but Lander explained:

> although biased against the king, and despite the fact that More tended to compose speeches for his characters in a manner condemned by present-day historians, his account of Richard's reign (with some exceptions) is plausible enough.

Plausible enough for the 'home counties' if not for 'the city cliques' in York, it would seem.[16]

In 1981 Charles Ross produced the most scholarly biography of Richard yet written. His *Richard III* followed his *Edward IV* (1974) in the outstanding 'Methuen English Monarchs' series, later to become the 'Yale English Monarchs'. Ross could not be accused of anti-northern prejudice, having been brought up in Yorkshire, and his studious thoroughness ensured that his life of Richard has stood the test of time. The Richard who emerged from Ross's studies was not 'the exemplar of a tyrant', nor was he unusually wicked. His downfall was caused by mistakes and 'errors of judgement rather than moral failures'. Ross famously concluded that, like everybody else, Richard was a child of his time, no more no less, and he 'was born into a violent age'. He seized the throne when his brother died in 'an unashamed bid for personal power'.

Like many medieval princes he was ruthless and unscrupulous in his methods. He had endured a violent and traumatic upbringing in which he had imbibed 'lessons in arbitrary procedures, even in regard to inheritance, which he did not forget'.

There were two features of the book that made a lasting impression. The first was a shifting of the blame for the calamitous usurpation in 1483 towards Edward IV, rather than wholly on Richard. The crisis that caused Richard to take the throne and dispose of his nephews was caused by his brother, Edward IV: 'Given the deep political tensions his own policies had helped to create, his premature death at the age of forty provided an invitation to dynastic disaster.' Ross was not lured by the temptation to indulge in a psychological portrait of Richard. The apparent puzzling dichotomy of a man with a pronounced loyalty to Edward IV and a manifest disloyalty to Edward's sons could not be resolved by resorting to the schizophrenic model. Richard was not complex and 'may not have been a particularly intelligent man'. He acted as he saw fit at the time, in his own interests; the mystery is only caused by our lack of information, not by Richard's character. Perhaps for this reason, that Richard was not to blame for the difficult situation caused by his brother's death, Ross also did much to cut the assumed link between the battle of Bosworth and the usurpation. Richard did not lose the battle because his enemies were able to exploit his lack of popularity, but rather because power had, through natural causes and poor political judgement on Edward's part, become dangerously concentrated in the hands of two magnates who had no reason to continue to support Richard. In fact, in Ross's assessment, Richard was successful in managing the nobility he inherited and, with better luck, might have gone on to create a successful regime.[17]

The second feature was a lofty disdain for Richard's modern supporters. If Tudor propaganda had blackened his name, 'Richard's reputation has suffered scarcely less from the attentions of his own defenders'. Writing at a time when the influence of Tey and Kendall was still strong, Ross took the view that defenders of Richard were largely a bunch of amateurs at war with the professionals. These 'historical novelists and the writers of detective stories' were a group with a strange preponderance of females, which Ross could only view with suspicion. The novelists were 'nearly all women writers, for whom the rehabilitation of the reputation of a long-dead king holds a strange and unexplained fascination'. By categorising Richard's defenders in such a pejorative way, Ross did much to ensure that academic 'professionals' would hesitate to ruin their credentials by challenging the Ross orthodoxy. When Ross declared that 'Markham was the philo-progenitive ancestor of Richard's modern defenders' he put himself in the Gairdner camp and unwittingly perpetuated the old rivalry between them.[18]

As the 500th anniversary of Richard's reign approached there were concerted efforts to present him in a more favourable light. Jeremy Potter, who went on, in his capacity as chairman of the Richard III Society, to successfully defend Richard in a court case staged for television in 1984, published *Good King Richard?* (1983). Making no claims of impartiality, he at least made a thorough study of the historiography of Richard and was able to demonstrate how difficult it was for commentators to free themselves from their own prejudices and preoccupations. P. W. Hammond and Anne Sutton, in *Richard III: the Road to Bosworth Field*, which appeared in 1985, presented many of the primary sources for the reign, particularly new evidence contained in the records of the Signet Office, known as British Library Harleian Manuscript 433, which Hammond had just completed editing with Rosemary Horrox. Hammond and Sutton set out to show that Richard III was a man of good character with 'a strong desire to do the right thing'. There were ambiguities in his personality but the charge of hypocrisy was unfounded. It was invoked to cloak the undesirable necessity of having to admit that Richard was not only learned, brave, loyal and just, but that he remained so until he was killed. Most writers, they lamented, 'prefer the certainty of condemnation'. Richard was a king 'of excellent intentions' who managed to secure the throne at the expense of the executions of four persons and the disappearance of two children in a coup 'coupled with a moral claim to the throne that was precise and complex on a point of canon law'. He was a man of piety and culture who loved music and jewels. Hammond and Sutton hoped 'to provide the material for an informed appraisal of his acts and character'. Both Hammond and Sutton were, like Potter, active members of the flourishing Richard III Society whose avowed aim was, and still is, to 'secure a re-assessment' of the character and career of the king in the belief that the traditional account is 'not supported by sufficient evidence nor reasonably tenable'.[19]

Rather than closing the ever-widening gap between defenders and detractors, however, these favourable accounts of Richard had little impact on the overall trend in academic circles. They fed the controversy, rather than providing a resolution, and inevitably provoked a reaction. While many academics no longer accepted the 'traditional' view, they were unwilling to collude in the whitewash of the reputation of a man whose innocence was far from proven. That the hostile approach to the study of Richard's reign continued to flourish was most notably demonstrated in the appearance of Desmond Seward's *Richard III: England's Black Legend*, in 1983. At least Seward made no attempt at a pretence of impartiality, describing Richard as 'the most terrifying man ever to occupy the English throne'. Richard 'early mastered the art of murder for political ends' and, like a mafia Godfather, used his northern 'hit-men' to usurp the throne and keep it. Once again we find the source of this heavy bias in a refusal to relinquish the good old Tudor version. Thomas More is credited with 'a brilliant reconstruction' that is 'not too far from the truth'. The Croyland chronicler, distinctly antipathetic towards Richard, is 'very knowledgeable and well informed'. Polydore Vergil is accepted as essentially 'correct', and the archetypal Tudor propagandist, Edward Hall, despite being 'treated with considerable reserve by modern historians' is followed closely because he 'could well have had access to sources of information which have since disappeared'. As Lander found More 'plausible enough', so Seward found Hall 'more than plausible'.[20]

Seward's case was so obviously flawed and partisan that it was relatively easy for other historians to distance themselves from it while maintaining a less than sympathetic approach to Richard. In 1991, Tony Pollard, in *Richard III and the Princes in the Tower*, described Seward's book as 'flamboyant' and 'mischievous'. Nevertheless, as he himself admitted, the picture that emerged from the pages of his own work 'more closely fitted the archetype of the wicked guardian than the pattern of the saintly brother'. There is a consciousness in Pollard's concluding remarks that two viable but entirely opposed views of Richard were in existence. Pollard's 'third story, as yet untold, which might offer a way of reconciling conflicting views' turns out to be remarkably close to the one posited by Sharon Turner in the early 19th century: Richard could have been good but was ruined by ambition. Richard's life was a tragedy because 'so much promise and potential was ruined by a ruthless disregard for the rights of others in the pursuit of power'. The pity is that 'a man of such apparent virtue as Richard should have destroyed both himself and so many others to satisfy his ambition'.[21]

Seward was by no means alone in rooting for the survival of the archetypal wicked uncle and the odious tyrant of Tudor tradition. Colin Richmond, in 1986, accounted for the success of the usurpation by arguing that Richard was far too bad for those around him to suspect what he would do. He was able to outmanoeuvre everybody and take them all by surprise because they were unaccustomed to such calculated atrocities. Richard was so skilful and so swift in obtaining his objectives that 'conventional politicians were swept aside in stunned disbelief'. In another article in 1993, Richmond repeated these claims and confirmed his belief that Richard may have disposed of his nephews even before he became king on 25 June 1483, perhaps on 22 June, because 'in these fateful days nothing was beyond him'. Despite Ross concluding that Richard's loss at Bosworth had little to do with the usurpation and more to do with bad luck, Richmond firmly linked the two together again. Defeat at Bosworth was a consequence of a loss of support caused by the unlawful and wicked act of usurpation: 'Even the lukewarmness of his northerners, manifest at Bosworth, may have had its origin in what he had done or was held to have done to the princes'.[22]

Rosemary Horrox, in a perceptive monograph published in 1989, showed that Richard did indeed lose support after the usurpation, and this caused him in the end to lose the throne, but that without the unexpected rebellion of the duke of Buckingham at the beginning of the reign he may have established a secure regime. During the usurpation, she argued, Richard stood for continuity. He wanted to be seen as, and may have believed himself to be, the only safeguard of Edward IV's achievements. After Buckingham's rebellion Richard realised, to his great surprise, that Edward's retainers could not be relied upon to support him. It was in response to this realisation that Richard had to place an emphasis on his own northern affinity and begin to distance himself from the former government. Richard now set out to show that he had come to reform the corruption rife during his brother's reign and to set right the manifold wrongs of that period. By distancing himself from Edward's legacy Richard weakened his support and played into the hands of Henry Tudor, who could now portray himself as the continuity candidate.[23]

Horrox accepted that the political establishment were taken off-guard and failed to realise that Richard was aiming at the throne. He was in the driving-seat, manipulating events and determined to stay ahead of his enemies. He was not evil and more than likely motivated by the thought that, as he was the adult male most closely associated with Edward IV, he had a responsibility to keep the show on the road. Although ambition cannot be ruled out, there can be no doubt that a child on the throne at this time would wreck everything the Yorkists had striven to achieve. Because he stood for the continuity of good governance established by his brother, he assumed that the local gentry connections established by Edward would remain loyal to him. The real turning point in the reign came when these networks supported Buckingham's rebellion. Richard was shocked by the behaviour of Edward's former retainers and was forced to garner support from outside the establishment and from within his own trusted affinity. It was this that cost him the throne in the end. Because his confidence in all but his own men was diminishing, there was an insecurity at the heart of his regime that made him 'ever less willing to gamble on the loyalty of men outside his immediate circle'. Richard's failure to widen his power base led to fears of treachery and a 'lack of enthusiasm for his cause' at Bosworth. The uncommitted were pushed into opposition when the door to advancement was closed to them. Richard did, however, come close to defeating Henry Tudor, and the result of the battle 'should not be taken as a considered verdict' on him. Nevertheless 'the battle did expose the extent to which Richard had failed to establish himself'.[24]

As to the questions central to the debate on Richard III – his motives for seizing the crown and the mystery of the disappearance of the princes in the Tower – Horrox is characteristically and judiciously circumspect. Given Richard's power and influence over Edward IV, 'it is possible that Gloucester simply yielded to temptation in 1483, first to dominate the minority and then, when that proved easy, to make himself king'. There were other factors that may have given him the motivation to usurp the throne: he may have feared a diminution of his power that the accession of Edward V would bring, but also he may well have believed that the factionalisation inherent in Woodville control of the heir posed such a threat to political stability that his own rule was preferable. He 'may have persuaded himself, in fact, that he was acting for the good of the realm'. He acted ruthlessly and drove events at every stage but 'his actions were perhaps not entirely a matter of cynical expediency'. The nephews met their fate during Buckingham's rebellion early in the reign when it seemed that the rebels were aiming to restore Edward V. This aim, and growing disaffection, 'provides the most plausible context for

Richard's putative murder of his nephews'. Faced with serious opposition Richard may have hoped to cut the ground from under the rebels' feet 'by having his nephews killed' and allowing it to be known that they were dead.[25]

There were crumbs of comfort here for Richard's supporters who felt increasingly emboldened to argue that Richard was indeed acting for the good of the realm and that he had not intended to murder his nephews. The overall response to Horrox's book, however, was disappointing for Ricardians. Here was an eminently plausible account based on reasonable assumptions allowed by the evidence and underscored by an awareness of the realities of medieval politics. While his actions 'were perhaps not entirely' a matter of cynical expediency, Horrox allowed for the possibility that Richard's behaviour was largely a matter of self-interest and opportunistic calculation. The gulf between the two Richard camps had been narrowed to some extent, perhaps to the furthest possible extent, but it remained very much a gulf. There was certainly no reason for those adhering strongly to the traditional view of Richard to mitigate their stance.

RECENT TRENDS

In 1993 John Gillingham edited a slim volume of essays under the title *Richard III: A Medieval Kingship*. In his introduction Gillingham accused Richard of threatening the hereditary basis of the monarchy. No king of England had aroused, Gillingham acknowledged, 'and continues to arouse' stronger passions – both for and against. This observation did not prevent Gillingham from reiterating the conclusions he had reached in an earlier work, *The Wars of the Roses*, published in 1981. Richard should have been content to play the role of protector to his nephew, as John of Gaunt had for Richard II. He seized the throne because he could not be content with a subordinate role. He was ruthless, violent and self-motivated. The usurpation was a bad mistake and created problems that had not been there before. He threw the whole institution of monarchy into jeopardy but, thankfully, 'he was removed, and removed swiftly'. Gillingham admitted that, 'Many thoughtful people will certainly regard my interpretation of Richard as just another hatchet job, the pathetic fag-end of the tradition of Sir Thomas More and Shakespeare.' Gillingham did not mind this opprobrium because he felt it necessary to pass judgement on Richard and avoid the mistake of suspending moral condemnation in the interests of impartiality. Gillingham found it impossible to be impartial and so justified his partiality. To say that Richard was 'a man of his times' as Ross had done, was to escape anachronism but to fall prey to 'chronocentrism', the belief that different standards governed human behaviour in the past. Richard's ruthlessness and violent acts shocked contemporaries just as much as they shock us. He was a tyrant, an unacceptable king, and this was why he was overthrown. 'The most significant feature of Richard III's reign is its brevity.'[26]

Two of the articles in the volume pour fuel on to this flame of anti-Ricardian resistance. In the chapters contributed by Michael Hicks and Colin Richmond, Richard III emerges as a complex man, but a very bad one too. Gairdner would have been proud of this vindication. Indeed the argument deployed by Gillingham, that it is morally incumbent upon us to accuse Richard of the evil he committed, takes us back to the days of Lingard in the early 19th century, and even back to Hall in the 16th century. Hicks is a disciple of Ross, and his work exhibits a similar unwillingness to credit Richard with anything more than a dissembling and calculating virtue. Hicks is of the view that Richard was 'complex and many-sided' but also a 'formidable egotist'. He was a strong personality, in control of his own affairs, and he alone should bear the responsibility for manipulating conventional procedures in contempt of the 'accepted norms of political conduct'. As with Gillingham, so Hicks also found that Richard's blessed removal was a triumph for the established system and vital for its survival. He made a fatal error in seizing the crown, and was 'as complete a failure as the most inept of English kings.'[27]

Colin Richmond blamed the motivation for the coup on Richard's 'paranoia'. He feared for his landed estate, for his vice-regal status in the north, for his political future and for his personal safety. These fears were groundless and the product of his 'insecure personality' or the influence of the duke of Buckingham. He succeeded in taking the throne because 'his novel brutality shocked everyone into submission.' The moment he ordered the murder of Hastings he had crossed the Rubicon and 'contemptuously threw down the gauntlet to the political establishment'. This was when he finally revealed 'what one is tempted to call his heart of darkness'. The message was 'as clear as that of Hitler on the Night of the Long Knives'. It may be a little surprising, possibly even refreshing, for the casual reader to discover that in the absence of conclusive evidence concerning Richard's motives, professional historians can fill the gaps with as many prejudices and mixed metaphors as they like. It must also be abundantly clear that both laudable and malign motives might be postulated but that agreement between the exponents of either will be impossible. However stark and grotesque the portrayal of Richard might be, its brutal grimness only adds to our knowledge of the writer of the portrait, and not to our knowledge of the king. We know that Colin Richmond thinks that Richard was like Hitler and, just for good measure, a gauntlet-throwing Julius Caesar as well, but this does not bring us any closer to knowing what Richard was really like.[28]

As with Hicks, Richmond took the view that Richard's demise was a necessary and direct consequence of the usurpation. Normality was restored by the advent of Henry Tudor amid the total destruction of the Yorkist dynasty. In *The Wars of the Roses*, 1997, Christine Carpenter followed the same line of argument. Richard's usurpation was a bad mistake that cost him and his dynasty everything. His reign was inevitably short. Because 'there was no reason at all for him to become king, Richard, even more than the general run of usurpers, had to buy support', and this led to a fragility at the heart of the regime. There was only so much Richard could give to win support and when he had reached the limits of his available resources the nobility looked elsewhere. Richard always reigned as a usurper and this fatally undermined his position. Defeat at Bosworth was a consequence of the usurpation. The disloyalty around Richard was a direct result of his attack on Edward IV's establishment. Victory for Henry Tudor was, in actual fact, a 'Yorkist restoration, the vindication of Edward IV's rule, which had been so rudely destroyed by his brother'. As for the vexed question of the motive for the usurpation, Richard probably panicked and Buckingham egged him on. Rather than being a strong and independent-minded leader, as preferred by Hicks, Carpenter saw him as 'a born subordinate who could not cope with independent command, a man susceptible to misleading advice'.[29]

As the new millennium unfolds, the Tudor tradition appears to be thriving in academic circles. Hicks has further contributed to the survival of the Black Legend by arguing that, while Richard is remembered 'as the most wicked of kings and uncles', his poor wife,

Anne Neville, was 'another victim that he used, exhausted, and inevitably discarded'. In this case, Hicks confidently asserts, 'Shakespeare was right'. There is a just a little hint of hysteria in some of these supposedly academic conclusions. The general population has come to associate the professional historian with an objectivity and reliability born from dispassionate research. When Hicks describes Richard's relationship with his wife, Anne, he manifestly departs from this paradigm and throws impartiality to the winds. Anne Neville was Richard's cousin once removed. There was, and is, absolutely no impediment to this union. Because Anne's sister, Isabel, was married to Richard's brother, Clarence, Hicks manages to declare that, 'in fifteenth-century parlance, Richard was Anne's brother and Anne was Richard's sister'. Their physical union 'was incestuous, sinful, prohibited, deeply shocking and probably incapable of being dispensed'. Richard could only validate the marriage by a papal dispensation, but he never obtained one. No one at the time knew that the necessary dispensations had not been granted and this explains why 'none of the critics of Richard III in his own time ever queried his marriage. Its invalidity is a modern discovery'. Neither Thomas More nor Shakespeare was canny enough to accuse Richard of incest. The 'modern discovery' turns out to be the absence of any record of a dispensation having been issued. The fact that this might suggest that contemporaries considered it a matter of no importance, and certainly not worth wasting any time over, is too banal for Hicks to contemplate. Historical fact is manipulated to support a conclusion already reached. Richard was a baddy.[30]

On the other side of the battlefield the Ricardian camp has become as entrenched as that of its opponents. What continues to inspire both sides is a desire to resolve the injustices deliberately perpetrated by a distortion of the available evidence. What needs to be rescued is not Richard's reputation, but the validity of historical interpretation. There will always be a market for partisan work on Richard III, to be thrown as crowd-pleasers to those behind the respective parapets, but each new addition to the opposing genres merely serves to erode confidence in the study of history itself. When writing about Richard it is vitally important to set prejudice aside and to draw conclusions that do not go beyond what the evidence can bear. Unfortunately publishers are less scrupulous about the quality of historical work than perhaps they once were. If the book has a market it is likely to be printed, regardless of its historical merits.[31]

Thankfully there is good work taking place as well. Anne Sutton and Livia Visser-Fuchs, among many others, have contributed valuable articles in *The Ricardian*, the journal of the Richard III Society, that have furthered our knowledge of various aspects of the life and reign of Richard. Tony Pollard, while continuing to believe that Richard failed to win the confidence of his subjects, destroyed the house of York and 'did not live up to the high ideals of Christianity and chivalry he claimed to espouse', nevertheless felt able to list a few of Richard's significant achievements and suggest that 'he might well have succeeded in establishing his own branch of the Yorkist dynasty on the throne'. Although Ricardians in general, almost by definition, will never accept that Richard was less than a maligned saint, medievalists are increasingly willing to acknowledge that Richard's efforts to rule justly may have been more than calculated expediency, and that his defeat at the battle of Bosworth was not necessarily a consequence of the usurpation.[32]

CONCLUSION

The battle of Bosworth in August 1485 has often been seen as a turning-point in English history. There is some justification for this view in that the Tudor dynasty shaped an era markedly different from that of its Lancastrian and Yorkist predecessors, but it would be a mistake to view Bosworth as the end of the factional quarrels that had plagued the country since 1450. The Wars of the Roses had ended decisively in 1471, not 1485. Nor was the battle of Bosworth a verdict on Richard's ability as king, nor on the moral case for the usurpation. The two events, the usurpation of 1483 and the battle of Bosworth two years later, are connected, but not because Bosworth was a response to the outrage caused by the murder of the princes in the Tower. Kingship was damaged by usurpation because a power that derived its authority from the religious and legal principles of sacred sovereignty, the very substance of royal rule, was weakened when that power was seized against the will of the monarch. To bind subjects under one authority, an element of transcendence was required. The king had to be elevated above the common herd, however high and mighty they might be, and sovereign power was enshrined in his person through the agency of God. The Almighty ruler of the universe assisted this process in three ways: He protected the sanctity of royal blood, passed on by hereditary succession; He conferred His grace on the monarch through the agency of the Church and its ministers at the coronation ceremony; and He showed His approval through marks of favour granted to the king, such as victory and prosperity. If another mortal interfered with these divinely ordained operations, that person undermined the sanctity of the office, and therefore its authority. He had stolen power and not inherited it; he had grasped what was not his to take and had adopted the instruments of its power but not its moral force. Instead of unifying, the royal power had become divisive.

What this meant in practice was that the new king would always be viewed by some as less of a king and more of a man. It was easier to conspire against such a man and to seek to displace him. On the rare occasions when a usurpation had occurred in English history it was always followed by uncertainty, rebellion and war. Edward III had solved this problem by turning everyone's attention towards France, and also having the advantage of being the legitimate son of the deposed monarch. In the case of Henry IV, he had had to face serious uprisings and defeat the rebels in battle. Edward IV had had to do the same, despite winning the throne at Towton. This battle alone was not sufficient to guarantee his acceptance. There were two further battles in 1464 and Edward was still deposed in 1469. Not until after the battles of Barnet and Tewkesbury in 1471 was he secure. With a legitimate right and victory in numerous battles, it nevertheless took Edward 10 years to establish himself on the throne. Richard's usurpation was always going to cause these difficulties in any case. To compound them, his claim to rule was weak. Henry Tudor's invasion would have been one of many rebellions that Richard would have needed to deal with before he, too, could feel secure. Henry Tudor's rather unexpected victory at Bosworth should also be seen as an act of usurpation. It was vitally important that the Tudors linked the usurpation of 1483 with Richard's death at Bosworth. By claiming that Henry had been an instrument of God's wrath against a usurper, he was able to disguise his own opportunistic power-grab as an act of justice. The Black Legend was an essential tool of Tudor propaganda because it masked a ludicrously flimsy claim to the throne. Henry Tudor's claim to the throne was even weaker than Richard's, and he had not set out to right a wrong or punish the cruel murderer of two innocent boys. He had merely exploited the weakness in the monarchy caused by Richard's own usurpation to chance his luck. This was what usurpation brought about: anyone could aim at the top once the protection of sanctity had been removed.

The taking of the throne in 1483 had weakened the institution of monarchy and invited threats, but these could be overcome. Buckingham's rebellion shortly afterwards had further weakened Richard by forcing him to reconfigure the agencies of his power and by narrowing the base from which he could do so. Again, this need not have caused him to lose the throne in 1485. Although the task of holding on to the crown had been made more difficult, there is no reason to believe that a victory at Bosworth would not have allowed a new dispensation of royal authority to emerge. The loss of Richard's son, Edward, and his wife Anne, in 1484 and 1485 respectively, were further blows that undermined the stability of Richard's kingship, but even these losses need not have been fatal to his cause. We know that the lack of enthusiasm of two magnates at Bosworth and the decisive treachery of William Stanley gave the victory to Henry, but even then it might have been possible to defeat the rebel army. Richard's attempt to attack Henry may have been his last option, but it very nearly succeeded according to the scant information we have.

Any king who had gained the throne by deposing another would have faced multiple problems and certainly would have had to fight to keep his prize. What Bosworth did was highlight the difficulties such a king would face. Henry Tudor could, and did, expect just as many problems in keeping the throne, and inevitably found himself having to fight a further battle. Monarchy was again damaged at Bosworth: a usurper had been toppled by a middle-ranking upstart. Henry was well aware of the fragility of his rule; his response to the manifold threats perpetuated a trend. He further reduced the power of the magnates and continued to promote and rely on members of the gentry. He enforced the statutes against private liveries and the hiring of military retainers that saw the king eventually gain a monopoly over the recruitment and deployment of soldiers. All this had been initiated by the Yorkist kings, both Edward and Richard, but it had required Henry Tudor's taking of the throne to make the necessary changes. They had to be made because the monarchy had been even further weakened by another violent coup.

There was continuity in other ways too. Henry Tudor had no experience in government and very little in exercising even aristocratic power. He had not been a great magnate in the way that Richard had been and had not had to manage landed estates and a great household. His response to the rapid change of circumstances in which he found himself was, naturally, to keep what he found and use the system that was already working. The use of the chancery and its officials in the royal household, rather than the cumbersome exchequer, and the exploitation of royal rights on his landed estates, was continued and developed. The promotion of men of ability, rather than of inherited rank, particularly lawyers, naturally appealed to Tudor's tastes and met his needs. The irony is that if Richard had usurped the throne in 1483 because he wanted the strong government of his brother to be maintained and not fall into the hands of a weak king surrounded by the wrong people, this was the outcome of the events of 1483–1485, not so much because of his own act of usurpation as because of his death in battle two years later. Strong kingship was indeed maintained and central authority the winner. Richard did not fail to achieve this objective, but he failed to secure it for himself.

It is impossible to judge Richard III as a ruler because his reign was too short to allow him to show what he could do. It would give us a very distorted picture of Edward IV if we were to judge him on the first two years of his reign, or even the first 10. Similarly, the reign of Henry Tudor would warrant barely a footnote in a book on 15th century history if he had lost the battle of Stoke in 1487. A longer reign of Richard would have seen a greater prominence given to the north and its people in national affairs and possibly a more aggressive foreign policy, but financial constraints and the lack of a legitimate heir may have had a significant impact on the character of the period. A fundamental problem would remain at the heart of the body politic and would be exposed at Richard's death. Any successor would find it difficult to be universally accepted. A peaceful succession from Richard to his chosen heir would be very unlikely. If Henry IV's usurpation could provide a cause for the rebellion of the duke of York 60 years later, then Richard III's seizure of the throne would surely cause difficulties for many years too. Henry Tudor was able to use Richard's coup as justification for his own. To portray Richard as an illegal intrusion was to shore up Tudor credentials. Richard declared his nephews illegitimate to justify seizing the crown. It was not the reason for the coup. Their illegitimacy was a convenient fiction to gloss over the usurpation. The same tactic was deployed by Henry Tudor. He did not attack Richard because Richard was not the rightful king. He wanted the throne, had the opportunity and then provided the narrative. The destruction of Richard's reputation was as necessary to the Tudor story as the Eleanor Butler pre-contract had been to Richard's. Henry was able to survive and keep his throne, not without considerable danger and difficulty, by making a good marriage to a daughter of Edward IV and, more important, producing an heir to the throne. The price of strong monarchy was the almost perpetual ignominy suffered by Richard III.

NOTES

INTODUCTION

1 I. Wood, *The Merovingian Kingdoms* (London, 1994), pp.224–31; the Latin reads: *hac die natus erat Ricardus Rex Angliae iii Apud Fotheringhay Anno Domini mcccclii*, facsimile reprinted in P. W. Hammond and A. F. Sutton, (eds), *Richard III: The Road to Bosworth Field* (London, 1985), p.22.

2 J. Gairdner, *Life of Richard III* (Cambridge, 1898), p.5.

3 P. A. Johnson, *Duke Richard of York* (Oxford, 1988), p.1.

4 A. Crawford, *The Yorkists* (London, 2007), pp.2–4.

5 I. Watts, *Henry VI and the Politics of Kingship* (Cambridge, 1996), pp.236–240.

6 *The Croyland Chronicle Continuations 1459–86*, N. Pronay and J. Cox (eds), (London, 1986). Also available online at the *Richard III Society Online Library of Primary Texts and Secondary Sources* (www.r3.org/bookcase/croyland).

7 *Chronicles of London*, C. L. Kingsford (ed.), (Stroud, 1977); Robert Fabyan, *New Chronicles of England and France*, H. Ellis (ed.), (London, 1811); *The Great Chronicle of London*, A. H. Thomas and I. D. Thornley (eds), (London, 1938). Also online at *The Richard III and Yorkist History Server* (www.r3.org/bookcase/fabyan).

8 Dominic Mancini, *The Usurpation of Richard III*, C. A. J. Armstrong (ed.), (Oxford, 1936, 2nd edn, 1969, 1984). On Mancini see A. J. Pollard, *Richard III and the Princes in the Tower* (Stroud, 1991), pp.7–9; A. J. Pollard, 'Dominic Mancini's account of the events of 1483', *Nottingham Medieval Studies*, 38 (1994), pp.152–63; C. Ross,

Richard III (London, 1981), pp.xli–xliii; K. Dockray, *Richard III: A Source Book* (Stroud, 1991), pp.xv–xvii.

9 Philippe de Commynes, *Memoirs*, J. Calmette and G. Durville (eds), (1924–5); modern edition by M. Jones (ed.), (London, 1972).

10 J. Gairdner (ed.), *The Paston Letters*, six vols (London, 1904, repr. 1984); N. Davis (ed.), *Paston Letters and Papers of the Fifteenth Century*, two vols (Oxford, 1971–6); N. Davis (ed.), *The Paston Letters, a selection in modern spelling* (Oxford, 1983); T. Stapleton (ed.), *The Plumpton Correspondence* (Camden Society, 1839), pp.45–8; C. L. Kingsford (ed.), *The Stonor Letters and Papers, 1290–1483* two vols (Camden Society, 3rd ser. xix–xxx, 1919); C. Carpenter (ed.), *Kingsford's Stonor Letters and Papers 1290–1483* (Cambridge, 1996); A. Hanham, *The Cely Letters, 1472–1488* (Early English Texts Society, 1975), esp. pp.184–5.

11 *Calendar of Patent Rolls, 1441–1509*, 8 vols (London, 1908–16); *Calendar of Close Rolls, 1461–85*, 3 vols (London, 1949–54), both available at British History Online, National Archives' Calendars of State Papers. R. E. Horrox and P. W. Hammond (eds), *British Library, Harleian MS 433*, 4 vols (1979–83); National Archives, *Duchy of Lancaster: Letters Patent and Warrants*; *Duchy of Lancaster Minute Book*; York Records, *Extracts from the Municipal Records of the City of York*, R. Davies (ed.), (Gloucester, 1976).

CHAPTER 1

1 P. A. Johnson, *Duke Richard of York* (Oxford, 1988), p.108.

2 J. Watts, *Henry VI and the Politics of Kingship* (Cambridge, 1996), p.104.

3 J. de Waurin, *Recueil des Croniques*, W. Hardy (ed.), (Rolls Series, 1864–91), v, 275.

4 J. S. Davies, *An English Chronicle* (Camden Society, 1856), p.89; William Gregory's 'Chronicle of London', in J. Gairdner (ed.), *The Historical Collections of a Citizen of London in the Fifteenth Century* (Camden Society, 1876), pp.205–7.

5 J. Gairdner (ed.), *The Paston Letters* (London, 1904), i. 525.

6 J. Gillingham, *The Wars of the Roses* (London, 2001), p.116.

7 John Whethamstede, Abbot of St Albans, H. T. Riley (ed.), *Registrum* (Roll Series, 1872–3), i. 376–8; also John Tiptoft, letter to the earl of Worcester, in P. A. Johnson, *Duke Richard of York* (Oxford, 1988), pp.213–4.

8 *Rotuli Parliamentorum* (London, 1767), v. 375–9, quoted in J. R. Lander, *The Wars of the Roses* (London, 1990), pp.79–80.

9 John Whethamstede, Abbot of St Albans, H. T. Riley (ed.), *Registrum* (Roll Series, 1872–3), i, 382; J. Stevenson (ed.), *Annales Rerum Anglicarum* (Rolls Series, 1864), 2, i, p.775.

10   H. Kleineke, *Edward IV* (Abingdon, 2009), p.44; C. Ross, *Edward IV* (London, 1974), p.22.
11   Gregory's Chronicle, *The Historical Collection of a Citizen of London*, J. Gairdner (ed.), (Camden Society, 1876), p.211.
12   H. Kleineke, *Edward IV* (Abingdon, 2009), p.45; J. Gillingham, *The Wars of the Roses* (London, 2001), pp.122–4; C. Ross, *Edward IV* (London, 1974), p.30.

CHAPTER 2

1   A. H. Thomas and I. D. Thornley (eds), *The Great Chronicle of London* (London, 1938), pp.194–6.
2   C. Ross, *Edward IV* (London, 1974), p.35.
3   J. R. Lander, *The Wars of the Roses* (Guild Publishing, 1990), pp.90–91; K. Dockray, *Henry VI, Margaret of Anjou and the Wars of the Roses: A Source Book* (Stroud, 2000), pp.111–12; C. Ross, *Edward IV* (London, 1974), p.34.
4   C. Ross, *Edward IV* (London, 1974), p.35.
5   J. Gillingham, *The Wars of the Roses* (London, 2001), pp.131–5; C. Ross, *Edward IV* (London, 1974), pp.36–8; K. Dockray, *Henry VI, Margaret of Anjou and the Wars of the Roses: A Source Book* (Stroud, 2000), p.112–5; J. R. Lander, *The Wars of the Roses* (London, 1990), pp.92–3; P. Bramley, *The Wars of the Roses: A Field Guide and Companion* (Stroud, 2007), pp.235–240.
6   Prosper di Camulio, *Calendar of State Papers, Milan*, A. B. Hinds (ed.), (London, 1912), i, 74.
7   R. Horrox, *Richard III: A Study in Service* (Cambridge, 1989), p.29; C. Ross, *Richard III* (London, 1981), pp.9–10.
8   A. J. Pollard, *Richard III and the Princes in the Tower* (Sutton, 1991), pp.42–5; A. J. Pollard, *Warwick the Kingmaker* (London, 2007), pp.110–14; M. Hicks, 'Richard, Duke of Gloucester: The Formative Years', in J. Gillingham (ed.), *Richard III: A Medieval Kingship* (London, 1993), p.23; S. Cunningham, *Richard III: A Royal Enigma* (National Archives, 2003), pp.5–9; C. Ross, *Richard III* (London, 1981), pp.6–8.
9   K. Dockray, *Edward IV: A Source Book* (Stroud, 1999), pp.33–5; A. Crawford, *The Yorkists* (London, 2007), p.22; A. J. Pollard, *Warwick the Kingmaker* (London, 2007), pp.49–51, 55.
10   D. Baldwin, *Elizabeth Woodville* (Stroud, 2002), pp.12–15; C. Ross, *Edward IV* (London, 1974), pp.85–86.

11   M. K. Jones, *Bosworth 1485: Psychology of a Battle* (Stroud, 2002), pp.73–6; A. J. Pollard, *Warwick the Kingmaker* (London, 2007), pp.65–7; H. Kleineke, *Edward IV* (Abingdon, 2009), p.92.

12   *Croyland Chronicle Continuations*, N. Pronay and J. Cox (eds), (London, 1986), p.552.

CHAPTER 3

1   S. Cunningham, *Richard III: A Royal Enigma* (National Archives, 2003), pp.13–14; R. Horrox, *Richard III: A Study in Service* (Cambridge, 1989), pp.30–32.

2   John Warkworth, *A Chronicle of the First Thirteen Years of the Reign of Edward the Fourth*, J. O. Halliwell (ed.), (Camden Society, 1839), p.8; 'Chronicle of the Rebellion in Lincolnshire 1470', in J. R. Lander, *Wars of the Roses* (London, 1990), p.122; A. J. Pollard, *Warwick the Kingmaker* (London, 2007), p.67; C. Carpenter, *The Wars of the Roses* (Cambridge, 1997), p.176.

3   *Proclamation at York: Calendar of Close Rolls 1468–1476*, (London, 1908) p.138; Grant from Richard, duke of Gloucester, to Reginald Vaughan, 10 Edward IV, signed at Hornby 26 March 1470, *Archaelogia Cambrensis* (3rd Series, 9,Cambridge, 1863), p.55; M. K. Jones, 'Richard III and the Stanleys', in *Richard III and the North*, R. Horrox (ed.), Studies in Regional and Local History, No. 6 (Hull University, 1986), esp. p.36 and fn. 52, p.46.

4   D. Hipshon, *Richard III and the Death of Chivalry* (Stroud, 2009), p.117–41; D. J. Clayton, *The Administration of the County Palatine of Chester, 1442–1485* (Chetham Soc. 3rd series, 35, 1990), p.98–109; for the Stanleys and the Harringtons in general, see: I. Grimble, *The Harrington Family* (London, 1957); B. Coward, *The Stanleys: Lords Stanley and Earls of Derby* (Chetham Soc. 3rd series, 30, 1983).

5   A. J. Pollard, *Richard III and the Princes in the Tower* (Stroud, 1991), p.48; A. J. Pollard, *Warwick the Kingmaker* (London, 2007), p.68.

6   'The Manner and Guiding of the Earl of Warwick at Angers', in *Chronicles of the White Rose of York*, J. A. Giles (ed.), (London, 1845), p.232–3; for Warwick's formal submission: *Milanese State Papers: Newsletters from France, June/July 1470* (Calendar of State Papers: Milan, London, 1913), vol. 1, p.140.

7   J. Warkworth, *A Chronicle of the First Thirteen Years of the Reign of Edward the Fourth*, J. O. Halliwell (ed.), (Camden Society, 1839), p.12.

8   J. Warkworth, *A Chronicle of the First Thirteen Years of the Reign of Edward the Fourth*, J. O. Halliwell (ed.), (Camden Society, 1839), p.10–11.

9   J. Warkworth, *A Chronicle of the First Thirteen Years of the Reign of Edward the Fourth*, J. O. Halliwell (ed.), (Camden Society, 1839), p.11; *Croyland Chronicle Continuations*, N. Pronay and J. Cox (eds), (London, 1986), p.554.

10   *The Historie of the Arrivall of Edward IV in England*, J. Bruce (ed.), (Camden Society, 1838), p.9.

11   *The Historie of the Arrivall of Edward IV in England*, J. Bruce (ed.), (Camden Society, 1838), pp.10–11.

12   *Calendar of Patent Rolls 1466–77* (London, 1909), p.241; dated 5 March 1471.

13   *The Historie of the Arrivall of Edward IV in England*, J. Bruce (ed.), (Camden Society, 1838), p.14; for Polydore Vergil see C. Ross, *Richard III* (London, 1981), p.20–21; see also H. Keineke, *Edward IV* (Abingdon, 2009), pp.114–5; C. Ross, *Edward IV* (London, 1974), pp.164–5; J. Gillingham, *The Wars of the Roses* (London, 1981), pp.193–4.

14   *The Historie of the Arrivall of Edward IV in England*, J. Bruce (ed.), (Camden Society, 1838), p.17; 'The Great Chronicle of London', in K. Dockray, *Edward IV: A Source Book* (Stroud, 1999), p.89.

15   Henry's words reported in a letter from Margaret of Burgundy to the dowager duchess of Burgundy, April 1471, and quoted in C. Ross, *Edward IV* (London, 1974), p.166; *Arrival*, p.17; *Croyland Chronicle*, p.555; *Warkworth* says 'took in ward', p.17.

16   W. G. Searle, *The History of the Queens' College* (Cambridge Antiquarian Society, 1867), p.92, reprinted in P. W. Hammond and A. F. Sutton, *Richard III: The Road to Bosworth Field* (London, 1985), p.68; R. Horrox, *Richard III: A Study in Service* (Cambridge, 1989), pp.35, 37–8, 41; M. K. Jones, 'Richard III as a Soldier', in J. Gillingham (ed.), *Richard III: A Medieval Kingship* (London, 1993), p.96; C. Ross, *Richard III* (London, 1981), pp.21–2; P. J. Watson 'A Review of the Sources for the Battle of Barnet', *Ricardian* (June 2000), vol. XII, no. 149, pp.61–2.

17   *The Historie of the Arrivall of Edward IV in England*, J. Bruce (ed.), (Camden Society, 1838), pp.29–31.

CHAPTER 4

1   R. Somerville, *History of the Duchy of Lancaster* (London, 1953), vol 1, pp.153, 240 ff.

2   C. Carpenter, 'Gentry and Community in Medieval England', *Journal of British Studies*, 33 (University of Chicago, 1994), pp.340–80.

3   C. Ross, *Richard III* (London, 1981), p.32; A. J. Pollard, *Richard III and the Princes in the Tower* (Stroud, 1991), pp.67–9.

4   R. Horrox, *Richard III: A Study in Service* (Cambridge, 1989), esp. pp.39–44; C. Ross, *Richard III* (London, 1981), pp.24–6; A. J. Pollard, *Richard III and the Princes in the Tower* (Stroud, 1991), pp.69–70.

5   The papal dispensation was issued on 22 April 1472: M. Hicks, *Anne Neville* (Stroud, 2007), p.133. Hicks constructs so many impediments to the marriage as to allow him to accuse Richard of 'serial incest'. For a riposte, see M. Barnfield, 'Diriment Impediments, Dispensations and Divorce: Richard III and Matrimony', *The Ricardian* (2007), vol. XVII, pp.84–98. Barnfield's argument is that a dispensation would need to cover all impediments and therefore, because the dispensation issued in 1472 only covers affinity, the matter of consanguinity must have been dispensed with previously. Charles Ross declared that 'worldly cynicism inspired the insertion of a clause ... guaranteeing Gloucester's title ... should the marriage later end in divorce', *Richard III* (London, 1981), p.28. In canon law the marriage was validated, whatever dispensations had or had not been acquired, by the marriage ceremony itself, but could be invalidated if either of the parties later sued for a divorce. Richard was simply, and routinely, protecting himself from this eventuality. A ceremony conducted by the Cardinal Archbishop of Canterbury, as in this case, was ample validation.

6   *Croyland Chronicle Continuations*, N. Pronay and J. Cox (eds), (London, 1986), p.557.

7   For Richard's illegitimate children, C. Ross *Richard III* (London, 1981), p.138. For his professed grief, P. W. Hammond and A. F. Sutton, *Richard III: the Road to Bosworth Field* (London, 1985), p.199. M. Hicks, *Anne Neville* (Stroud, 2007), who, throughout the book, describes the union as 'incestuous' and Richard as 'a serial practitioner' of incest (e.g. pp.205–6), also accuses him of being 'ruthless and cruel' towards her, and asserts that Anne died 'unregretted' (p. 212). These assertions pay scant regard to historical objectivity.

8   *Croyland Chronicle Continuations*, N. Pronay and J. Cox (eds), (London, 1986), p.561; C. Ross, *Edward IV* (London, 1974), pp.239–42; H. Kleineke, *Edward IV* (Abingdon, 2009), pp.145–7.

9   *Dominic Mancini*, p.63, in K. Dockray, *Edward IV: A Source Book* (Stroud, 1999), p.103.

10 C. Ross, *Richard III* (London, 1981), pp.33–4; see also R. Horrox, *Richard III: A Study in Service* (Cambridge, 1989), p.57.

11 M. K. Jones, *Bosworth 1485* (Stroud, 2002), pp.79–83; P. A. Johnson, *Duke Richard of York 1411–1460* (Oxford, 1988), pp.47–9.

12 A. J. Pollard, *Richard III and the Princes in the Tower* (Stroud, 1991), p.83; C. Ross, *Richard III* (London, 1981), p.35.

13 *British Library Harleian MSS 433*, P. W. Hammond and R. E. Horrox (eds), (1979–83) vol 1. pp.72, 74, 78, for the appointments of the Huddlestons, p.77 for Robert

Harrington; National Archives, DL 42/20/46 for the appointments of James Harrington. I. Grimble, *The Harrington Family* (London, 1957), pp.44–61.

14 National Archives, DL 42/20/54, for Thomas Pilkington. See also J. Pilkington, 'The early history of the Lancashire family of Pilkington and its branches', *Transactions of the Historic Society of Lancashire and Cheshire*, 45 (1983), pp.159–216; T. D. Whitaker, *An History of the Original Parish of Whalley* (York Archaeological Society, 1878); R. Horrox, 'Pilkington family' *Oxford Dictionary of National Biography* (Oxford, 2004).

15 *Calendar of Patent Rolls, 1476–85* (London, 1909) pp.213, 289, 313, 343, 398, etc.

16 M. Hicks, 'Richard Duke of Gloucester: the Formative Years', in J. Gillingham (ed.), *Richard III: A Medieval Kingship* (London, 1993), pp.30–31, for the text of the indenture.

17 For the proclamation: *Calendar of Close Rolls, Edward IV* (London, 1949), vol. 1. no. 1155; D. Hipshon, *Richard III and the Death of Chivalry* (Stroud, 2009), pp.139–40; M. K. Jones, 'Richard III and the Stanleys', in R. Horrox (ed.), *Richard III and the North*, Studies in Regional and Local History, no. 6 (Hull University, 1986), pp.38–40.

18 For Richard and Scotland: A. J. Pollard, *Richard III and the Princes in the Tower* (Stroud, 1991), p.74; Philippe de Commynes, *Memoirs*, in J. R. Lander, *The Wars of the Roses*, (London, 1990), p.155.

19 For the campaign: C. Ross, *Edward IV*, (London, 1974), pp.226–38; H. Keineke, *Edward IV* (Abingdon, 2009), pp.138–43.

20 For an elaborate view of the effect of Picquigny on Richard see: M. K. Jones, *Bosworth 1485: Psychology of a Battle* (Stroud, 2002), p.85.

21 D. Hipshon, *Richard III and the Death of Chivalry* (Stroud, 2009), pp.143–4; M. K. Jones, *Bosworth 1485: the Psychology of a Battle* (Stroud, 2002), p.54; P. W. Hammond and A. F. Sutton, *Richard III: The Road to Bosworth Field* (London, 1985), pp.64–7.

22 The statutes for Queens' College Cambridge and for Middleham are in P. W. Hammond and A. F. Sutton, *Richard III: The Road to Bosworth Field* (London, 1985), pp.68, 76.

23 C. Ross, *Edward IV* (London, 1974), pp.278–95; H. Kleineke, *Edward IV* (Abingdon, 2009), pp.149–53.

24 Edward IV to Sixtus, *Calendar of State Papers: Venice* R. Brown (ed.), (London, 1864), no. 483; *Croyland Chronicle Continuations*, N. Pronay and J. Cox (eds), (London, 1986), p.563; C. Ross, *Richard III* (London, 1981), p.47; for the text of the grant of the county palatine, etc.: P. W. Hammond and A. F. Sutton, *Richard III: The Road to Bosworth Field* (London, 1985), pp.89–91.

CHAPTER 5

1   R. Horrox, *Richard III: A Study in Service* (Cambridge, 1989), p.92; for the account that follows: *Croyland Chronicle Continuations*, N. Pronay and J. Cox (eds), (London, 1986), pp.564–7; Dominic Mancini, *The Usurpation of Richard III*, C. A. J. Armstrong (ed.), (Oxford, 1936), pp.85–115.

2   L. Pidgeon, 'Antony Wydevile, Lord Scales and Rivers: Family, Friends and Affinity, Part 2.' *Ricardian* (2006), vol. XVI, pp.42, 45.

3   Bishop Russell quoted in C. Ross, *Richard III* (London, 1981), p.75; A. Crawford, *The Yorkists* (London, 2007), pp.119–20.

4   The letter to York is in *York Civic Records*, A. Raine (ed.), (Yorkshire Archaeological Society Record Series, 1939), vol. 1, pp.73–4, reprinted in K. Dockray, *Richard III: A Source Book* (Stroud, 1997), p.56; the proclamation is in *York Civic Records*, vol. 1, p.75 and reprinted in P. W. Hammond and A. F. Sutton, *Richard III: The Road to Bosworth Field* (London, 1985), pp.108–9.

5   *Great Chronicle of London*, A. H. Thomas and I. D. Thornley (eds), (London, 1938), pp.231–3.

6   Philippe de Commynes, *Memoirs*, M. Jones (trans.) (Harmondsworth, 1972), pp.353–4; C. Ross, *Richard III* (London, 1981), pp. 88–92; D. Baldwin, *Elizabeth Woodville* (Sutton, 2002), pp.107–8; A. Crawford, *The Yorkists* (London, 2007), pp.131–2.

7   H. A. Kelly, 'The Case against Edward IV's Marriage and Offspring: Secrecy; Witchcraft; Secrecy; Precontract', *The Ricardian* (Sept 1998), vol. XI, no. 142, pp.326–39.

8   *The Great Chronicle of London*, A. H. Thomas and I. D. Thorney (eds), (London, 1938), p.232; P. W. Hammond and A. F. Sutton, *Richard III: The Road to Bosworth Field* (London, 1985), p.114.

9   *The Great Chronicle of London*, A. H. Thomas and I. D. Thorney (eds), (London, 1938), p.234; Dominic Mancini, *The Usurpation of Richard III*, C. A. J. Armstrong (ed.), (Oxford, 1936), p.93.

10 For the *Cely Memorandum* and the *Croyland Chronicle* see K. Dockray, *Richard III: A Source Book* (Stroud, 1997), pp.76, 78.

11 Foreign observers collected in J. Gillingham (ed.), *Richard III: A Medieval Kingship* (London, 1993), pp.16–17; Jan Allertz and Robert Ricard, in A. J. Pollard, *Richard III and the Princes in the Tower* (Stroud, 1991), p.122.

12 A. J. Pollard, *Richard III and the Princes in the Tower* (Stroud, 1991), p.123; Bodleian Library, Ashmolean Manuscript, 1448, folio 287; R. F. Green, 'The Historical Notes of a London Citizen, 1483–88', *English Historical Review*, Vol. 96 (1981), p.588; the

entry in the *Anlaby Cartulary* is given in J. Gillingham (ed.), *Richard III: A Medieval Kingship* (London, 1993), p.54.

13   Sir Thomas More, *The History of King Richard III*, R. S. Sylvester (ed.), (Yale, 1986), p.86. For the bones and their analysis, see A. J. Pollard, *Richard III and the Princes in the Tower* (Stroud, 1991), pp.124–7.

14   L. Visser-Fuchs, Review Article, 'What Niclas Von Popplau Really Wrote About Richard III', *The Ricardian*, vol. XI, no. 145 (June 1999), p.529.

CHAPTER 6

1   A. Raine (ed.), *York Civic Records* (Yorkshire Archaeological Society, 1941), pp.78–9; also online at www. richard111.com/York.htm (23 August 1483).

2   K. Dockray, *Richard III: A Source Book* (Stroud, 1997), pp.70–71.

3   A. Hanham, *Richard III and his Early Historians 1483–1535* (Oxford, 1975), p.50.

4   Thomas More, *The History of King Richard III*, R. S. Sylvester (ed.), *Complete Works* (Yale, 1963), II, p.91.

5   L. Gill, *Richard III and Buckingham's Rebellion* (Stroud, 1999), p.64; S. Cunningham, *Richard III: A Royal Enigma* (National Archives, 2003), pp.51–2; C. Ross, *Richard III* (London, 1981), p.115.

6   *Croyland Chronicle Continuations*, N. Pronay and J. Cox (eds), (London, 1986), p.568.

7   C. Ross, *Richard III* (London, 1981), p.112. Ross declares, 'It is much more likely that the rebellion was a direct result of the outrage and resentment felt by Edward's loyal servants of Richard's treatment of his heirs.' Ross himself cites many examples of rebels whose last thought would have been of the princes. He overstates the case for the political awareness and responsiveness of local communities.

8   The letter is reproduced in S. Cunningham, *Richard III: A Royal Enigma* (National Archives, 2003), p.55. The translation given there strangely omits the telling phrase 'of him that had the best cause to be true'.

9   *Croyland Chronicle Continuations*, N. Pronay and J. Cox (eds), (London, 1986), p.570.

CHAPTER 7

1   *Titulus Regius: Rotuli Parliamentorum*, J. Strachey *et al* (eds), (London, 1777), vol 6, pp.240–42. See also P. W. Hammond and A. F. Sutton, *Richard III: The Road to*

Bosworth Field (London, 1985), pp.155–9. Dominic Mancini, *The Usurpation of Richard III*, C. A. J. Armstrong (ed.), (Oxford, 1969), p.95. The idea that the *Titulus Regius* incorporated a modified version of the original petition was first suggested to me by Rosemary Horrox.

2   *British Library Harleian Manuscript 433*, R. E. Horrox and P. W. Hammond (eds), (1979), vol. 3, p.107.

3   J. B. Sheppard (ed.), *Christ Church Letters* (Camden Society, 1877), p.46.

4   *British Library Harleian Manuscript 433*, R. E. Horrox and P. W. Hammond (eds), (1979–83), vol. 2, pp.48–9.

5   *Calendar of Patent Rolls 1476–85* (London, 1909), p.413; A. F. Sutton, '"A curious searcher of our public weal": Richard III, piety, chivalry and the concept of the good prince', in P. W. Hammond (ed.), *Richard III: Loyalty, Lordship and Law* (Gloucester, 1986), p.64; C. Ross, *Richard III* (London, 1981), p.174; A. J. Pollard, *Richard III and the Princes in the Tower* (Stroud, 1991), p.154; H. Kleineke, 'Richard III and the Origins of the Court of Requests', *Ricardian* (2007), vol. XVII, pp.22–32.

6   R. Horrox, 'The Government of Richard III', in J. Gillingham (ed.), *Richard III: A Medieval Kingship* (London, 1993), p.69.

7   C. Ross, *Richard III* (London, 1981), pp.187–90.

8   See Emma J. Bolden, 'Richard III: Central Government and Administration', *The Ricardian* (2000), vol. XII, no. 149, pp.71–81.

9   *Croyland Chronicle Continuations*, N. Pronay and J. Cox (eds), (London, 1986), p.570.

10 A. Grant, 'Foreign Affairs Under Richard III', in J. Gillingham (ed.), *Richard III: A Medieval Kingship* (London, 1993), pp.113–32; C. Ross, *Richard III* (London, 1981), pp.191–209; A. J. Pollard, *Richard III and the Princes in the Tower* (Stroud, 1991), pp.158–62.

11 A. J. Pollard, *Richard III and the Princes in the Tower* (Stroud, 1991), p.167.

12 C. Ross, *Richard III* (London, 1981), p.134.

13 Nicholas von Poppelau, quoted in L. Vissier-Fuchs, Review Article, *The Ricardian*, vol. XI, no. 145, (June 1999), pp.528–9.

14 M. K. Jones, *The Psychology of a Battle: Bosworth 1485* (Stroud, 2002), pp.121–6.

15 Richard III's Book of Hours, *Lambeth Palace Library MS 474*, ff. 181–3, translated and printed by P. W. Hammond and Anne F. Sutton, *Richard III: the Road to Bosworth Field* (London, 1985), pp.191–3. See also J. Hughes, *The Religious Life of Richard III* (Oxford, 1997), p.24 for a rather quirky view. He states that this prayer 'reinforced a grandiose self-image defined in terms of hostility, misunderstanding and rejection'.

16 *York House Books*, Books 2/4, f. 163b, printed in P. W. Hammond and Anne F. Sutton, *Richard III: the Road to Bosworth Field* (London, 1985), pp.205–6.

17 For the motto see A. F. Sutton, 'A curious searcher for our weal public: Richard III, Piety, Chivalry and the Concept of the "Good Prince"', in P. W. Hammond (ed.), *Richard III: Loyalty, Lordship and Law* (Gloucester, 1986), p.62.

18 J. S. Roskell, 'William Catesby, Councillor to Richard III', *Bulletin of the John Rylands Library*, vol. 42, no. 1 (Sept. 1959), pp.162–4; *The Croyland Chronicle Continuations, 1459–1486*, N. Pronay and J. Cox (eds), (London, 1986), p.572.

19 R. Horrox, *Richard III: A Study in Service* (Cambridge, 1989), pp.276–7, 289–90.

20 I am very grateful to Richard Holmes, chairman of the Battlefield Trust, and Glenn Foard, the leader of the team from English Heritage, for this information.

21 P. W. Hammond and A. F. Sutton, *Richard III: The Road to Bosworth Field* (London, 1985), pp.216–19.

CHAPTER 8

1   K. B. McFarlane, 'Bastard Feudalism', in *England in the Fifteenth Century, Collected Essays*, (Oxford, 1981), ch. II. See especially the Introduction by G. L. Harriss. See also C. Carpenter, *The Wars of the Roses* (Cambridge, 1997), pp.49–53.

2   C. Carpenter, *The Wars of the Roses* (Cambridge, 1997), p.54.

3   J. L. Watts, *Henry VI and the Politics of Kingship* (Cambridge, 1996), pp.60–80, 91–101; C. Given-Wilson, *The English Nobility in the Later Middle Ages* (London, 1987).

4   H. Castor, *Blood and Roses* (London, 2004), p.12.

5   C. Carpenter, *The Wars of the Roses* (Cambridge, 1997), p.35.

6   C. Ross, *Richard III* (London, 1981), pp.153–4.

7   A. J. Pollard, *North-Eastern England During the Wars of the Roses* (Oxford, 1990), pp.358–60.

8   R. Horrox, *Richard III: A Study in Service* (Cambridge, 1989), pp.220–21.

9   A. Crawford, 'The Private Life of John Howard', in P. W. Hammond (ed.), *Richard III: Lordship, Loyalty and Law* (Gloucester, 1986), pp.21–2.

10 R. Horrox, *Richard III: A Study in Service* (Cambridge, 1989), pp.221–3.

11 *British Library, Harleian MS 433*, R. E. Horrox and P. W. Hammond (eds), (1979–83), vol. I, p.242, II, pp.10–11; III, p.144.

12 The National Archives, DL 42/20, 46v; DL 29/90/1653.

13 T. D. Whitaker, *A History of the Original Parish of Whalley* (3rd edn, Lancaster, 1878), vol. V, p.509; D. Hipshon, *Richard III and the Death of Chivalry* (Stroud, 2009), pp.117–41, 199–202.

14 For a survey of the literature and a summary of recent work on the gentry class in the 15th century, see P. Coss, *The Origins of the English Gentry* (Cambridge, 2005), pp.1–10.

15 J. S. Roskell, 'William Catesby, Councillor to Richard III', *Bulletin of the John Rylands Library*, vol. 42, no. 1 (Sept. 1959), pp.150–71; S. Payling, '"Never desire to be grete about princes, for it is daungeros": the rise and fall of the fifteenth century Catesbys', in J. Bertram (ed.), *The Catesby Family and their Brasses at Ashby St Ledgers* (London, 2006), pp.1–13.

16 R. S. Sylvester (ed.), *The Complete Works of Saint Thomas More* (Yale, 1963), vol II, p.45; B. P. Wolffe, 'When and Why did Hastings Lose His Head?', *English Historical Review* (Oct 1974), vol. 89, pp.835–44; *Calendar of Patent Rolls 1476–85* (London, 1897–1901), p.348.

17 *Calendar of Charter Rolls 1476–1485*, (London, 1916–17), vol. v, p.415; *A Descriptive Catalogue of Ancient Deeds* (London, 1890–1906), vol. iv, A10182; S. Payling, *The Catesby Family* (London, 2006), p.13.

18 *British Library, Harleian MS 433*, R. E. Horrox and P. W. Hammond (eds), (London, 1979–83), vol. II, p.25; R. Horrox, *Richard III: A Study in Service* (Cambridge, 1989), pp.58, 64; C. Ross, *Richard III* (London, 1981), pp.56, 57–8. R. Horrox, *Oxford Dictionary of National Biography* (Oxford, 2004), Article 22990.

19 *York Civic Records*, vol. I, 73; *The Great Chronicle of London*, A. H. Thomas and I. D. Thornley (eds), (London, 1938), p.567.

20 A. R. Myers, *The Household of Edward IV* (Manchester, 1959), pp.103–4.

21 *Calendar of Patent Rolls 1476–85* (London, 1908–16), pp.472, 512; *British Library, Harleian MS 433*, R. E. Horrox and P. W. Hammond (eds), (1979–83), vol. I, p.233.

CHAPTER 9

1 C. D. Ross, *Richard III* (London, 1981), pp.xxii–xxxiv; K. Dockray, *Richard III: A Source Book* (Stroud, 1997), pp.xxii–xxv.

2 Polydore Vergil, *English History*, H. Ellis (ed.), (Camden Society, 1844), pp.187–90; K. Dockray, *Richard III: A Source Book* (Stroud, 1997), pp.80–81; J. R. Lander, *The Wars of the Roses* (London, 1990), pp.180–81.

3 C. D. Ross, *The Rous Roll* (Gloucester, 1980); C. D. Ross, *Richard III* (London, 1981), p.xxii.

4 A. Hanham, *Richard III and his Early Historians* (Oxford, 1975), esp. pp.118–27; J. Potter, *Good King Richard?* (London, 1983), pp.88–9.

5 C. D. Ross, *Richard III* (London, 1981), p.xxvi.

6 R. S. Sylvester (ed.), Sir Thomas More, *The History of King Richard the Third* (Yale, 1963); K. Dockray, *Richard III: A Source Book* (Stroud, 1997), p.xxiv.

7 J. Potter, *Good King Richard?* (London, 1983), pp.175–83.

8   P. W. Hammond, 'The Reputation of Richard III', in J. Gillingham (ed.), *Richard III: A Medieval Kingship* (London, 1993), pp.142–3; J. Potter, *Good King Richard?* (London, 1983), pp.193–6.

9   A. J. Pollard, *Richard III and the Princes in the Tower* (Stroud, 1991), p.217.

10   C. A. Halsted, *Richard III as Duke of Gloucester and King of England* (London, 1844); K. Dockray, *Richard III: A Source Book* (Stroud, 1997), p.xxix; J. Potter, *Good King Richard?* (London, 1983), pp.196–201; C. D. Ross, *Richard III* (London, 1981), p.l.

11   J. Gairdner, *History of the Life and Reign of Richard the Third*, 2nd edn (London, 1898), pp.xi–xiii, l.

12   Sir John Millais' portrait, 'The Princes in the Tower' (1878), is at Royal Holloway College, Egham, Surrey. It has been reproduced in A. J. Pollard, *Richard III and the Princes in the Tower* (Stroud, 1991), p.142.

13   C. R. Markham, *Richard III: His Life and Character* (London, 1906); K. Dockray, *Richard III: A Source Book* (Stroud, 1991), pp.xxx–xxi; C. D. Ross, *Richard III* (London, 1981), p.li; P. W. Hammond, 'The Reputation of Richard III', in J. Gillingham (ed.), *Richard III: a Medieval Kingship* (London, 1993), pp.144–5; J. Potter, *Good King Richard?* (London, 1983), pp.216–21.

14   A. Bryant, *Freedom's Own Island* (London, 1980), pp.19–22.

15   W. S. Churchill, *A History of the English-Speaking Peoples* (London, 1956), vol. 1. pp.380–91.

16   J. R. Lander, *Government and Community: England 1450–1509* (London, 1980), p.330; *The Wars of the Roses* (London, 1990), pp.173, 185.

17   C. D. Ross, *Richard III* (London, 1981), pp.43, 157–69, 228–9.

18   C. D. Ross, *Richard III* (London, 1981), p.li.

19   P. W. Hammond and Anne F. Sutton, *Richard III: the Road to Bosworth Field* (London, 1985), pp.16–17; J. Potter, *Good King Richard?* (London, 1983), p.258.

20   D. Seward, *Richard III: England's Black Legend* (London, 1983), pp.21, 117; *The Wars of the Roses* (London, 1995), pp.278–9.

21   A. J. Pollard, *Richard III and the Princes in the Tower* (Stroud, 1991), pp.212, 219.

22   C. Richmond, '1485 and All That, or what was going on at the Battle of Bosworth?', in *Richard III: Loyalty, Lordship and Law*, P. W. Hammond (ed.), (Gloucester, 1986), p.183; '1483: the Year of Decision (or Taking the Throne), in *Richard III: A Medieval Kingship*, J. Gillingham (ed.), (London, 1993), p.53.

23   R. Horrox, *Richard III: A Study in Service* (Cambridge, 1989), esp. pp.22–3, 138–40, 178–81.

24   R. Horrox, *Richard III: A Study in Service* (Cambridge, 1989), pp.290, 297, 317–19.

25   R. Horrox, *Richard III: A Study in Service* (Cambridge, 1989), pp.128–9, 151.

26   J. Gillingham, *Richard III: A Medieval Kingship* (London, 1993), pp.4–14, 18–19.

27 M. Hicks, 'Richard Duke of Gloucester: The Formative Years', in J. Gillingham (ed.), *Richard III: A Medieval Kingship* (London, 1993), p.37; M. Hicks, *Richard III* (Stroud, 2000), p.19.

28 C. Richmond, '1483: The Year of Decision (Or Taking the Throne)', in J. Gillingham (ed.), *Richard III: A Medieval Kingship* (London, 1993), pp.45, 51.

29 C. Carpenter, *The Wars of the Roses* (Cambridge, 1997), esp. pp.208–14, 218; see also H. Castor, *Blood and Roses* (London, 2004), pp.288–9, 293.

30 M. Hicks, *Anne Neville* (Stroud, 2007), esp. pp.132, 146.

31 Some recent examples include A. Carson, *Richard III: the Maligned King* (Stroud, 2008) and J. Wilkinson, *The Young King To Be* (Stroud, 2008).

32 M. K. Jones, *Bosworth 1485* (Stroud, 2002); A. J. Pollard, *Late Medieval England 1399–1509* (Harlow, 2000), pp.347–8. Helen Castor follows Carpenter in believing that Bosworth *was* a consequence of the fragility of Richard's regime: *Blood and Roses* (2004), p 293.

FURTHER READING

POLITICS AND SOCIETY IN THE 15TH CENTURY

The background to the medieval period can be easily approached through J. Gillingham and R. Griffith, *Medieval Britain: a Very Short Introduction* (Oxford, 2000), first published in 1984 as *The Oxford Illustrated History of Britain*. For a detailed and comprehensive survey of the 15th century in an accessible form, the best place to start is A. J. Pollard, *Late Medieval England 1399–1509* (Longman, 2000). M. Rubin, *The Hollow Crown* (Penguin, 2005), covers a wider field but chapters 4–6 deal with the relevant period. The reign of Henry VI is comprehensively covered by R. A. Griffith, *The Reign of Henry VI* (fist published by the University of California, 1981 and now by The National Book Network, 2005), and B. P. Wolffe (Methuen, 1983 and now Yale, 2001). J. L. Watts, *Henry VI and the Politics of Kingship* (Cambridge, 1996), has given the long reign a new political perspective. The wider political scene has been surveyed in J. R. Lander, *The Limitations of English Monarchy in the Later Middle Ages* (Toronto University, 1989), and more recently by M. Hicks, *English Political Culture in the Fifteenth Century* (Routledge, 2002).

The nobility in the 15th century is a subject given incisive treatment by the great medievalist K. B. McFarlane, *The Nobility of Later Medieval England* (Oxford, 1973). The 14th century background to the subject is covered by C. Given-Wilson, *The English Nobility in the Later Middle Ages*

(Routledge, 1987, 1996) which also considers the status of the gentry and discusses the impact of McFarlane's work. His legacy was further considered in R. H. Britnell and A. J. Pollard (eds), *The McFarlane Legacy: Studies in Late Medieval Politics and Society* (Sutton, 1995). The drama of the 15th century from the point of view of the gentry is vividly captured through the eyes of the Paston family in H. Castor, *Blood and Roses* (Faber, 2004).The gentry have received considerable scrutiny in recent times. The tidiest summary of the best work is in M. C. Carpenter, 'Gentry and Community in Medieval England', *Journal of British Studies*, 33 (1994). The most recent work is by M. Mercer, *The Medieval Gentry: Power, Leadership and Choice during the Wars of the Roses* (Hambledon Continuum, 2010).

For the wider cultural aspects of the period there are important essays in R. Horrox (ed.), *Fifteenth Century Attitudes* (Cambridge, 1994), covering a range of topics including law, education, women and the different ranks of society. Additional aspects are covered by K. Dockray and P. Fleming, *People, Places and Perspectives* (Nonsuch, 2005). The social dimension and the lives of the rural community are given thorough treatment in C. Dyer, *Standards of Living in the Later Middle Ages* (Cambridge, 1989) and in R. Britnell and J. Hatcher (eds), *Progress and Problems in Medieval England* (Cambridge, 1996). Other aspects can be found in D. J. Clayton, R. G. Davies and P. McNiven (eds), *Trade, Devotion and Governance* (Sutton, 1994). The religious dimension is examined in E. Duffy, *The Stripping of the Altars: Traditional Religion in England, 1400–1580* (Yale, 2005), and in both C. Harper-Bill, *The Pre-Reformation in England, 1400–1530* (Longman, 1989), and R. N. Swanson, *Catholic England* (Manchester University, 1995).

THE WARS OF THE ROSES AND THE YORKISTS

The politics of the Wars of the Roses is definitively analysed in C. Carpenter, *The Wars of the Roses* (Cambridge, 1997). The historical issues concerning the origins of the conflict and the motives of the protagonists are debated in A. J. Pollard (ed.), *The Wars of the Roses* (Palgrave, 2001). A more narrative treatment can be found in J. Gillingham, *The Wars of the Roses* (Phoenix Press, 1981). A similar approach using the chronicles of the period appears in E. Hallam, *Chronicles of the Wars of the Roses*

(Guild Publishing, 1988). The most relevant sources are presented in K. Dockray, *Henry VI, Margaret of Anjou and the Wars of the Roses: A Source Book* (Sutton, 2000). For the details of the individual battles and their sites the best guide is P. Bramley, *The Wars of the Roses: a Field Guide and Companion* (Sutton, 2007).

The reigns of the Yorkist kings are succinctly and judiciously considered in A. Crawford, *The Yorkists* (Hambledon Continuum, 2007). The reign of Edward IV was comprehensively examined by C. Ross, *Edward IV* (Methuen, 1974 and Yale, 1997) and has recently been re-assessed by H. Kleineke, *Edward IV* (Routledge, 2009), while a more detailed examination of the careers of the leading protagonists is provided by H. Maurer, *Margaret of Anjou* (Boydell, 2005) and A. J. Pollard, *Warwick the Kingmaker* (Hambledon Continuum, 2007). Further detail from original records is given by K. Dockray, *Edward IV: A Source Book* (Sutton, 1999).

Richard's family have received the attention of historians. His brother, Clarence, is considered by M. Hicks, *False, Fleeting, Perjur'd Clarence* (Sutton, 1980). The same author has also examined the lives of the Woodvilles and Richard's nephew, Edward V, in 'The Changing Role of the Wydevilles in Yorkist Politics to 1483', in C. Ross (ed.), *Patronage, Pedigree and Power* (Sutton, 1979), and *Edward V* (Sutton, 2003). Edward IV's wife, Elizabeth Woodville, has received thorough scrutiny by D. Baldwin, *Elizabeth Woodville* (Sutton, 2002). The life of Richard's mother was placed in context by C. A. J. Armstrong, 'The Piety of Cecily, Duchess of York: A Study in Late Medieval Culture', in *England, France and Burgundy in the Fifteenth Century* (Hambledon, 1983). Richard's father, Richard duke of York, is best approached through T. B. Pugh, 'Richard Plantagenet, Duke of York as King's Lieutenant in France and Ireland', in J. G. Rowse (ed.), *Aspects of Late Medieval Government and Society* (Toronto, 1986) and P. A. Johnson, *Duke Richard of York, 1411–1460* (Oxford, 1988). The life of Richard's sister, Margaret, is examined by C. Weightman, *Margaret of York, Duchess of Burgundy, 1446–1503* (Sutton, 1989).

THE REIGN OF RICHARD III

P. M. Kendall's ground-breaking study of the life and reign of Richard in *Richard III* (Allen & Unwin, 1955 and W. W. Norton, 2002), is still worth reading despite its obvious bias and use of a little historical imagination. The first credible biography was produced by C. Ross, *Richard III* (Methuen, 1981 and Yale, 1999). R. Horrox, *Richard III: a Study in Service* (Cambridge, 1989), is still the main work of reference for any serious study of the reign. A well-illustrated and insightful study followed with A. J. Pollard, *Richard III and the Princes in the Tower* (Sutton, 1991). A short work focusing on the documents in the National Archives was produced by S. Cunningham, *Richard III: a Royal Enigma* (National Archives, 2003). An excellent collection of essays covering different aspects of the reign can be found in P. W. Hammond (ed.), *Richard III: Loyalty, Lordship and Law* (Richard III and Yorkist History Trust, 1986), with further contributions by leading historians in J. Gillingham (ed.), *Richard III: a Medieval Kingship* (Collins & Brown, 1993). Buckingham's rebellion and its consequences are dissected by L. Gill, *Richard III and Buckingham's Rebellion* (Sutton, 1999). Further consideration of this episode can be found in an article by P. Morgan, 'The Death of Edward V and the Rebellion of 1483', *History Review*, 68 (1995). Some interesting reflections on the reign are to be found in M. K. Jones, *Bosworth 1485: Psychology of a Battle* (Sutton, 2000), though recent archaeological discoveries have revealed what Jones could not know. These finds have shown that the earlier work of P. J. Foss, *The Field of Redemore: the Battle of Bosworth 1485* (Kairos Press, 1998) was somewhat prescient.

The historiography of Richard's posthumous reputation can be found in A. Hanham, *Richard III and his Early Historians* (Oxford, 1975), and in J. Potter, *Good King Richard?* (Constable, 1983). The northern dimension to Richard's career is best approached through R. E. Horrox (ed.), *Richard III and the North* (Hull University, 1986). A narrative account of Richard's life using primary sources was provided by P. W. Hammond and A. F. Sutton, *Richard III: the Road to Bosworth Field* (Sutton, 1985). K. Dockray, *Richard III: A Source Book* (Sutton, 1997), provides a selection of additional primary evidence with short commentaries on its significance.

INDEX

Abbeville, governor of 58
Abingdon 88
Abyssinian 227
Accord, Act of 35, 37, 46, 47
Agincourt 6, 7, 35, 104, 112
Aire, River 51
Albany, Alexander, duke of 115, 116, 172
Alkmaar 78
Allertz, Jan 138
Ambion Hill 182
American 231
Amiens 79, 111
Amounderness, Lancs. , 71, 73, 91
Andre, Bernard 216
Anlaby Cartulary 139
Anne Boleyn 134
Anne of Beaujeu 172
Anne, duchess of Buckingham, aunt of Richard 31, 33, 84, 154

Anne, duchess of Exeter, sister of Richard 6, 23, 62, 84, 154
Anne, wife of Richard, *see Neville*
Aquitaine 55
Arctic 227
Argentine, Dr John 15, 119, 137
Armstrong, C. A. J. 15
Arras, Treaty of 116, 171
Arrivall, chronicle 81, 85, 87, 89
Arundel, earl of, *see Fitzalan*
Arundel, Sir Thomas 154
Ashford, Kent 153
Ashmolean Musuem, Oxford 138
Ashton, Sir Ralph 159
Aspall, Sir Robert 39
Attila the Hun 41
Audley, John lord 60, 199
Austen, Jane 220

Bacon, Sir Francis 218, 219, 220
Balderstone, Isabella or Isabel 73, 105
Balderstone, Jane 73, 105
Banbury 63, 83, 84
Barnard Castle 57, 98, 105, 205
Barnet, battle of 86, 87, 89, 111, 194, 245
Barnoldswick, Yorks. , 56
Bath and Wells, bishop of, *see* *Stillington*
Bath, earl of, *see Chandee*
Bath, Order of 54
Baynard's Castle 47, 49, 56, 132, 133, 206
Beauchamp, Anne, countess of Warwick 95, 96, 98
Beauchamp, Richard, bishop of Salisbury 48
Beaufort, Cardinal, Henry 9
Beaufort, Edmund, 2nd duke of Somerset 10, 11, 19, 20, 22, 23, 24, 25, 26, 27
Beaufort, Edmund, 4th duke of Somerset 43, 79, 83, 85, 89
Beaufort, Henry, 3rd duke of Somerset 26, 27, 28, 29, 30, 38, 43, 51, 52, 56, 61
Beaufort, Joan 5, 6, 7, 95
Beaufort, John, marquess of Dorset, son of 2nd duke of Somerset 25, 83, 84, 85
Beaufort, Margaret, mother of Henry Tudor 148, 149, 151, 161, 196
Beaujeu, Anne of 172

Beaumont, Elizabeth 197. *See also Harrington, Elizabeth*
Beaumont, John, 1st Viscount 32
Beaumont, William, 2nd Viscount 83, 86
Bedford, George, duke of, son of John Neville 62, 69, 98
Bedford, Jacquetta, duchess of 62, 64
Bedford, John, duke of, brother of Henry V 8, 9, 20, 21, 62
Benedictine monasticism 3
Berkeley, Sir William 181
Berkeley, William, earl of Nottingham 147, 195, 199
Berkshire 16, 151, 153, 195
Berwick 54, 115, 116, 117, 126, 170
Beverley 80
Bishop's Lynn 77
Black Legend 236, 241, 245
Black Prince, Edward the 35
Blackburn, Lancs. , 71, 73, 91
Blanche of Lancaster 92
Blore Heath, battle of 27, 28, 41, 181
Blount, James 181
Blount, John, lord Mountjoy 200
Blount, Walter, lord Mountjoy 60
Bodleian Library, Oxford 138
Bodrugan, Henry 160
Bolingbroke, Henry, *see Henry IV*
Bolingbroke, Lincs. , lordship of 56

Bologna 175

Bona of Savoy 59

Bordeaux 19

Bosworth Field, battle of 1, 2, 27, 42, 147, 173–5, 180–3, 193–5, 197–9, 204, 205, 208–10, 213–5, 218

Bourchier, family 7

Bourchier, Henry, earl of Essex 62

Bourchier, Thomas, archbishop of Canterbury 36, 37, 47, 48, 56, 62, 99, 131, 203

Bourchier, William, viscount 62

Bowland, Forest of 71, 94, 96, 197

Brackenbury, Sir Robert 159, 206, 213, 215

Bradford 96

Brandon, Sir William 181

Brecon Castle 148, 151

Breze, Pierre de 54

Bridgewater 64

Brierley, Yorks. , 105

Bristol 64, 83, 138

British Library 17, 235, *also see Harleian*

British Museum 14

Brittany, duchy of 148, 161, 170, 171, 172, 173, 180, 181, 204, 205

Brittany, duke of, *see Francis*

Brook, John, lord Cobham 199

Bruges 43, 53, 79

Bryant, Arthur 228, 229, 231

Buck, Sir George 217, 218, 219, 220, 222

Buckingham, duchess of, *see Anne*

Buckingham, dukes of, *see Stafford*

Buckinghamshire 64, 159

Burford 80

Burgh, Sir Thomas 70

Burgundy, Burgundian 42, 43, 44, 50, 53, 54, 60, 77, 79, 87, 100, 110, 111, 114, 116, 121, 138, 170, 172, 182, 183

Burgundy, Charles the Bold, duke of 78, 100, 110, 112

Burgundy, John the Fearless, duke of 53

Burgundy, Margaret, duchess of, *see Margaret*

Burgundy, Maximilian of Austria, duke of 172

Burgundy, Phillip the Good, duke of 44, 50, 52, 53, 78

Burley, William 26

Bury St Edmunds 72

Butler, James, earl of Wiltshire 28, 30, 38, 40, 41, 51, 52

Butler, Lady Eleanor 132, 133, 165, 248

Byng, Admiral 219

Caernarvon 196

Caesar, Julius 241

Calais 26, 27, 28, 30, 32, 54, 58, 60, 63, 74, 89, 99, 110, 122, 170, 181, 200

Cambridge 51, 56, 87, 114, 175, 179, 215, 227

Cambridge, Richard, earl of 7, 35

Camulio, Prospero di 52

Canterbury, Archbishop of, *see Bourchier*

Canterbury, city of 54, 63, Christ Church 147

Carlisle 54

Carmeliano, Pietro 215, 216

Carpenter, Christine 241

Castelli, Cardinal 212

Castillon, battle of 19, 20, 21, 33, 199

Castle Rising 67

Castleford 51

Catesby, Sir William 139, 160, 162, 174, 180, 202, 203–206

Cato, Angelo, Archbishop of Vienne 15, 16

Cecily, duchess of York, *see Neville*

Cely, family 16, George 137

Chandee, Philibert de, earl of Bath 173

Channel, English 20, 43, 79, 126, 173

Charels I 211

Charles VII, king of France 9, 10, 20, 50, 53, 102, 112

Charles VIII, king of France 111 (as Dauphin), 171, 172, 173

Chepstow 64

Chertsey Abbey 141, 175

Cheshire 67, 71, 88, 96, 107, 108, 182, 197

Chester, earldom of 21, 145

Cheyne, Sir John 153, family of 159

Childeric II 3

Chlothar III 3

Christ 177, 178

Churchill, Sir Winston 209, 229, 230, 231, 232

Cinque Ports 58

Cirencester 88

Clarence, George, duke of, brother of Richard 4, 23, 30, 43, 44, 62, 63, 99

Clarence, Lionel of Antwerp, duke of 35, 55

Clerkenwell 176

Clifford, John 27, 38, 39, 43, 51; estates of 96

Clifford, Thomas 25, 27

Clitheroe 67, 71

Cobham, Eleanor, duchess of Gloucester 134

Cobham, John, lord, *see Brook*

Codnor, Henry, lord, *see Grey*

Collingbourne, William 180, 181

Columbus, Christopher 227

Commynes, Philippe de 16, 58, 60, 110, 111, 132, 137, 138, 141

Constable, Marmaduke 159

Conyers, Sir John 57, 63

Coppini, papal legate 41

Corfe, Dorset 96

Cornwall 88, 85, 153, 154, 159, 200, 206

Cottingham, Yorks. , 96

Council of the North 147, 193

Courtenay, earls of Devon, lands of 159,

Courtenay, John, earl of Devon, younger brother of Thomas 83, 84, 85, 89

Courtenay, Peter, *see Exeter, bishop of*

Courtenay, Sir Edward 154

Courtenay, Thomas, earl of Devon 28, 38, 51, 52

Coutenay, Henry 57

Coventry 27, 30, 32, 63, 64, 75, 83, 143, 156

Crevecouer, Philippe de, Seignuer d'Esquerdes 173

Cromer 80

Croyland Chronicle 13–14, 41, 48, 66, 77, 87, 90, 97, 100, 116, 117, 119, 122, 124, 127, 128, 137, 141, 150, 151, 154, 158, 160, 172, 174, 180, 182, 183, 236

Cumberland 69, 72, 75, 94, 95, 96, 104, 106, 108, 117, 159, 197, 205

Dacre, Elizabeth 104

Dacre, family of 57, 104, 105

Dacre, Humphrey, lord Dacre of Gilsland 54, 57, 104, 105, 159, 199, 206

Dadlington 182

Dales, Yorkshire 222

Danzig 138

Dartford 11

Dartmouth 73

Dean, Forest of 64

Debenham, Gilbert 160

Derby, earl of, *see Stanley, Thomas*

Derby, earldom of 92

Derbyshire 96

Despenser, family of 58, 96, 97

Devereux, Walter, lord Ferrers of Chartley 48, 60, 159, 199

Devon 74, 88, 151, 154, 159

Devon, earl of, *see Courtenay, and also Stafford*

Devon, earldom of 154, 159, 206

Dighton, John 139

Dinham, John lord 159, 200, 207

Divisie Chronicle 138, 141

Docket, John 175

Doncaster 91

Dorset, 88, 96, 126, 151, 153, 159

Dorset, marquess of, *see Grey and Beaufort*

Douglas, James, earl of 172

Dover 153

Dublin 5, 34

Dudley, John, lord *see Sutton*

Durham, bishopric 147

Durham, County 6, 54, 56, 98, 159, 172

Dutch 78, 138, 141

East Anglia 51, 67, 160, 163, 181, 194

Edgecote, battle of 63, 64

Edinburgh 116, 117

Edingburh, Treaty of 110, 114

Edmund, earl of Lancaster, son of Henry III 92

Edmund, earl of Rutland, brother of Richard 10, 23, 28, 38, 39, 43, 51, 102, 113

Edward I 92

Edward II 35, 140, 141, 211

Edward III 6, 7, 10, 35, 53, 55, 92, 121, 150, 245

Edward V 2, 15, 50, 61, 86, 119–21, 123, 126, 128–33, 135–7, 139–41, 145, 149, 151, 165, 167, 179, 187, 203, 213, 220, 223, 238, as prince of Wales 22, 153, 214

Edward, brother of Richard, as earl of March 10, 23, 28, 30, 32, 34, 37, 38, 40, 43, 46, 47; as duke of York 7, 42, 47, 48; as King Edward IV 1, 2, 12–14, 47–56, 58–100, 106–24, 126, 128, 130–8, 140, 143–5, 149–54, 157, 160, 162, 163, 165, 166, 169–71, 174, 175, 179–81, 186, 187, 190–9, 202, 203, 205–7, 211–3, 216, 217, 233, 234, 237, 238, 241, 245, 247, 248

Edward, of Middleham, son of Richard III 99, 101, 144, 162, 172, 246

Edward, Prince of Wales, son of Edward IV 119, 153, *see also Edward V* and *Princes in the Tower*

Edward, Prince of Wales, son of Henry VI 21, 22, 32, 33, 43, 52, 74, 75, 80, 81, 83, 84, 89, 96, 97, 216

Edward, Prince of Wales, son of Henry VI 21, 42, 43, 81, 89, 96, 214, 216

Edwardian, era 225

Egremont, *see Percy, Thomas*

Elizabeth I 4

Elizabeth of York, daughter of Edward IV 69, 111, 149, 151, 161, 174, 180, 186, 213

Elizabeth Woodville, *see Woodville*

Elizabeth, duchess of Suffolk, sister of Richard 10, 23, 69, 84, 147

Elizabethan 209

Ely, bishop of *see Morton*

Empingham, Rutland 70

England 1, 3, 4, 6, 9, 13, 14, 15, 16, 20, 24, 30, 32, 33, 34, 36, 44, 47, 51, 52, 54, 55, 58, 59, 60, 68, 73, 74, 78, 79, 80, 81, 89, 92, 93, 94, 95, 97, 100, 102, 110, 111, 112, 113, 114, 115, 116, 126, 129, 132, 134, 138, 151, 153, 157, 159, 161, 163, 165, 170, 171, 172, 173, 176, 180, 182, 183, 185, 188, 193, 196, 204, 209, 211, 212, 214, 216, 220, 221, 222, 225, 226, 228, 229, 230, 231, 236, 239

Esau 177

Essex, county of 56, 62, 89, 95, 151, 159, 181

Essex, earl of, *see Bourchier*

Eton 175

Europe, European 12, 16, 44, 53, 59, 65, 79, 100, 161, 170, 171, 175, 176, 188, 221

Exchequer 56, 145, 169, 199, 204, 247

Exeter, bishop of, George Neville (until 1461) 37, 47, 48, 58, Peter Courtenay 154, 161

Exeter, city of 88, 156

Exeter, duchess of, *see Anne*

Exeter, duke of, *see Holland*

Fabian, or Fabyan, Robert 14, 46, 47

Farleigh Hungerford, Wilts. , 96

Fastolf, John 34

Fauconberg, lord, *see Neville, William*

Fauconberg, Thomas, Bastard of 79, 80, 89

Fenland 13, 41

Fenny Drayton 182

Ferdinand of Aragon 137

Ferrers, lord *see Devereux*

Ferrybridge 51

Fitzalan, Thomas, lord Maltravers 195

Fitzalan, William, earl of Arundel 28, 51, 195, 199

Fitzhugh, Anne, daughter of Henry 104

Fitzhugh, family of 57, 104, 105

Fitzhugh, Henry, lord 104

Fitzhugh, Richard, lord 105, 159, 199

Fitzwalter, *see Radcliffe*

Flanders, Flemish 79, 85, 183

Flushing 80

Fogge, Sir John 153

Forest, Miles 139

Fortescue, Sir John 181, 186

Fotheringhay 3, 4, 11, 23, 113, 115, 176, 174

Fowler, Thomas 162

France 6, 8, 9, 10, 14, 15, 16, 19, 20, 21, 33, 36, 38, 40, 44, 50, 53, 54, 59, 62, 73, 83, 84, 102, 108, 109, 110, 111, 112, 113, 114, 115, 116, 132, 137, 161, 170, 171, 172, 173, 176, 179, 188, 199, 204, 245

Francia 3

Francis II, duke of Brittany 80, 161, 171, 172

Frank, Edward 159

Frederick III, Holy Roman Emperor 100, 141, 175

Gairdner, James 224, 225, 226, 227, 232, 235, 240

Garter, Order of 53, 55, 105, 106, 196

Gascony 9, 10, 19, 20

Gaunt, John of, duke of Lancaster 6, 35, 55, 92, 95, 100, 239

Gaunt, John of, *see Lancaster*

George I 219
George II 219
German 230
Gibbon, Edward 220
Gideon 48
Gillingham, John 239, 240
Gloucester, city of 88, 89, 141
    (cathedral), 143, 144, 148,
    215
Gloucester, duchess of, see Cobham
Gloucester, Humphrey, duke of,
    brother of Henry V 8, 55,
    129, 134
Gloucestershire 72, 73, 96, 159
Golden Fleece, Order of 53
Grantham 156
Great Britain 225, 228, 229
Great Chronicle of London 14,
    85, 134, 136, 140, 141,
    146
Great Seal 1, 17, 93, 114, 154,
    155
Green, J. R. 225
Greenwich 56
Gregory, William, chronicle of
    41, 42
Grey, Edmund, earl of Kent 147,
    199
Grey, Henry, lord Grey of Codnor
    199
Grey, John, lord Grey of Powys
    199
Grey, Sir John, 1ˢᵗ husband of
    Elizabeth Woodville 73
Grey, Sir Richard, son of
    Elizabeth Woodville 59,

120, 122, 124, 125, 130,
    131, 135
Grey, Thomas, marquess of
    Dorset, son of Elizabeth
    Woodville 59, 62, 121, 122,
    123, 153, 154, 161, 192,
    204
Greyfriars, Leicester 183
Greystoke, family of 57, 104, 105
Greystoke, Ralph, lord 199
Gruthuyse, Louis de 78, 79, 80
Guildhall, London 132, 106
Guines 30
Gunthorpe, John 126

Habsburg 175
Halifax, Lord 227
Hall, Edward 149, 212, 217,
    236, 240
Halsted, Caroline 222, 223, 224,
    226, 228, 232
Halton 67, 71
Hammes 181
Hammond, P. W. 235
Hampshire 151, 153, 159, 161
Hanse, towns 78, 79
Hanseatic League 78, 79, 87
Harleian, British Library MS 433
    17, 235
Harrington, Anne, daughter of
    John 72, 109, 197
Harrington, Elizabeth, daughter
    of John 72, 109, 197
Harrington, family of 71, 72, 73,
    82, 103, 104, 107, 108,
    109, 196, 197, 198

Harrington, James, 2nd son of Thomas 57, 72, 73, 82, 83, 91, 104, 105, 107, 108, 109, 112, 197, 198

Harrington, John, clerk of the council 167

Harrington, John, eldest son of Thomas 197

Harrington, John, son of James 197

Harrington, Margaret, sister of William Harrington of Lathom 104

Harrington, Robert, 3rd son of Thomas 57, 72, 73, 91, 104, 105, 107, 108, 109, 112, 128, 197

Harrington, Sir William 104

Harrington, Thomas 72,

Harrington, William, of Lathom 104

Hastings, Richard, lord Willoughby 200

Hastings, William lord 60, 61, 77, 81, 83, 84, 86, 88, 94, 105, 111, 121, 122, 127, 128, 129, 130, 131, 135, 147, 148, 160, 167, 191, 192, 195, 196, 203, 204, 205, 240

Haute, Sir Richard 128, 131, 153, 206

Haute, Sir William 153

Hedgeley Moor, battle of 61

Helmsley, Yorks. , 96

Henry III 92

Henry IV 6, 35, 46, 47, 48, 49, 55, 80, 93, 174, 213, 245, 247

Henry V 6, 7, 8, 9, 21, 35, 38, 41, 55, 62, 112, 127, 175, 228

Henry VI 8, 9, 10, 12, 20, 21, 26, 30, 33, 35, 37, 38, 39, 40, 42, 43, 44, 46, 47, 49, 50, 52, 54, 55, 59, 60, 61, 64, 74, 75, 76, 77, 79, 90, 85, 86, 89, 90, 91,127, 141, 145, 175, 186, 190, 191, 202, 209, 213, 214, 215, 216, 228

Henry VII, *see Tudor*

Henry VIII 134, 212, 216, 217, 227

Herbert, Sir Richard 63, 64

Herbert, Sir Thomas 64

Herbert, William, earl of Huntingdon 62, 99, 163

Herbert, William, earl of Pembroke 48, 60, 62, 63, 64, 68, 163

Hereford 34, 40, 41

Herefordshire 73, 126

Hertfordshire 96

Hicks, Michael 240, 241, 242

Hitler 230, 232, 240, 241

Holderness 80

Holinshed, Raphael 212

Holland 78, 79, 80

Holland, Anne, daughter of duchess of Exeter 62

Holland, Henry, duke of Exeter 23, 28, 38, 51, 52, 54, 79, 83, 84, 86, 87

Home Counties 229

Hornby Castle, Lancs. 71, 72, 73, 82, 83, 105, 107, 108, 109, 197, 198

Horrox, Rosemary 120, 235, 237, 238, 239

House of York 4, 7, 12, 19, 20, 40, 72, 140, 157, 179, 243

Howard, Elizabeth, countess of Oxford 95

Howard, John, duke of Norfolk 60, 126, 134, 147, 160, 163, 181, 182, 191, 194, 195

Howard, Thomas, earl of Surrey 147, 182, 194, 218

Huddleston, family of 71, 72, 104, 96

Huddleston, John 57, 72, 104, 112, 159

Huddleston, Richard 104

Huddleston, Thomas159

Hull 38, 80, 96

Humber, River 117

Hume, David 220

Hundred Years War 9, 12, 20, 21, 25, 183, 201

Hungary 176

Hungerford, estates of 96

Hungerford, Sir Walter 153

Hungerford, Thomas 57

Hungerford, Wilts. , 96

Huntingdonshire 204

Hussey, Sir William 201

Hutton, John 159

Indian 227

Ireland 8, 28, 30, 33, 55

Isabel, daughter of Anne Mortimer 7

Isabel, daughter of Warwick, see Neville

Isabella of Castille 137, 171

Italy, Italian 15, 44, 101, 119, 137, 212, 215

Jacob 177

Jacquetta of Luxemburg, dowager duchess of Bedford 62, 64

James I 4, 217, 218, 219

James II 211

James III of Scotland 110, 114, 115, 172

Jersey 54

Joan of Arc 53

John, illegitimate son of Richard, 99, 155, 156, 200

John, King 141, 210

Jones, Michael 102

Katherine, illegitimate daughter of Richard 99, 163, 198

Katherine, queen, wife of Henry V 41

Kendall, John 144, 160, 202

Kendall, Paul Murray 107, 231, 232, 234

Kent 51, 89, 148, 151, 153, 154, 157, 159, 167

Kent, earl of, see Neville, William and Grey, Edward

Kidwelly, Morgan 160

Kimbolton, Hunts. , 204

King's College Cambridge 175

Kingmaker, Warwick the, *see Neville, Richard*
Knaresborough 96, 106

Lancashire 67, 68, 71, 72, 73, 88, 91, 92, 93, 94, 96, 104, 107, 108, 159, 196, 197
Lancaster, 1st earl of, *see Edmund*
Lancaster, city of 72
Lancaster, duchy of 17, 55, 56, 58, 67, 71, 80, 87, 91–94, 106, 126, 169, 191, 196, 198, 203
Lancaster, duke of, *see Gaunt*
Lancaster, earldom 92
Lancaster, Henry, 1st duke of 92
Landais, Pierre 172, 173
Lander, J. R. 233, 236
Langley, Edmund, *see York*
Langton, Thomas, bishop of St David's (later Salisbury)146, 147, 166
Latimer, Richard Neville, lord 99
Latin 3, 13, 14, 78, 214
Leeds 96
Leicester 23, 83, 143, 148, 156, 181, 182, 183, 209
Leicester, earldom of 92
Leicestershire 60, 160, 172
Leodegar, St Ledger 3
Lille 15
Lincoln, bishop of, *see Russell*
Lincoln, city of 8, 144, 155, 157
Lincoln, earl of, *see Pole*
Lincolnshire, county of 13, 56, 60
Lingard, John 220, 221, 240

Lionel, (of Antwerp) duke of Clarence 7, 35, 55
Lisle, Edward Grey, viscount 147, 199
Liverpool 67
Lochmaben 172
London 3, 11, 14–16, 23, 26, 32, 33–36, 38, 40–44, 46–48, 50, 51, 54, 56, 60, 63, 65, 70, 81, 83–86, 88–90, 93, 97, 100, 115, 119, 120–122, 125–127, 129, 132, 134, 136–138, 140, 143, 145–148, 151, 156, 171, 178–181, 206, 215, 224, 229
Lonsdale, Lancs. , 71
Lorraine, duke of 110
Losecoat Field, battle of 69–70, 81
Louis XI, king of France 15, 16, 50, 58, 59, 73, 79, 109, 110, 111, 114, 170, 171
Lovell, Francis lord 57, 57, 105, 147, 159, 163, 180, 195, 204, 207
Lovell, Minster 148
Low Countries 78
Ludford, Rout of 28, 29, 33, 60
Ludgate Hill 26
Ludlow 11, 27, 28, 30, 31, 34, 43, 119, 120
Lumley, Thomas lord 159, 199
Lune, River 72

Magdalen College, Oxford 144
Maltravers, Thomas lord 195

Mancini, Dominic 15–16, 101, 103, 119, 120, 121, 122, 123, 124, 129, 130, 132, 136, 137, 165, 203, 206

March, earl of, *see Edward IV and Mortimer, Roger*

March, earldom of 169, 192, 203

March, Scottish, East 58, 115, 126, 193

March, Scottish, West 54, 58, 77, 91, 104, 110, 114, 117, 193, 199, 206

March, Welsh 8, 40, 51, 68, 87, 126, 169, 196, 203

Margaret of Anjou, wife of Henry VI 10, 20, 26, 30, 50, 54, 73, 74, 95, 145, 202

Margaret, duchess of Burgundy, sister of Richard 23, 30, 84, 100, 111, 114

Market Bosworth 182

Market Drayton 27

Markham, Sir Clements 225, 226, 227, 228, 231, 232, 235

Mary of Burgundy, daughter of Charles the Bold 100

Mary, Queen of Scots 4

Mauleverer, William 159

Maximilian, Archduke of Austria and duke of Burgundy 100, 172

McFarlane, K. B. 185

Metcalfe, Thomas 57; family of 105

Micklegate Bar, York 39

Middleham 4, 27, 57, 63, 64, 94, 95, 97, 98, 99, 101, 103, 105, 114, 172, 175, 179, 193, 222

Milan, duke of, *see Sforza*

Milan, Milanese 52

Milewater, John 87

Milford Haven 181

Millais, Sir John Everett 225

Minorca 219

Minster Lovell 148

Molinet, Jean 138, 141

Montacute, Alice, wife of the earl of Salisbury 5

Montagu, John, marquess of, *see Neville*

Montagu, lands 96

Montereau 53

Montgomery, Sir Thomas 201

More, Sir Thomas 139, 140, 149, 203, 204, 209, 212, 216, 217, 218, 220, 221, 224, 225, 227, 228, 229, 230, 233, 236, 239, 242

Mortimer, Anne 7, 35

Mortimer, Edmund, 5th earl of March 7

Mortimer, Roger, 4th earl of March 35

Mortimer's Cross, battle of 40, 41, 43, 60, 74, 81

Morton, John, bishop of Ely 128, 130, 148, 151, 216

Morton, Robert 148

Mowbray, John, duke of Norfolk 48, 51, 52, lands of 163, 194

Musgrave, family of 105
Musgrave, John 159

Nancy, Lorraine 100
Nazi 229
Nene, River 3
Netherlands 43, 45, 48, 63, 85
Neville, Anne, daughter of
    Warwick and wife of
    Richard 57, 62, 74, 84,
    96–9, 172, 174, 180, 242,
    246
Neville, Anne, duchess of
    Buckingham, sister of Cecily
    31
Neville, Cecily, duchess of York
    4, 5–6, 7, 9, 10, 11, 22, 30,
    31, 33, 34, 38, 42, 43, 84,
    102, 132
Neville, Eleanor, sister of duchess
    Cecily 5
Neville, Eleanor, sister of
    Warwick 71
Neville, George, brother of
    Warwick, bishop of Exeter
    (until 1461), chancellor and
    archbishop of York 5, 37,
    47, 48, 57, 58, 63, 85
Neville, George, duke of Bedford,
    son of John marquess
    Montagu 98, 99
Neville, Isabel, daughter of
    Warwick 62, 63, 65, 75, 96,
    97, 98, 100
Neville, John, brother of
    Warwick, marquess

Montagu 42, 43, 58, 69, 70,
    76, 82, 84, 86, 87, earl of
    Northumberland 58, 69, 70
Neville, John, lord 38
Neville, Katherine, sister of
    duchess Cecily 5
Neville, Margaret, countess of
    Oxford, sister of Warwick
    74
Neville, Ralph, 1st earl of
    Westmorland 5, 6, 7, 95
Neville, Ralph, 2nd earl of
    Westmorland 95, 107, 162,
    193, 194, 199
Neville, Ralph, 3rd earl of
    Westmorland 95
Neville, Richard, earl of Salisbury
    5, 22, 27, 28, 30, 31, 32,
    34, 38, 39, 43, 48, 95, 96
Neville, Richard, earl of Warwick
    22, 26, 27, 28, 30, 32, 33,
    34, 36, 37, 39, 40, 42, 43,
    46, 48, 51, 56, 57, 58,
    59–63, 64, 65, 67, 68, 69,
    70, 71, 72, 73–75, 76, 77,
    79, 81, 82, 83, 84, 86, 87,
    88, 89, 91, 92, 94, 95, 96,
    97, 98, 103, 104, 105, 106,
    136, 186, 187, 189, 202
Neville, Richard, *see Latimer*
Neville, Thomas 37, 38, 39
Neville, William, lord
    Fauconberg, earl of Kent 51,
    59
Newcastle 171, 172
Newcastle-under-Lyme 27

Norfolk 3, 16, 33, 67, 77, 78, 80, 194
Norfolk, duke of, *see Mowbray and Howard*
Normandy 9, 10, 11, 54, 102
Norrey, family of 195
Northampton 64, 120, 123, 124
Northampton, battle of 31–4, 39, 41, 64, 199
Northamptonshire 3, 60, 202–4
Northcroft, George 140
Northumberland, county of 69, 70, 106
Northumberland, earldom of, *see Percy and Neville, John*
Nottingham 51, 64, 82, 87, 91, 115, 143, 171, 172, 181
Nottingham, earl of, *see Berkeley*

Olivier, Lawrence 228
Olney, Bucks. , 64, 65
Oman, Sir Charles 225
Orleans, Louis, duke of 172, 173
Oxford 144, 147, 156, 227
Oxford, earl of, *see Vere*
Oxfordshire 16, 153, 195

Padua 175
Parliament, 25, 26, 29, 36, 37, 40, 46, 49, 64, 65, 93, 98, 99, 101, 126, 127, 131, 132, 133, 158, 160, 164–6, 168, 170, 188, 191, 204, 223, 230
Parr, family of 87, 103, 104, 105
Parr, John 87

Parr, Mabel 104
Parr, Sir William 57, 82, 87, 91, 104
Parr, Thomas 87
Paston, family 15, 201, John 33, 34, Clement 41
Pembroke, earldom of, *see Herbert or Tudor, Jasper*
Pennines 73, 197
Penrith 57, 94, 104
Percy, family 39, 58, 69, 76, 81, 106, 118, 192
Percy, Henry, 2nd earl of Northumberland 25
Percy, Henry, 3rd earl of Northumberland 27, 28, 38, 51, 52, 56
Percy, Henry, 4th earl of Northumberland 69, 70, 75, 81, 82, 97, 105–7, 115, 116, 126, 135, 147, 162, 163, 181, 183, 184, 192, 193, 205
Percy, Sir Ralph 61
Percy, Thomas, lord Egremont 32
Peru 226, 227
Peterborough 3
Philibert de Chandee 173
Philippa, daughter of Lionel duke of Clarence 35
Pickering, Yorks. , 56, 96
Picquigny, and Treaty of 109, 110, 111, 171
Pilkington, Elizabeth 104
Pilkington, family of 71, 73, 103, 104, 105, 196

Pilkington, Sir Charles 72, 73, 91, 105, 128

Pilkington, Sir John 72, 73, 91, 105

Pilkington, Sir Thomas 71, 104, 112

Pius VII, Pope 221

Plummer, Charles 185

Plumpton, family 16

Pole, Elizabeth de la, duchess of Suffolk, *see Elizabeth*

Pole, John de la, duke of Suffolk 51, 199

Pole, John de la, earl of Lincoln 37, 147, 162, 193, 195, 198

Pollard, A. J. 236, 237

Pont de l'Arche 173

Pontefract 39, 51, 82, 96, 99, 113, 114, 125, 143, 144, 154, 175, 205, 206

Pontoise 102, 112

Poppelau, Nicholas von 141, 142, 175, 176

Potter, J. 15, 235

Princes in the Tower 1, 2, 14, 15, 17, 132, 136–42, 145, 150–54, 165, 176, 209, 214, 224, 225, 228, 232, 234, 236–8, 244

Privy Seal 17, 126

Public Record Office, now National Archives 238

Queens' College Cambridge 87, 175, 179

Raby, County Durham 6, 94

Radcliffe, John, lord Fitzwalter 48

Raleigh, Sir Walter 218

Ramsey, James 225

Ratcliffe, Richard 105, 129, 139, 159, 174, 180, 201, 205, 206

Ravenspur 80

Readeption of Henry VI 75, 78, 79, 86, 109, 202

Reading 59

Redbank 34

Redemoor 182

Redesdale, Robin of 63

Redmane, Edward 159, 202

Redmane, Richard 202

Reformation 219

Renaissance, Italian 12, 44, 176, 213

Rennes Cathedral 161

Ricardians 15, 220, 224, 229, 231, 239, 243

Ricart, Robert 138

Richard II 20, 35, 49, 80, 93, 140, 174, 175, 239

Richard III,
  18th year 77–80
  Admiral and Great Chamberlain of England 94
  assessment of 244–8
  Battle of Barnet, role in 87
  benefices, abolition of 168
  Berwick, capture of 116
  birth 3
  Bosworth 181–4
  brother of a king 53

Buckingham, execution of 156
Buckingham's rebellion, reasons for 153–4
Buckingham's rebellion, response to 154–6
Burgundy, first flight to 42–45
Catesby, rise and role of 203–5
chief steward of Wales and the earldom of March 68
chivalry 176
Clarence, conflict with 97–8
Clarence, role in reconciliation with Edward 84
Clarence's fall, attitude to 100–103
Constable of England 68
coronation 143
Council of the North 193
countess of Oxford's and countess of Warwick's estates, seizure of 96
coup at Stony Stratford 123–4
crown lands, management of 169
Cumberland, granted palatinate powers in 117
death 183
duchy of Lancaster, beginning of association with 56
duchy of Lancaster, chief steward of in the north 92
early years 5
Edwardian regime, denigration of 162
exile during Warwick's rebellion 77

exile, return from 80
father 6–11
finance 168–170
flight of father 28–31
foreign relations 170–173
French expedition 110
Gloucester, created duke of 55
Hastings, execution of 127–9
Henry Percy, relations with 107, 195
Henry Tudor, threat from 181
Hornby Castle, appearance at, 72
Hornby dispute 108–9, 197
illegitimate children 99
justiciar of north Wales 68
law, concern for 166–8
loan, need for 170
London, move to 34
lord of the north 107
loyalty 179
marriage to Anne Neville 97
master forester 94
mother 5–6
motivation 179–80
nobility, changing role of 191–2
northern affinity, creation of 94–6, 104–5
northern plantations, reasons for and extent of 157–60
Parliament 164
Picquigny, Treaty of, attitude towards 109–10
poor requests, appointment of clerk of 167

prayer 177
Princes, responsibility of fate of 139–42
progress, royal 143–4
Protector 126–7
Queens' College Cambridge 175
Ratcliffe, rise and role of 205
reburial of father 113–4
recent views on 243
reign, place of in political history 186
religious foundations 175
reputation, posthumous, battle for 217–239
return to England 54
Scottish war 114–16
son, birth of 99
son, death of 172
Stanley, first clash with 70–73
Stanley, relations with 107–8, 196
support, level of 147
Tewkesbury, first command at 88–9
throne, taking of 134–5
Titulus Regius 164–6
Tudor legend, creation of 208–217
usurpation of the throne 120–125
Warwick's rebellion 65
western March, warden of 77
withdrawal from court 103
York, visit to as king 146

Richard III Society 235, 243
Richmond, Colin 237, 240, 241
Richmond, earl of, see Tudor
Richmond, north Yorks. 56, 96, 101, 205, earldom of 20, 149
Rivers, earl Rivers, see Woodville, Richard and Anthony
Robin, see Redesdale
Rochdale 91
Rochefort. Guillaume de 137
Roos, Thomas lord 38, 54
Ross, Charles 101, 117, 233, 234, 235, 237, 240
Rotherham, Thomas, archbishop of York 126, 128, 130, 145, 147
Rotterdam 138
Rouen 5, 102, 165
Rous, John 137, 183, 214, 215, 216
Rowse, A. L. 232
Royal Geographical Society 227
Royal Society 227
Royal Society of Antiquaries 227
Russell, John, bishop of Lincoln 126, 127, 144
Rutland, county of 70
Rutland, earl of see Edmund

Salisbury, Alice Montagu, countess of 31
Salisbury, bishop of, see Beauchamp and Woodville, Lionel
Salisbury, city of 57, 156
Salisbury, earl of, see Neville, Richard

Sandal, castle 39, 193
Sarum Rite 3
Saville, John 159
Say, Sir John 67, 68
Scarborough 96
Scotland 38, 41, 52, 54, 77, 110,
    113, 114, 115, 116, 117,
    118, 168, 169, 170, 171,
    172, 199, 202
Scrope, Agnes, daughter of Henry
    lord Scrope 205
Scrope, family of 57, 105
Scrope, Henry, lord Scrope of
    Bolton 205
Scrope, John, lord Scrope of
    Bolton 159, 199
Scrope, Thomas, lord Scrope of
    Masham 159
Seine valley 173
Sellyng, William 147
Severn, River 88
Seward, Desmond 236, 237
Sforza, Francesco, duke of Milan
    52
Shakespeare 1, 2, 40, 208–12,
    214, 217, 218, 221–2,
    224–5, 227, 239, 242
Sharp, Henry 13
Shaw, Dr Ralph 131, 132
Shaw, Sir Edmund 136
Sheffield 3
Sheriff Hutton 57, 94, 172, 193
Shrewsbury, battle of 174
Shrewsbury, city of 11, 34
Shrewsbury, earl of, see Talbot
Shropshire, county of 27, 126, 181

Sicily 92
Signet 17, 155, 235
Silesia 141, 175
Sixtus IV, Pope 117
Skipton in Craven 96
Slaydburn, parson of 197, 198
Sluys 43, 53
Somerset, county of, 64, 88, 126,
    151, 153
Somerset, dukes of, see Beaufort
Somme 79, 111
South America 227
Southampton, castle 159
Southampton, Plot 7
Southwark 34
St Albans, 1st battle of 21, 23–25,
    32, 33, 39, 41, 52, 74; 2nd
    battle of 41–42, 43, 46, 59,
    60
St Edward the Confessor 48, 86
St George 88, chapel of 88, 175
St John, Order of 176
St John's Field 47
St Leger, Sir Thomas 154
St Martin, church of, London 97
St Omer 59
St Paul's Cathedral, 11, 25, 26,
    48, 85, 87, 126, 131, 180
St Quentin 79
Stafford, Anne, countess of 150
Stafford, Edmund, earl of 150
Stafford, Henry, duke of
    Buckingham 62, 111, 112,
    121–3, 124, 125, 126, 128,
    129, 130, 132, 133, 134,
    138, 139, 143, 147–52,

155, 156, 157, 160, 161,
162, 163, 165, 167, 180,
191, 194, 195, 196, 197,
198, 201, 203, 204, 205,
206, 207, 237, 238, 240,
241, 246
Stafford, Humphrey, duke of
Buckingham 24, 25, 28, 31,
32, 33
Stafford, Humphrey, earl of 25
Stafford, Humphrey, earl of
Devon 63, 64, 69
Stafford, Margaret 5
Stamford, Lincs. , 70
Stanley, Edward, younger son of
Thomas 72, 197
Stanley, family 27, 28, 67, 72,
94, 152, 156, 181, 182,
192, 196, 198, 204
Stanley, George, lord Strange,
elder son of Thomas 181,
196, 204
Stanley, John 72
Stanley, Sir William 27, 28, 152,
163, 209, 246
Stanley, Thomas, lord 27, 28, 67,
69, 70–73, 75, 82, 83, 94,
105, 106, 107, 108, 109,
116, 118, 126, 128, 135,
147, 159, 163, 181, 183,
184, 195, 196, 197, 198,
earl of Derby 204
Staplers, Company of 26
Stillington, Robert, bishop of
Bath and Wells 132, 147
Stoke Golding 182

Stoke, battle of 183, 195, 247
Stonor, family 16, 195
Stonor, Sir William 153, 181
Stony Stratford 123, 124, 125,
138, 130, 131, 137, 153
Strange, lord *see Stanley, George*
Strangways, family 105
Stuart 4, 219
Stubbs, Bishop William 225
Sturgeon, John 162
Sudeley, Gloucs. , 96
Suffolk, county of 56, 181, 194
Suffolk, duke of, *see Pole*
Surrey 148, 153, 159
Surrey, earl of, *see Howard*
Sussex, county of 8, 148, 151,
153, 159
Sutton, Anne 235, 243
Sutton, John, lord Dudley 25,
199
Swiss 100, 110
Swynford, Katherine 6

Tahitians 226
Talbot, George, earl of
Shrewsbury 198–9
Talbot, John, earl of Shrewsbury
19, 20, 32, 75, 199, family
of 156
Talbot, Sir Gilbert 199
Tanner, Lawrence 140
Tewkesbury Abbey 89
Tewkesbury, battle of 87, 88, 89,
90, 94, 97, 111, 154, 245
Texel 78
Tey, Josephine 231, 234

Thames, River 34, 47, 163,
    Valley 163, 195
Thomas, of Woodstock, duke of
    Gloucester 55, 121, 150
Tickhill 96
Titulus Regius 132, 133, 164, 165
Tours 137
Tower of London 22, 24, 32, 74,
    77, 86, 87, 89, 90, 101,
    121, 127, 128, 130, 131,
    132, 136, 137, 138, 140,
    150, 151, 183, 209, 213,
    219, 225, 226, 228, 244
Towton, battle of 49–53, 54, 58,
    60, 74, 75, 81, 82, 245
Trent, River 94, 96, 126
Trollope, Sir Andrew 28
Tudor, Edmund 20
Tudor, Henry, earl of Richmond
    and King Henry VII 2, 15,
    74, 148–52, 154, 156, 161,
    170–76, 180–84, 186, 193,
    194, 198, 199, 204, 208,
    210, 213, 214, 216, 218,
    229, 230, 231, 237, 238,
    241, 245, 247
Tudor, Jasper, earl of Pembroke
    20, 38, 40, 41, 54, 74, 88
Tudor, Owen 40, 41, 74
Turks 12, 175, 176
Turner, Sharon 221
Tyburn 100
Tyrell, Sir James 139, 140, 160,
    201, 206, 213

Urbino, Italy 212

Valera, Mosen Diego de 137
Vaughan, Sir Thomas 124, 125,
    128, 131, 206
Veere, town 78
Vere, John de, earl of Oxford 63,
    74, 80, 83, 84, 86, 87, 95,
    105, 163, 181, 182, 183,
    194
Vergil, Polydore 84, 139, 146,
    182, 183, 212, 213, 214,
    216, 217, 222, 236
Victorian 224, 225
Visser-Fuchs, Livia 243

Wakefield, battle of 38–9, 41, 42,
    43, 46, 48, 51, 197
Wales 8, 38, 40, 54, 56, 60, 63,
    68, 69, 70, 87, 88, 89, 92,
    93, 94, 122, 126, 146, 148,
    152, 156, 163, 193, 196,
    197, 198, 199, 229
Wallingford 195
Walpole, Horace 219, 220, 221,
    226, 232
Walpole, Sir Robert 219
Walsingham 58, 63
Warbeck, Perkin 138
Warkworth, John 63, 70, 75, 77,
    78, 87, 90
Wars of the Roses 2, 4, 5, 8, 9,
    12, 19, 21, 24, 152, 185,
    186, 190, 201, 202, 132,
    133, 239, 241, 244
Warwick Castle 4, 57, 64, 143
Warwick, countess of, *see*
    Beauchamp

Warwick, earl of, *see Neville, Richard*

Warwickshire 60, 160, 183, 202, 203, 214

Wash, the 3

Waurin, Jean de 87, and Plate 4

Wax Chandlers 179

Wedrington, John 106, 107

Weinreich, Caspar 138

Welles, John 148

Welles, Richard lord 70

Welles, Sir Robert 70

Wenlock, John, lord 25, 60, 89

Wensleydale, Yorks. 4

Wesley, John 220

Westminster 37, 48, 65, 77, 86, 100, 131, 134, 150, 172, 193

Westminster Abbey 48, 49, 86, 140, 143, 151, 174, 175

Westmorland, county of 105, 108, 197, 206

Westmorland, earls of, *see Neville*

Weymouth 88

Whethamstede, Abbot John 41

Wigmore, castle of 40

Willoughby, Sir Robert 154

Wiltshire 88, 96, 126, 151, 153, 154, 159, 161, 180, 206

Wiltshire, earl of, *see Butler*

Wiltshire, earldom of 56

Windsor 88, 100, 141, 175

Wirral 34

Woodstock 144

Woodville, Anne 62

Woodville, Anthony, earl Rivers 63, 77, 78, 80, 81, 84, 86, 87, 120, 122, 123, 124, 125, 130, 131, 135, 159, 163, 167, 192, 194, 206

Woodville, Elizabeth, wife of Edward IV 58, 59, 61, 86, 128, 132, 133, 134, 149, 153, 160, 165, 174

Woodville, Katherine 62, 122

Woodville, Lionel, bishop of Salisbury 146, 147, 148, 153, 161

Woodville, Mary 62

Woodville, Richard, earl Rivers, father of Elizabeth 62, 63, 64, 68

Woodville, Sir Edward, 116, 121, 126, 130

Woodville, Sir John 63, 64

Worcester 141, 215

World War 227, Second 227, 228

Wright, Professor William 140

York Minster 144, 145

York, 1st duke of, Edmund Langley 7, 35, 55

York, 2nd duke of, Edward 7, 112

York, 3rd duke of, Richard, father of Richard III 4, 6–11, 13, 21–31, 33–40, 42, 44, 45, 47, 53, 65, 72, 81, 82, 102, 109, 112, 113, 114, 130–2, 165, 179, 186–7, 189, 202, 212, 247

York, 4th duke of, Edward, *see Edward IV*

York, 5th duke of, Richard,
  nephew of Richard III, *see
  also Princes in the Tower* 125,
  134, 136, 138, 140, 194
York, archbishop of *see Neville,
  George, and Rotherham*
York, city of 9, 17, 39, 41, 52,
  57, 64, 65, 70, 71, 80, 81,
  108, 120, 129, 134, 143,
  144–6, 148, 154, 175, 178,
  193, 233

Yorkshire 3, 8, 16, 51, 56, 58,
  63, 69, 71, 72, 73, 75, 94,
  95, 96, 99, 101, 106, 107,
  108, 144, 154, 159, 172,
  193, 197, 222, 228, 233
Zeeland 78, 79
Zouche, Margaret, wife of
  William Catesby 202
Zouche, William lord 159, 199,
  202, 207.